WITHDRAWN

2272

2443

2562
br. m. s

VAR.10°E

2468

2542

2640

y. br. m

2766

2464

2868

2752
br. m

2615

3023
br. m

6

SANDWICH ISLANDS

MOLOKAI
Kalawao

Halawa Pt

PAILOLO CHANNEL

Waihku Hbr
Kahului Hbr
Spreckelsville
Haiku

NAPILI B.

Napili B.

AU CHAN

184

21.8

Lahaina

MAUI

Kauiki Hd

Haleakala

Hana Hbr
(Kapueokahi)

malalaea Bay

10082

50

Makena

Molokini I.

63   752

iki Pt

ALALAKEIKI CHAN

KAHOOLAWE

1261   ALENUIHAHA CHANNEL

441

Upolu Pt.
205

Kauhala Pt
42

Mahukona
341

130

KAWAIHAE BAY   AF-10

Mauna Kea
13805

Alia Pt
40
HILO BAY

Keahole Pt.

Mt. Hualalai
8275

F. 10

27 Leleiwei Pt

Kailua Bay

H A W A I I

Keauhou Bay

Mauna Loa
13675

Kealakekua Bay

Kilauea

C. Kumukahi

Punaluu
Honuapo

2875

180

Kaalualu

55

Ka Lae

30

60

60

30

90

VAR.9°E

VAR.8°E

2650

HAWAII:

RECIPROCITY OR ANNEXATION

Hawaii:

RECIPROCITY OR ANNEXATION

∴

BY MERZE TATE

EAST LANSING

Michigan State University Press

1968

To My Brothers

CONTENTS

PART II.
Reciprocity with Pearl Harbor, Independence, and Annexation

Contents ix

Contents

ACKNOWLEDGEMENTS

For assistance in securing the information contained in this study an expression of appreciation is due the staffs of the Diplomatic, Legal, and Fiscal Division, the Navy Department, and the Central Search Room of the Archives of the United States, and especially to Miss Camille Hannon in the last named section; to Miss Agnes Conrad, Archivist, Public Archives of the State of Hawaii, and her efficient staff always eager to assist with the most detailed problem; to the late Michael W. Standish, Chief Archivist, and Miss Pamela S. Cocks, Senior Archivist, National Archives of New Zealand, who appeared delighted to search for and find unusual information concerning New Zealand's relations with the Hawaiian Islands and the attitude of Premier Richard Seddon toward their annexation to the United States; to Miss Janet Bell, Curator of the Hawaiian Collection in the University of Hawaii Library; to Mrs. Willowdean Handy and Miss Bernice Judd, formerly in charge of the Hawaiian Historical Society Library, and the Hawaiian Mission Children's Society Library, respectively, whose collections now repose together in the Mission-Historical Library in Honolulu; to Miss Ella M. Hymans, Supervisor of the Rare Book Collection of the General Library of the University of Michigan, who graciously arranged to make the Stephen Spaulding collection available to me for extra hours during the summer of 1957; to the Directors and staffs of the manuscript division of the Harvard College Library and of the Baker Library of the Harvard University Graduate School of Business Administration; to the officers and staff of the Library of Congress, especially to those in the Jefferson Reading Room, Newspaper, Manuscript, and Government Publications Reading Rooms; to the staff of the Main Reading Room of the British Museum; and to the officers in charge of the Central Reading Room of the British Public Record Office. I am especially indebted to Dr. Jacob Adler, Professor of Economics and Business, University of Hawaii, for permission not only to quote his published articles but to cite and quote his Ph.D. dissertation, Claus Spreckels, Sugar King

of Hawaii: Interaction of an Entrepreneur with an Island Economy,
*before its publication by the University of Hawaii Press. Mrs. Lucille
H. Watson typed the manuscript and Mrs. Ethel Harris Grubbs
assisted in indexing.*

*Finally, without financial assistance from the American Council
of Learned Societies, the Rockefeller Foundation, the Washington
Evening Star, Dr. James M. Nabrit, Jr., President, and Dr. Stanton
L. Wormley, Vice President of Howard University, in the form of
grants-in-aid of research for related projects, this study would not
have reached a stage worthy of publication.*

Howard University   MERZE TATE

ABBREVIATIONS

Adm.	British Admiralty Archives in the Public Record Office.
AH	Public Archives of the State of Hawaii.
NANZ	National Archives of New Zealand.
CO	British Colonial Office Archives in the Public Record Office.
FO	British Foreign Office Archives in the Public Record Office.
FO & Ex.	Foreign Office and Executive File, Archives of Hawaii.
For. Rels.	U.S. Dept. of State, *Papers Relating to the Foreign Relations of the United States.*
HHS	Hawaiian Historical Society.
Min. For. Rels.	Hawaiian Minister of Foreign Relations.
RHAS	Royal Hawaiian Agricultural Society.
USDS	United States Department of State Archives.

Introduction

I

BACKGROUND OF AMERICAN
INTEREST

Early American Contacts

THE earliest American contacts with the Hawaiian Islands were commercial and these continued to predominate and influence United States relations with the archipelago until annexation was consummated. A small Boston trading craft, the *Columbia*, under the command of Captain Robert Gray in the course of his voyage from the northern Pacific coast to China and his circumnavigation of the world, arrived at the Islands on August 24, 1789, remained twenty-four days, "salted down five puncheons of pork, and sailed with one hundred and fifty hogs on deck." Captain Gray's visit established a precedent for vessels sailing between Oregon and Canton. Practically every ship that visited the Pacific coast in the closing years of the eighteenth century put in at "the Islands," which proved a delightful rest station. By 1800 the transpacific fur trade was monopolized by New England craft seeking the mid-ocean haven.

Three Bostonians, Captains Nathan Winship, Jonathan Winship, and William Heath Davis monopolized for the first ten years the sandalwood trade that flourished in the Sandwich Islands between 1812 and 1829.[1] Although the avaricious traffic in this product, which was highly prized in China as incense and for making delicate pieces of furniture, caused the island population to decrease and the sandalwood forests to disappear, "it represented the beginning of American interest in the Islands and of American concern for the fate of the archipelago."[2] A small but influential group in the United States became concerned over the strategic location, the conversion of the inhabitants, and the commercial advantages of the mid-Pacific Kingdom.

After the War of 1812 various American trading houses regu-

larly stationed representatives at Honolulu, and that town's significance as a trading center increased when, in 1804, Kamehameha I
took up residence in Waikiki, where produce from other islands was
transshipped. James Hunnewell of Boston conducted a regular retail
store there for about ten months in 1817–18. Five years later there
were four American mercantile establishments: that of Hunnewell;
John C. Jones, agent for Marshall and Wildes; "Nor'west John" De
Wolf, from Rhode Island; and one from New York, probably that
of John Ebbets, who represented the house of John Jacob Astor
and Son.

The Anglo-American conflict spelled the eclipse of British pelagic
whaling, and Americans then extended their search for new grounds
in the Pacific. In 1818, after increased numbers of Europeans had
entered the whaling industry, causing a depletion of this mammal
in the North Atlantic and the known grounds of the South Pacific,
Captain George W. Garner, in the Nantucket *Globe*, steering west
from the old tracts, discovered what he called the "Off-shore Ground"
in 5° to 10° south latitude and 105° to 125° west longitude, where
whales teemed in countless numbers. Within ten years more than
fifty ships were whaling in this locality. The crews of two whale
ships, the *Balaena* of New Bedford and the *Equator* of Nantucket,
killed a whale off Kealakekua Bay, Hawaii, in September 1819, and
during the next two months two other whalers visited the Islands,
the vanguard of a vast fleet to use the ports.[3]

Another impetus to the industry was given by the opening of
the Arctic fishery. During the late 1820's the whaling industry replaced the traffic in sandalwood as the chief commercial activity in
the Pacific. Six-sevenths of the world's whaling fleet operated in that
ocean, and the majority of the ships concerned came from New
England. The recurrent visits of large fleets of whale ships to
Hawaiian ports were a significant factor in shaping the history of
the Islands and their people. Favorite ports of call were Honolulu,
on Oahu; Lahaina, on Maui; Hilo, on Hawaii; and Waimea, on Kauai
—with a preponderant preference for Honolulu. During the twenty-
year period of 1824–43 approximately seventeen hundred whaling
ships arrived at Honolulu, an average of about eighty-five annually,
nearly fourteen hundred of which were American, while slightly
more than three hundred were British.[4]

The golden age—when the Hawaiian Kingdom enjoyed its greatest prosperity from the whalers—coincided with the long reign of

Kamehameha III (1825–54). The average number of vessels stopping at the Islands annually from 1843 to 1855 was four hundred and nineteen, the great majority being American.[5] A zenith was reached in the whaling industry during the late 1850's. By that time activities in several other fields served to bind the Hawaiian Islands and their people closer to the United States.

Thus in the early nineteenth century, "sandalwood, geography, and fresh provisions made the islands a vital link in a closely articulated trade route, between Boston, the Northwest Coast, and Canton."[6] By the 1840's, the Sandwich Islands were an economic, commercial, and religious frontier. Although removed from the Atlantic seaboard by thousands of miles of water requiring five to six months to traverse, Hawaii had become an outpost of New England. Besides the Hudson's Bay Company's agency, there were in Honolulu six business houses. Of these, four were American, one British, and one French. The little community might not have been quite as Yankee as a Boston suburb, yet the town was certainly more American than European.

Cultural Influences

MISSIONARY endeavors were a significant, if not a preponderant, magnet in drawing Hawaii from the British into the American sphere of influence. Although the missionaries' primary interest was nonpolitical, their direct and intimate association with both the chiefs and the commoners gave them a personal ascendancy over the Hawaiian mind, and consciously or unconsciously presented to it an American point of view. Although evangelism was the primary function of the Congregational and Presbyterian missionaries who journeyed to the Sandwich Islands under the auspices of the American Board of Commissioners for Foreign Missions, they immediately set about to systematize the Hawaiian language, to prepare a literature to be used in the churches and schools, and to develop an educational system. Teaching and printing played a large and significant role in the Christianizing process. Through the printed word, the missionaries gained access to the hearts and minds of their pupils: religious concepts and ideas were incorporated in the reading material, and teachers converted as they taught.

The achievements of the mission press are indeed impressive.

The mission had three presses in operation by 1840 and had printed one hundred million pages, covering perhaps fifty different works. The entire Bible had been printed in the Hawaiian language by May 10, 1839. Thirteen separate works in the Hawaiian language were published by the Oahu Mission's press in Honolulu and six others by the press at Lahainaluna during the year ending May, 1840.[7] The volumes written or translated and printed by that year embraced a wider range of literature than that which constituted the library of many young people in progressive New England in the 1830's, to say nothing of the less fortunate parts of the United States and the world. By 1873 not less than one hundred and fifty different works, as well as thirteen magazines and an *Almanac*, 1834–62, had been prepared and printed—in excess of two hundred million pages.[8] Credit must be given the Sandwich Islands missionaries for making a substantial beginning in the development of printed Hawaiian literature.[9]

The educational work of the missionaries, initiated first among the chiefs, their children, and the advisers, developed through several stages, eventually offering primary and secondary education and manual training to a large percentage of the Islands' population. A high school was established at Lahainaluna, or Upper Lahaina, on Maui, to "instruct men of piety and promising talents" in order that they might become assistant teachers. At the request of the chiefs, a family or boarding school was opened in Honolulu in 1839 for the education of their children, and remained under mission supervision until 1846, when it was placed under the Ministry of Public Instruction and designated the "Royal School." Punahou School, later known as Oahu College, developed into a preparatory school, elementary and secondary, and performed a distinctive service through the education of a significant proportion of Hawaii's business and professional leaders. In instituting several manual-labor schools, the missionaries were forty years ahead of their contemporaries in the United States. The educational work of the Sandwich Islands Mission up to 1840, when it surrendered the administration of the common schools to the Government, was of incalculable value in disseminating knowledge to all classes of people in the Kingdom, in planting and nurturing religious concepts and some of the better features of Western civilization, and in laying the foundation for a system of public instruction in the English language.[10]

In the technical, mechanical, and industrial fields, the efforts and performance of the missionaries were commendable. Hiram Bingham's pioneer company, which arrived in 1820, included a printer, a teacher and a skilled mechanic, and a prosperous Massachusetts farmer, and carried a supply of seeds and agricultural implements, the most important tools of various mechanical arts, surgical instruments, and a twenty-year-old Ramage printing press. These Puritans were the first in Hawaii to yoke oxen. By introducing foreign plants, milling sugar and molasses, and starting spinning and weaving cottage industries, they demonstrated their interest in teaching Hawaiians new trades. In the construction of stone churches and schoolhouses, to supplant the native grass structures, missionaries laid the plans and superintended the work. Realizing their limited resources and numbers, they appealed, in a memorial drafted in July, 1836, to the American Board or some society formed on similar principles to send agricultural and industrial teachers. Thus, one hundred and thirteen years before President Truman's "bold new program" for making the benefits of American scientific know-how and industrial progress available for the advancement of undeveloped areas of the world, the Sandwich Island missionaries demonstrated a genuine and prophetic acquaintance with the requirements of a people lacking skill, enterprise, and industry. The missionaries' schools served as the first American technical mission overseas; their tireless labors and simple instruction in the agricultural, mechanical, and manual fields represented the first chapter in the prelude to Point Four.[11]

The unique achievements and moral victories of the Sandwich Islands Mission were possible because its members, as a whole, were men and women of superior ability and training. Even more important were their intense convictions, their profound altruistic enthusiasm, and a triumphant certainty of success in their divine task. For the first quarter of a century after its advent in 1820, this Christian Mission was by far the predominating white influence in the Islands, and for another twenty-five years "it so assimilated and moulded the other growing white elements as to secure their practical cooperation." In the words of the Rev. Sereno E. Bishop, son of the Rev. Artemas Bishop of the first reinforcement, "the whole community, both native and foreign, became subject to their controlling moral and social influence. With the natives the yielding was trustful and willing. With the restive and violent whites it was quite otherwise, yet conclusive and effectual."[12]

The return of missionary couples in the late 1840's to the United

States for their children's education, combined with the movement of population toward California and Oregon and the swing of world interest into the Pacific region, created in 1848 a "grand crisis" for the Sandwich Islands Mission. The problem was finally resolved by the American Board's revision of its original policies concerning secular pursuits, the acquisition of property, and citizenship. Mission property, including herds, was divided, and the missionaries were encouraged to become naturalized Hawaiians and remain in the Islands. As a further inducement, provision was made for the college education of mission children at Punahou, for which the Hawaiian Government agreed to grant land.[13] These decisions changed the course of the Kingdom's history and brought the nation more and more under American influence. Out of the seventy-seven married couples who sojourned in the Islands, forty-two families continued to be represented by descendants. Among them the grandson of the Rev. Asa Thurston, the son of the Rev. Daniel Dole, the son of the Rev. William P. Alexander, and the sons of two secular agents of the mission, Amos Starr Cooke and Samuel N. Castle, became powerful in the economic and political life of Hawaii and influenced tremendously its destiny.

Political Role of Americans

THE major credit for the predominating political influence of the United States in Hawaii "is almost universally given to the missionaries—and rightly so."[14] In the beginning the members of the mission were in a strict sense *amici curiae*, remaining in the background, prompting, teaching, and guiding the rulers. From the peculiar nature and structure of the Government, and the fact that the dominant chiefs were zealous advocates of the church, "it came to pass that church and state were actively for a time united." The churches, schools, teachers—the whole system of religious order and influence —depended in no small degree upon the support and sanction of the Government.

Missionary prompting was behind three laws of December 8, 1827: murder was prohibited on penalty of death, and theft and adultery on penalty of confinement in irons. The Hawaiian Declaration of Rights plainly showed the influence of both the Bible and the United States Declaration of Independence.

Decidedly against the ancient system of government by 1838, certain missionaries, newcomers to the Islands, spoke out sharply in the *Kuma Hawaii* (*Hawaiian Teacher*). The *Hawaiian Spectator*, among whose founders and first contributors were several missionaries, also emphasized the "importance and bearing of other efforts for converting the world, besides such as are generally termed missionary efforts; such as gradual change of their laws and political institutions."[15] Thus the evangelists, before officially advising the chiefs, resorted to the press as a medium of instituting needed reforms.

Soon, however, members of the mission openly joined the service of King Kamehameha III, often severing their connections with the American Board to serve the Government full time. The Rev. William Richards was prevailed upon in 1838 to accept an appointment as "chaplain, teacher and translator" to the King. During his first year with the Government the clergyman devoted a little less than three months' time to the King and chiefs and continued to do "a large share of the native preaching in the church which he had served so many years."[16] Eventually, Dr. Gerrit P. Judd, Richard Armstrong, and Lorrin Andrews followed Richards' example in entering this new sphere of endeavor which promised to increase their usefulness and in which they hoped to enjoy the same confidence that they had had under the immediate direction of the American Board.

American laymen with legal background were also drawn into the service of the Hawaiian Government. The first, John Ricord, appointed Attorney General on March 9, 1844, helped to interpret the Constitution of 1840 and prepared drafts of the three organic acts, providing for the Privy Council, the Executive Department, and the Judiciary. He created the Courts of Chancery, Probate, and Admiralty, and provided them with a body of law by which their adjudication should be governed. This was accomplished by adopting the common and civil law as administered especially in Great Britain and the United States, and by attempting to make court decisions conform to practices and precedents in these countries. Ricord also contributed his legal and literary talents to the initial work of the Land Commission. In interpreting and reforming the Constitution to meet the exigencies of a small kingdom having intercourse with the great powers and their citizens, he adopted so far as possible the principles of the British constitution and attempted to assimilate Hawaiian laws, influenced by American practices, to British models.[17]

The second man taken into service was William Little Lee, who, on a stopover en route to Oregon in 1846, was persuaded to remain and head the prospective judicial system. At the age of twenty-six, only seven weeks after reaching Hawaiian soil, Lee became one of the leading men of the Kingdom. Before his premature death on May 28, 1857, he was reported "to control almost every important action of the government."[18] As Chief Justice of the newly created Superior Court, he emphasized the interpretation and enforcement of the law, with dignified and unostentatious guidance. His abilities were still further recognized by appointment to the Privy Council and to membership on the Land Commission. When the Legislative Council requested him to draft civil and criminal codes, Lee, drawing liberally from the proposed penal codes of Massachusetts and Louisiana, drafted one which remained the permanent basis of Hawaiian criminal law.[19] He also participated in the preparation of the civil code, which was not completed until after his death. He was elected a member of the House of Representatives, from which judges were not excluded until the adoption of the Constitution of 1864, and he served ably as the Speaker of that chamber. Judge Lee, representing the House of Representatives on the three-member commission which drafted the Constitution of 1852, did much of the preparation of that instrument, which represents his democratic point of view. After its adoption, Lee was appointed Chief Justice of a reconstituted Supreme Court and held this position, as well as that of Chancellor of the Kingdom, until his death.[20] This American served both Kamehameha III and Kamehameha IV "with a talent, integrity, and devotion" to "Their Majesties' interest and the cause of justice, never surpassed."[21]

Elisha H. Allen, a practicing lawyer in Maine before he was named to the consulate in Honolulu, was appointed Minister of Finance by Kamehameha III, a post which he retained until he succeeded Lee as Chief Justice and Chancellor of the Kingdom. He was held in high esteem by the young King. Allen's greater period of service to Hawaii came, however, in the mid-1860's, when with Minister of Foreign Affairs Robert C. Wyllie he controlled government policy.

In September, 1845, Lorrin Andrews, a missionary educator without legal training, was appointed by Kekuanaoa, the progressive governor of Oahu, to act as his substitute in his court in Honolulu in all cases between or affecting the interests of foreigners, whether alien or naturalized. It was Andrews' integrity and his facility with the Hawaiian language that recommended him to the King and chiefs. The mild yet firm manner in which he administered the duties of his office not only created a favorable impression upon the public but also won him the esteem of those convicted. Under an act to organize the Judiciary, passed in April 1846, he was officially designated a judge of original and appellate jurisdiction. When the Superior Court of Law and Equity was created the following year, Andrews, along with John Ii, was appointed associate justice of a tribunal that was substantially a supreme court in all but name. In 1854 he was named a probate judge, having concurrent jurisdiction with the judges of the Supreme Court in hearing and determining probate and divorce cases in which native Hawaiians were involved. The former missionary's "correct knowledge of the native language" rendered "him particularly fitted" to fill this post.[19] In the Privy Council, to which he was appointed in 1846, Andrews served for several years as secretary, and to him we are indebted for the early records of that body kept in both English and Hawaiian.

On the death of William Richards, Kamehameha III's councilors were of the opinion that since the mission had done so much for the nation, a missionary should be appointed to the vacancy in the Ministry of Public Education. The Rev. Richard Armstrong's fifteen years' acquaintance with Hawaiian life, language, and customs, his deep concern for the welfare of the nation, his editorship of two native-language newspapers, and his zeal for the cause of education made him the natural choice for the vacant post. Moreover, fears were expressed that if he declined the position the then existing public instruction system would probably be abolished for want of a suitable man.[23] In 1848 Armstrong accepted the position and was vigilant in his defense of the common schools, which he considered the "poor man's college," for "the little education he gets is there." Instruction of boys in the elements of agriculture and of girls in homemaking he viewed as fundamental, and he made strenuous efforts to have some sort of manual labor connected with every school. His general plan was to "aim at the improvement of the heart, the head and the body, at once."[24] Through extensive tours of inspection, Armstrong kept in touch with the outlying areas. He encouraged the teaching of English, insofar as possible with the limited sources available, and he recommended an appropriation to aid in the support of English-language schools. He also favored and promoted the expansion of Punahou School into Oahu College, because it would eliminate the expense and risk of sending youths in pursuit of a liberal education to the Americas or Europe, and would create a class of learned men on the Islands.[25] The legislation enacted between 1848 and 1855 recognized the principle that public schools should be conducted at public expense, in keeping with American practice. Armstrong's services to his adopted country extended beyond the field of religion and education to include matters of land distribution and utilization. Realizing that the first steps toward democracy should be in granting the people undisputed right to the land they occupied, he, along with Judd, Lee, and Wyllie, convinced the King and chiefs, and in 1848, Kamehameha III granted the *Mahele*, or division of the lands of the Kingdom.

Of the eight outstanding foreign officials who served Kamehameha III—Richards, Judd, Wyllie, Ricord, Andrews, Lee, Armstrong, and Allen—all but Wyllie were Americans and four had previously been connected with the Sandwich Islands Mission. Undeniably, missionary personnel provided the leadership in the formative days of the Hawaiian constitutional monarchy. Richards, Judd, Armstrong, and, to a lesser extent, Andrews, were instrumental in bringing about a new political and economic organization in the Hawaiian Kingdom, having played a vital role in instituting the Declaration of Rights, the Constitution of 1840, the *Mahele*, financial and juridical reforms, and the school laws, all of which were strongly influenced by American ideals and practice. Thus missionary work which began with proclaiming the gospel eventually led to the reorganization of the national polity.

In spite of the preponderance of American commercial and business interests in the Hawaiian Kingdom, the ubiquitous moral and social influence of the Puritan missionaries, and the predominance of Americans in government, certain factors tended to militate against American prestige in the Islands. One was the lack of unity among the Americans themselves. There was a division, from 1824 on, between the missionary and anti-missionary parties, who at times waged outright war on each other. Hawaiians observed the unedifying spectacle of American citizens attacking the persons and homes of revered clergymen. Petitions and memorials prepared and sponsored by American malcontents and directed against their countrymen were not uncommon. In addition, certain members of the British diplomatic corps exploited American racial prejudice and slavery in order to stir up antipathy against "Yankees."

This was not difficult. Returning from London in 1850, the two impressionable teen-age royal princes had been subjected to offensive racial prejudice when they visited the United States with **Dr. Judd**. In contrast, on the Continent and in England they were accorded the courtesies and honors befitting royal visitors. The violent slavery controversy on the mainland, the "bleeding Kansas" episode, and the Civil War, which appeared to demonstrate the weakness and vulnerability of the American democratic system, did not add to the esteem and admiration of the United States in the Islands. Moreover, the behavior of irresponsible residents provided a basis for British and French contentions that Americans were hostile to the Hawaiian race.

Throughout his reign of thirty years, Kamehameha III generally relied on the advice and counsel of American missionaries for problems of state. They were his most loyal subjects and faithful supporters. However, Prince Alexander Liholiho, who ascended the throne as Kamehameha IV on December 15, 1854, definitely had anti-missionary feelings. The new King immediately reappointed all the ministers who were in office when his predecessor died. The following year, the office of Minister of Public Instruction was abolished, and for it was substituted a board of education consisting of a president and two other directors: Prince Lot Kamehameha and Elisha H. Allen. As president of the board, Richard Armstrong continued as head of the school system, but ceased to be a member of the Cabinet. Ostensibly this change was made to enable Armstrong to devote all his time and energy to the public schools, but the ulterior motive appeared to be the desire to remove missionary influence from the inner circle of government. This influence waned after 1855, and never again did American missionaries—or those of any other nationality—hold high cabinet positions or wield the power of a William Richards or Gerrit P. Judd. In the summer of that year no member of the Cabinet had ever been connected with the American Mission, and an Englishman, Charles Gordon Hopkins, replaced Edwin O. Hall, a former secular agent of the Sandwich Islands Mission, as editor of the *Polynesian*, the official organ of the Government. Thereafter, that journal constantly sought to depress American and elevate British character. The effect of the new management of this newspaper was to diminish the favorable opinion of the Hawaiian people toward the United States.[26] Finally, when David L. Gregg, formerly United States Commissioner, was forced to resign his post as Hawaiian Minister of Finance in late August, 1862, the King's Cabinet contained not a single American. The veteran Robert C. Wyllie was the commanding figure in government.

Annexation of the Pacific archipelago to the United States was seldom mentioned and never officially considered in the first half of the nineteenth century; after 1850 the subject was frequently discussed both in Hawaii and on the mainland. The United States Government made no official propositions providing for union before 1854, but it was determined to resist strenuously any attempt on the part of Great Britain or France to obtain possession of the Islands, and refused to enter with the governments of those countries into a tripartite agreement regarding Hawaii. In the spring and summer of that year a treaty of annexation was laboriously negotiated and thoroughly considered for nearly three months by the Privy Council, but it remained unratified by the ailing Kamehameha III and was withdrawn by his successor. During the period of negotiations British Consul General William Miller repeatedly raised the question of American racial prejudice and slavery to frighten and deter the Hawaiian chiefs, the Crown Prince, and the King. The treaty's statehood article, insisted upon by Foreign Minister Wyllie and Judge Lee in an effort to shield the inhabitants of the Islands from slavery, made the treaty unacceptable to President Franklin Pierce.[27] Even with statehood Prince Alexander Liholiho did not favor the union of Hawaii with the United States, and at the beginning of his reign several Americans who were known to have been active in or to have shown sympathy for the annexation movement were removed from office. Thereafter, numerous suggestions for annexation emanated from various sources, but never from a Hawaiian sovereign.

Thus, by the late 1850's American political influence in the counsels of the King and chiefs had sharply diminished. But, as the whaling industry had replaced the traffic in sandalwood in the late 1820's, the cultivation of sugar, with its concomitant activities, superseded whaling in the 1860's, and in this new field of economic endeavor Americans were to remain dominant.[28]

NOTES

1. Samuel E. Morison, "Boston Traders in the Hawaiian Islands, 1794," Massachusetts Historical Society, *Proceedings*, LIV (1920–21), 11, 16.
2. Harold Whitman Bradley, *The American Frontier in Hawaii: The Pioneers, 1789–1843* (Palo Alto, 1942), pp. 119–20.
3. Alexander Starbuck, *History of the American Whale Fishery from Its Earliest Inception to the Year 1876* (Waltham, Mass., 1878), p. 96.
4. Ralph S. Kuykendall, "American Interests and American Influence in Hawaii in 1842," HHS Thirty-Ninth *Report*, 1930 (Honolulu, 1931), p. 49.
5. Raymond A. Rydell, *Cape Horn to the Pacific* (Berkeley and Los Angeles, 1952), pp. 70, 73.
6. Morison, p. 14.
7. *Missionary Herald* (Boston), organ of and published by the American Board of Commissioners for Foreign Missions, XXXV (1839), 145–46, XXXVII (1841), 145.
8. Rufus Anderson, *History of the Sandwich Islands Mission* (Boston, 1870), pp. 390–97; Anderson, *The Hawaiian Islands: Their Progress and Condition under Missionary Labors* (Boston and New York, 1864), pp. 262–68.
9. See my "The Sandwich Islands Missionaries Create a Literature," *Church History*, XXI (1962), 182–202, for a catalogue of publications, see pp. 197–202.
10. See my "The Sandwich Islands Missionaries Lay the Foundation for a System of Public Instruction in Hawaii," *Journal of Negro Education*, XXX (1961), 396–405.
11. See my "Sandwich Islands Missionaries: The First American Point Four Agents," HHS Seventieth *Report*, 1961 (Honolulu, 1962), pp. 7–23.
12. S. E. Bishop, "The American Missionaries Here," *Pacific Commercial Advertiser* (Honolulu), July 2, 1906, p. 81.
13. Rufus Anderson to the Sandwich Islands Mission, July 19, 1848, and May 8, 1850, *General Letters of the ABCFM* (Honolulu, 1834–59), pp. 9–10, 30. Printed as leaflets, leaves, or broadsides for circulation among members of the mission. Pages refer to each letter, not to the volume. See my "The 'Grand Crisis' for the Sandwich Islands Mission and the Year of Decision," *Journal of Religious Thought*, XX (1963), 43–52.
14. Kuykendall, p. 55. For a general treatment of the subject, see my "The Early Political Influence of the Sandwich Islands Missionaries," *Journal of Religious Thought*, XVII (1960), 117–32.
15. *Hawaiian Spectator*, I (1838), frontispiece. See the first issue of Jan., 1838, pp. 55–57, for a considered view of conditions in Hawaii written by Rev. Artemas Bishop. These early issues of the *Hawaiian Spectator* are in the Spaulding Collection, University of Michigan Library, but not in the Library of Congress.
16. Richards to Rufus Anderson, Aug. 1, 1838, Letters of the American Board (Harvard College Library), Vol. CXXXV, No. 83; William Richards, "Report to the Sandwich Islands Mission on His First Year in Government Service, 1838–1839," HHS Fifty-First *Report*, 1942 (Honolulu, 1943), p. 68.
17. W. R. Castle, "Sketch of Constitutional History of Hawaii," HHS Twenty-Third *Report*, 1914 (Honolulu, 1915), p. 16. For further information on

Ricord, see the pamphlet *Motion in the Hawaiian Parliament, Made by R. C. Wyllie . . . to Release John Ricord . . . from a Debt Standing against Him in the Books of the King's Treasury . . .* (Honolulu, 1853), and a manuscript title on John Ricord by A. F. Judd, II, read before the Bar Association of Hawaii, June 20, 1923 (Hawaiian Mission Children's Society Library, Honolulu).

18. David L. Gregg to Sec. of State William L. Marcy, March 9, 1857, No. 207, USDS, Dispatches, Hawaii, VIII.

19. *Penal Code of the Hawaiian Islands, Passed by the House of Nobles and Representatives on the 21st of June, A.D. 1850; to Which Are Appended the Other Acts Passed by the House of Nobles and Representatives during Their General Session for 1850* (Honolulu, 1850); cf. pp. iii–iv for Lee's report on the preparation of the code, and the *Polynesian* (Honolulu), Aug. 3, 10, 17, 1850, for "an Act Establishing a Penal Code."

20. Thomas M. Spaulding, "Chief Justice William Little Lee," *Honolulu Mercury*, II (1930), 346–47, and Thomas M. Spaulding, "William Little Lee," *Dictionary of American Biography*, XI, 135.

21. Wyllie to Ricord, Dec. 1854, AH, FO & Ex., Misc. Foreign file.

22. King Kamehameha IV to Privy Council, Dec. 25, 1854, AH, Local Officials.

23. Armstrong to Ruben A. Chapman, Dec. 8, 1847, Armstrong-Chapman Papers, Library of Congress. Armstrong's concern and anxiety for the future of the Hawaiian Kingdom runs through his correspondence with his brother-in-law, Judge Chapman of Massachusetts. See especially his letters of March 3, 1843, Sept. 18, 1844, Oct. 5, 1846, and Oct. 11, 1847.

24. Armstrong to Chapman, Sept. 8, 1848, Armstrong-Chapman Papers; cf. *Report of President of Board of Education, 1856* (Honolulu, 1856), p. 5. This plan was carried by Armstrong's son, Gen. Samuel C. Armstrong, to Hampton Institute, whence Booker T. Washington went to train the head, the hand, and the heart of Negroes at Tuskegee Institute. The idea was borrowed by Mahatma Gandhi for his basic education of the masses of India.

25. *Report of the Minister of Public Instruction, 1856* (Honolulu, 1856), p. 5; Benjamin O. Wist, *A Century of Public Education in Hawaii* (Honolulu, 1940), pp. 60–61.

26. Gregg to Marcy, May 3, 1856, No. 163, USDS, Dispatches, Hawaii, IV.

27. See my "Slavery and Racism as Deterrents to the Annexation of Hawaii, 1854–1855," *Journal of Negro History*, XLVII (1962), pp. 10–11, 17–18.

28. Rydell, p. 73. For a similar but more comprehensive treatment of early American interest and influence in the Sandwich Islands, see my *The United States and the Hawaiian Kingdom* (New Haven, 1965), pp. 1–26. The permission of the Yale University Press to reproduce parts of those pages is hereby acknowledged.

Part I

HAWAIIAN SUGAR, PROSPERITY,

AND RECIPROCITY TO

1881

Indies died in 1827, more than a hundred acres of cane were under cultivation. The following year a new venture in sugar production and utilization was undertaken when the Governor, either by lease or partnership, allowed William French, Stephen Reynolds, John C. Jones, and John Ebbets to distill rum in a sugar house converted into a distillery. The resident missionaries, however, refused to allow their oxen to haul the cane, and Queen Regent Kaahumanu cancelled the Manoa lease and had sweet potatoes planted on the land.[3]

Two factors retarded the development of the Hawaiian sugar industry: the lucrative whaling business and the feudal system of land tenure. The first extensive cultivation of the plant on a more or less permanent plantation was begun in 1835 by William Ladd, Allan Brinsmade, and William Hooper, who obtained a fifty-year lease on about one thousand acres of land at Koloa, on the island of Kauai. Lack of implements and draft animals added to the difficulties in getting started. The ground was broken by plows drawn by humans who were paid twelve and one-half cents a day plus food. The novelty of wage payments attracted retainers away from the chiefs' estates, and the large plantation also demonstrated the advantages of large-scale sugar culture as compared with haphazard growing on small tracts.

The first sugar mill at Koloa was a crude wooden press, but by the end of 1837 an iron mill was in operation, and in 1841 an improved mill run by water power was installed. The plantation produced 5,039 pounds of sugar and 400 gallons of molasses from one acre of plant cane in 1838, an immense yield for those days. However, failure to realize that growing and refining operations had to be combined led to the abandonment of the enterprise after a few years.

Meanwhile, in 1838, American missionaries stationed on Kauai set up a sugar mill. In that year twenty crude mills run by animal power and two run by water power were in operation. The cane was fed by hand, one stalk at a time. The rollers were sometimes of wood, and the kettles in which the juice was boiled were whalers' try-pots.[4] Many mills were erected in the Islands during the following decade, especially on Maui, Oahu, and Kauai, the tendency being to replace many small mills with larger and more efficient ones, and small fields of cane with big plantations under centralized management. In 1848 Dr. Robert W. Wood and A. H. Spencer bought out Ladd and Company. By combining growing and refining processes, the new firm soon prospered. Spencer later became the Honolulu representative of the German H. Hackfeld Company which handled trade goods in Hawaii and sandalwood throughout Polynesia.

There are records that indicate the export of Hawaiian sugar to California as early as 1827 and to Australia in 1833. In February of the former year Captain F. W. Beechey of H.B.M.S. *Blossom*, visiting Honolulu, wrote to a gentleman in California: "The Sandwich Islanders think of sending a cargo of sugar to your coast in a few months—the sugar has been made here, and looks very good indeed."[5] Nine years later, in 1836, only four tons were exported; by 1876 the figure had risen to approximately thirteen thousand tons. In addition, a large quantity of sugar was consumed locally and sold to visiting ships and whalers. In the forty-year period before reciprocity, the Hawaiian sugar industry made much progress in dealing with problems of land, irrigation, labor, technology, financing, and marketing.

The first sugar refined in Hawaii was poor in quality, and it was not until 1842 that a fair marketable grade was produced. Although the volume of production increased between 1843 and 1850, the quality of the refined product improved but slightly. It was evident that raw sugar could be produced in the Islands equal, if not superior, to that grown in other parts of the world, but "the sugar of superior quality was more often the result of chance than of skillful operations."[6]

Prior to 1843 sparsely settled California did not afford an adequate market even for the small amount of sugar produced in the Sandwich Islands, and planters there shipped their sugars not only to the West Coast but to Chile and Australia. The hazardous sea passage often resulted in heavy losses. Also in the forties marketing standards were difficult to establish. Much of the Hawaiian sugar exported during 1849, being superior to competing sugars from Manila and Central America, had a price advantage in the California market of two or three cents a pound, and Island producers were anxious to maintain this advantage.

Hawaiian agriculture, including sugar production, was favorably affected by the *Mahele* (division of land) of 1848 and by the discovery of gold in California in the same year and in Australia in 1850. Hordes of newcomers dropped in at the Islands, a few with plenty of cash and get-rich-quick schemes, but most of them poor. Some headed for the new El Dorados, some, like William G. Irwin, remained. This influx of capital and the transfer of monies from one industry to another produced a money economy for Hawaii that quickly supplanted what remained of the barter economy. Moreover, the rush of gold seekers into California caused a critical food shortage in that area. All prices, especially those of vegetables, rose, and the favorably located Hawaiian producers were the first to reap a rich harvest. But the high prices also resulted in the dumping on the California market of foreign produce and low-grade sugars, which under normal conditions would not have been sold abroad. Consequently, the reputation of Sandwich Islands sugar suffered for a time, since the inferior grades were placed almost on a par with Hawaiian sugars.

As a result of the general economic prosperity and awakening, the Royal Hawaiian Agricultural Society was organized on August 12, 1850, at Maunakilika, Oahu. The organization was composed largely of Americans, many of whom were influential in the affairs of the Kingdom. In addition to the members residing on Oahu, there were delegates from all the Islands, and even life members residing in Boston and vicinity, including Henry A. Peirce, James F. B. Marshall, and Captain Charles Brewer, all of whom had either large investments in sugar plantations in Hawaii or in a line of freighters operating between Boston and Pacific ports. The society conducted systematic investigations in order to arouse and increase interest in agriculture and to create greater zeal among those who had been cultivating the soil without spectacular or even profitable results. One of the first acts of the organization was to announce awards for the most productive acre of sugar cane, the best keg of sugar, the best gallon of syrup, as well as the finest fruits, most perfect livestock, best grains of coffee and cereals, best potatoes, best woven cloth and mats, and so forth. The cooperation of all was urged and appeals were made to missionaries to assist in the organization of auxiliary societies on each of the larger islands.[7]

Enterprising white men, both old residents and newcomers, ventured into the Islands' sugar industry. Some of these pioneers brought capital to invest, while others came poor and pushed their way up through pluck and perseverance. Among these were many energetic Americans, but there were also Englishmen, Scotsmen, Irishmen, Norwegians, Germans, Portuguese, and Spaniards who acquired large tracts of land. A typical investor was Henry A. Peirce who had returned to Boston in 1842 after a successful business career with C. Brewer and Company. He visited the Islands in 1849 on a trading voyage to China. While in Hawaii he was struck with the possibility of developing a sugar plantation on Kauai in the vicinity of Nawili-wili Bay, and in association with Judge William L. Lee and Charles R. Bishop, proceeded to organize the firm of H. A. Peirce and Company. Later James F. B. Marshall joined the enterprise as a partner and manager of the Lihue Plantation. Half of the original capital of sixteen thousand dollars was contributed by Peirce, but before any sugar was produced, several times the original amount was invested in land, equipment, and the construction of buildings. The editor of the *Polynesian* singled out the Lihue Plantation as an excellent example of the method by which a sugar plantation should be established.[8] The first cane crop harvested in 1853 amounted to a little over one hundred tons; that of 1854, reduced by rotting caused by unseasonable storms, fell from an expected four hundred tons to fifty. Eventually, however, with efficient management and adequate capital, the Lihue Plantation developed into a profitable, permanent enterprise.[9] It led in the introduction of steam power in 1853 and thereafter steam replaced water and animal power on many plantations. The first extensive use of irrigation occurred at Lihue. There, the manager, William H. Rice, supervised in 1856 the digging of a ditch about ten miles long, including tunnels. Seven years later there were several ditches cut along the foot of the hills, for conveying and distributing the waters of the mountain streams to sugar plantations in the vicinity of Wailuku.

In contrast to Henry Peirce, a much smaller investor with very little accumulated capital, was the Rev. Richard Armstrong, who bought some six hundred acres of land, later increased to twelve hundred, on the island of Maui where he had once pastored. He obtained the services of David S. Rice, a "full-grown yankee" with "all the go-ahead of his native land in him," to plant cane on his land. Sugar could be raised for about three cents per pound and it brought seven to nine cents in the market. Although Armstrong's surplus for investment was very small, he could invest it in sugar land at twelve and a half per cent and be safe. In 1848 the average produce of an acre of cane was worth over one hundred dollars.[10]

In less than two years the farmers of Hawaii were doing well. Those who had been struggling with debt were "in funds" and some had "sold out at immense profit." At the beginning of the year 1850 there were sugar plantations worth thirty to forty thousand dollars. Land was in great demand. Land selling for one dollar an acre in 1849 now brought five. Sugar that had sold for five or six cents per pound before the gold rush now sold for fifteen cents. Thus, land rose in value and was sold both to Hawaiians and foreigners as rapidly as they applied for it.

The boom in Hawaii collapsed in 1851, and in the same year a severe drought occurred in the Islands. The sugar and coffee planters suffered from a general depression which gripped the whole Kingdom in 1851–52. The export of sugar in 1851 amounted to only 21,000 pounds in comparison with the three-quarters of a million pounds shipped in 1850. Only 27,190 pounds of coffee were exported in 1851 in sharp contrast to 208,428 pounds in 1850. But this crisis was only a temporary setback, for the settlement of California and Oregon provided a convenient and continually expanding market for Hawaiian agricultural products.

Moreover, the arrival in the Islands in 1851 of David M. Weston, of Boston, an expert mechanic induced by Henry A. Peirce to go out to set up the mill at Lihue, proved to be a significant event in the history of the sugar industry. Peirce also sent along some superior machinery for his mill. The following year two hundred and ninety-three Chinese coolies arrived, thus initiating the importation of alien labor. Weston's distinguished contribution to the Hawaiian sugar enterprise was the application of centrifugal separators for drying of sugar and freeing it from molasses. His first small machine went into operation in October, 1851 on the Koloa Plantation of Messrs. Wood and Spencer. Larger ones were ordered and their use resulted in a revolution in sugar manufacture. The new process greatly improved the quality of Island sugars without affecting quantity; thus the sugar produced brought a higher price. The centrifugal machine as finally developed performed in a few minutes a task which formerly required weeks and was then only accomplished with great waste, often as much as forty-five per cent.[11] In addition, Weston directed the starting of a foundry and machine shop in 1853 which proved to be a significant factor in accelerating the development of sugar production and also added a much needed industry to the Islands' economy. This foundry became the well-known Honolulu Iron Works.[12]

The application of improved machinery and implements, including Samuel Burbank's heavy, deep plough, particularly effective in cane fields,[13] and the importation of Chinese labor, aided in setting the infant industry on its feet. Moreover, the Hawaiian Government attempted through legislation to give an impetus to agricultural pursuits. A law of 1850 exempted from custom duties all sugar and coffee mills, steam engines, and other machinery and implements imported into the Kingdom for use in agronomy. The same act gave a similar exemption to seeds and plants and to livestock introduced for the purpose of improving the breeds of animals.[14] A superior variety of cane—called Lahaina cane, after the port of entry on Maui —was introduced in 1854 from Tahiti.

The statistics for the acreage under cane cultivation on the seven largest plantations in 1852 and 1853 indicate the increasing popularity of and confidence in the industry and also forecast its future growth:

SUGAR PLANTATION ACREAGE IN 1852 AND 1853		
PLANTATIONS AT	ACRES 1852	ACRES 1853
Lihue, Kauai	200	580
Koloa, Kauai	240	650
Honuaula, Maui	250	300
Makawao, Maui	325	500
Hana, Maui	45	130
Waimea, Hawaii	50	50
Hilo, Hawaii	540	540
	1,650	2,750

Polynesian, Oct. 23, 1852, July 30, 1853.

The *Polynesian*, figuring the average yield at one ton, or 2,000 pounds per acre, estimated the 1852 crop at 3,300,000 and that of 1853 at 5,480,000 pounds. With the price of sugar at five cents per pound, the crop of 1852 was valued at $165,000, and that of 1853 at $274,000. The journal observed that tens of thousands of acres of good land were lying uncultivated in different sections of the Islands, only needing capital and enterprise to increase the export of sugar to millions of dollars instead of a few thousand.[15] Such capital and enterprise were soon forthcoming.

By 1854 sugar had come to be looked upon as Hawaii's most promising crop. Coffee was doing well, with an export of 91,090 pounds, and it was believed that these two staples, given proper attention, could provide the exports needed to place Hawaii's economy on a sound basis. In the same year an improved mill commenced operation at Koloa, with a new train of boilers and clarifiers, and a new waterwheel built by Weston. The Koloa crop of three hundred tons produced a revenue of $46,000 at an expense of $15,000. The

cultivation of sugar cane not only continued to attract general interest
and capital, but a greater confidence in its success was evident. One
of the first firms to become directly interested in the enterprise and
to make considerable investment in it was C. Brewer and Company,
which had been founded by James Hunnewell and by him handed
on to Peirce and Brewer. In 1856 Charles Brewer 2nd and Captain
James Makee bought the East Mauian Haliimaile Plantation belonging to Stephen Reynolds, which was thereafter generally referred to
as the Brewer Plantation.[16]

The early years of sugar cultivation had been crucial ones, with
inexperienced plantation owners frequently having to cope with
drought, pests, and shortages of labor and capital. For the most part,
however, the sugar industry was favored by excellent soil, climate,
topography, and sources of water for irrigation, by adequate capital,
efficient management and marketing, and later by imported, cheap
labor, by the great United States market opened up by a reciprocity
treaty, and by absolute security of life and property.

Scientific methods of cultivation and processing, introduced mainly
by Americans, increased the average yield from one ton per acre in
1856 to two and a half tons in 1872, and four and a half tons in 1905,
with individual irrigated plantations averaging ten tons to the acre.[17]
There were particular areas in the Islands, such as the Wailuku
Valley of Maui, which in 1866 and in the 1870's produced six, eight,
ten, twelve, and even thirteen thousand pounds of sugar to the acre
on unfertilized soil.[18]

The chief obstacles to trade were the high tariff on sugar imported
into the United States and the competition of cheap sugars from
Manila, China, and Central America, where the cost of production
was not so high; consequently, the large importation into the West
coast from these areas in the early fifties almost excluded Hawaiian
products. To overcome these difficulties, efforts were directed toward
securing a reciprocity agreement with the United States which would
open the great American market to Hawaiian goods free of duty.

First Proposals of Reciprocity

THE first efforts to secure a reciprocity agreement were made by
Hawaii in September, 1848, immediately after the Mexican War

settlement had definitely ceded California to the United States. Theodore Shillaber, an American merchant largely engaged in foreign trade at the Islands and well-acquainted with their internal commerce, was sent from Honolulu to San Francisco as special commissioner to negotiate an agreement with the governor of California whereby Hawaiian agricultural products might be admitted into that territory at five per cent ad valorem, the same rate at which American merchandise was admitted to the Hawaiian Kingdom. He was also instructed that "all the privileges of any kind allowed to vessels under the American flag in Hawaiian ports, should be allowed to vessels under the Hawaiian flag, in American ports."

Minister of Foreign Affairs Robert C. Wyllie, in commissioning Shillaber, advanced the same arguments for reciprocity that were to become hackneyed over the following four decades. "The effects of such a reciprocity," the Minister wrote, "would be greatly to promote the agriculture, commerce and shipping of the Islands, and to introduce profitable industry generally among the natives." The opening of the markets of California and Oregon would promote the development of the Islands' resources, banish idleness and vice, "increase the consumption of American goods here, and cement by the strong tie of the greatest mutual interest the friendly relationships that have subsisted between the two states for the last 26 years." Wyllie emphasized that "nearly three-fourths of the Foreign Shipping trading to these Islands, and of foreign goods imported, are of American origin or on American account." Regardless of how premature the mission might appear, the Minister of Foreign Affairs wished on the part of the Hawaiian King's Government "to welcome the United States in their nearer approach to the shores of this independent Kingdom" and "to lay the foundation of lasting friendship."[19] Since, under the Constitution of the United States, Governor Mason of California could not assume to commence even the preliminaries of a negotiation of a treaty with a foreign power unless he had been especially authorized for that purpose by the federal government, nothing came of the proposal. Wyllie, however, sought to gain the same ends through commercial treaty negotiations which he was conducting with the United States Commissioner, Anthony Ten Eyck, to whom he submitted a draft of a reciprocity agreement on October 13, 1848.

Later in the same month, in Washington D.C., James Jackson Jarves and Secretary of State James Buchanan discussed difficulties at the Sandwich Islands relating to land titles of Americans. Jarves expressed the opinion that the Hawaiian King might be induced to allow Americans to sell their properties to other aliens or, upon the relinquishment of the King's rights, to convey freehold titles in the town of Honolulu, provided the United States "were willing to grant privileges equal in value to Hawaiian citizens, by way of admission of their sugar, coffee, &c, free into the U.S." Buchanan was anxious to negotiate a commercial treaty and was willing that "it should be upon a *perfect basis of reciprocity, as to duties, rights &c.*" If American goods were to be admitted free to the Islands, Hawaiian products should be admitted free into the United States.[20] The Jarves-Clayton Treaty of December 20, 1849, however, did not provide for reciprocal duty-free admission of products.

During the boom of 1849–50 the need for a free market was not so evident and was not pressed. But "Tacitus," in a letter to the *Polynesian* of December 22, 1849, advocated the negotiation of a reciprocal agreement with the United States for the admission of Hawaiian sugar, molasses, and other products into the Pacific coast area in exchange for admitting free American products into Hawaii. The depression of 1851–52 emphasized the necessity of such action. The *Polynesian* returned to the subject and published two editorials urging that an energetic effort be made to obtain "An Important Desideratum," a reciprocity agreement with the United States. The editor observed: "We can make sugar of the very best quality, but we want a market for it, unencumbered by a burdensome duty of 30 per cent." He considered that the permanent interests of the Islands depended upon the development of their agricultural resources and insisted that California and Oregon were the natural markets for Hawaiian products. He proposed a convention of planters and businessmen to further the object of reciprocity which would have the effect of concentrating their opinions and views, and might induce the Government to send a special agent to Washington D.C. to propose the arrangement to the United States Government. The *Polynesian* invited discussion of the subject and opened its columns for the purpose.[21]

Minister Wyllie again brought up the subject of reciprocity in January, 1852, this time with Luther Severance, the United States Commissioner, who discussed the practicability of admitting Hawaiian sugar into California and Oregon free of duty in exchange for the free admission to the Islands of flour, salmon, lumber, and other products of the Pacific coast. This arrangement, he believed, would be beneficial to the people on both sides, would "give a great impulse to the sugar cultivation of the Islands," and would not affect the planters of Louisiana. The Commissioner presumed that a treaty stipulation was not necessary, that the desired results could be achieved by an act of Congress, and that the President's recommendation of such "at the present session would be hailed with joy by the planters here and readily concurred in by the Hawaiian Government."[22]

In a dispatch of February 14, Severance urged the importance of the cultivation of sugar to the island Kingdom as a means of paying for its large imports of foreign goods. On March 1, Wyllie transmitted to the Commissioner an act of the King and Privy Council proposing a reciprocal repeal of certain duties of the Government of the United States and of the Hawaiian Kingdom. In forwarding this to the State Department, Severance explained that the Hawaiian Government was not contemplating the admission of Hawaiian sugar into the Atlantic ports of the United States. The Pacific ports, with their rapidly increasing population, would take all the sugar which could be produced on the Islands for many years to come. Nor was the unqualified repeal of American duties on sugar desired by the Hawaiians, for this would leave them still to compete with sugar from China and the Philippines, and little would be gained by the proposed arrangement if it had the effect of admitting Spanish sugar into American ports free.[23]

Meanwhile, a February 28 meeting of the board of managers of the Royal Hawaiian Agricultural Society prepared a petition calling upon the Hawaiian Government to open negotiations with the United States which would secure the introduction of certain staples of each country—stipulated in the resolution—into each others' ports free of duty.[24]

Acting in response to this petition, King Kamehameha III and his Council agreed upon a measure providing that American flour, fish, coal, lumber, staves, and heading would be admitted free of duty into Hawaii if the United States reciprocally admitted free of duty Hawaiian sugar, syrup of sugar, molasses, and coffee. Severance endorsed this proposal, stating that "it is considered almost a matter of life or death with those who have invested their means in sugar estates." He was of the opinion that if acted upon favorably by the Congress then in session, it would infuse new life into the languishing plantations at the Islands and confer a corresponding benefit upon all other branches of business.[25] Washington, however, was unresponsive and no agreement resulted from the overtures.

Negotiations of 1855–1857

THE tantalizingly good markets of California and Oregon could be secured either by a reciprocity treaty or by the annexation of Hawaii to the United States. Both plans had been proposed and rejected. Annexation was favored not only by sugar and coffee planters and livestock interests in Hawaii, but by advocates of "manifest destiny" in the United States and their supporters in the Islands.

With the accession of Kamehameha IV (Alexander Liholiho) on December 15, 1854, the negotiations for annexation to the United States, which had been in progress with Commissioner David L. Gregg, were terminated, and substituted for them were proposals for a treaty of reciprocity and a tripartite or quadripartite guarantee of Hawaiian independence.

The new Sovereign was interested in both reciprocity and the preservation of his Kingdom's independence. The two problems were interrelated. He feared that the predominance of American interest in the Islands might result in their annexation; therefore, he wished to counteract such influences and to remove "the causes of discontent at home."[26] Realizing that the Hawaiian sugar industry was seriously hampered by the high tariff of the United States, that it suffered from the competition of sugar from the Philippines, and that such a situation influenced many sugar planters—American by birth or parentage —to favor annexation, he was interested in reciprocity in trade as a substitute for annexation, and coupled it with another facet of his policy, a quadripartite treaty with the United States, Great Britain, and France to respect and maintain the independence of Hawaii.

Chief Justice and Chancellor William L. Lee, one of the most powerful and highly respected government officials and the King's most trusted adviser, was planning to visit the United States for rest and medical advice and was entrusted with the important two-fold mission. His ability and prestige qualified him to conduct negotiations with Secretary of State William L. Marcy and with the Ministers of Great Britain and France in Washington.

The mission was given special consideration in five Cabinet Council meetings,[27] and, in the general instructions issued by Wyllie, Lee was authorized to negotiate a tripartite treaty "for the preservation of the King's Sovereignty and of the Independence of the Hawaiian people as a distinct nationality, hostile to no nation and equally friendly to all." He was also "to negotiate, if possible, such a Treaty of reciprocity, as will benefit the agriculture and trade of the Kingdom, remove the argument for annexation to the United States founded on self interest, and yet not infringe any of the King's existing Treaties with other Foreign nations."[28]

Minister Wyllie notified Gregg of Lee's appointment and solicited assistance to secure a reciprocity treaty similar to the project of 1852. The Commissioner pointed out to Marcy that the great drawback of agricultural interests in the Islands arose from duties on sugar and molasses in American ports, and he indicated that a judicious system of reciprocity would be mutually advantageous. He was satisfied that such a reciprocity could not affect the interests of Louisiana or Texas, as the sugar trade at San Francisco was chiefly with Manila, China, the East Indies, and the Hawaiian Islands, and this state of things would probably continue to exist.

Aside from commercial considerations, there were strong political reasons which induced the Hawaiian Government to seek the removal of the duties on sugar, syrup, and molasses in United States ports. Under the operation of the existing American tariff nearly all Hawaiian planters were, as Gregg observed, "inclined to favor such a change of government as would be likely to relieve them from the depressing effect of imposts upon their productions, in the only markets, to which, from the nature of circumstances, they must always look for their best customers. Hence arises a strong and influential party in favor of 'annexation' to the U.S. But this is chiefly a party of foreigners—to a large extent American foreigners—orderly and peaceable it will be admitted—but still impelled to favor a new political order by the numerous advantages they may reasonably hope to derive from it."[29]

The influence of this group of planters was evident in the activities of the powerful Royal Hawaiian Agricultural Society. Messrs. R. W. Wood, B. F. Snow, and S. N. Castle, a committee of the board of managers, waited on Gregg the morning of March 14 and communicated to him the proceedings and resolutions of their body at a meeting held the previous evening on the subject of reciprocity in certain articles of trade. Among the four resolutions, a copy of which was also sent to Minister Wyllie, was one stating the opinion that "it would greatly conduce to the interest of citizens of the United States engaged in agriculture in the Hawaiian Islands, if the Government of the United States would accept the Reciprocity Act passed by the Legislature of the 25th of May 1852 . . . ." The committee also believed that reciprocity would greatly add to the wealth of the inhabitants of the United States.

These resolutions and a letter of introduction strongly endorsing Judge Lee were sent by Gregg to Secretary Marcy. The Commissioner emphasized that time was an important object with the Hawaiian Government. This was "emphatically true," especially in regard to removing all causes of discontent, either real or fancied, which might afford a pretense of disturbance or revolution. Though there was no "real cause or actual grievance, and no government is less exacting upon foreign residents than that of these Islands," observed Gregg, there might be room "to complain that great natural advantages of position, of soil, and of climate, are suffered to lie dormant for want of the ability or the disposition to turn them to profitable account. Our people are never disposed to brook with patience any thing which falls behind their own indomitable energy, perseverance and enterprise."[30]

The United States Consul in Honolulu, D. A. Ogden, also communicated with Secretary Marcy, stating that in his opinion a reciprocity arrangement with Hawaii would result in "an extensive and profitable trade confined to the Pacific Coast and Islands and without prejudice to the trade and production of the Atlantic States." Another important consequence would be "the rapid and permanent settlement of the agricultural portion of the Islands, by citizens of the U.S., a fact which would forever prevent their falling into other hands while it would prepare the way for their final annexation to the Union should such a result be desired hereafter." Moreover, a free trade policy "would produce a very favorable impression and kindly feeling toward the Government, institutions and people of the U.S. on the part of the Government and people here, and result in a still closer identification of feeling and interest commercially and socially, than now exists."[31]

In a letter introducing Justice Lee to Senator Charles Sumner, Elisha Allen indicated that a modification of treaty stipulations would be of service not only to Hawaii "but equally so to the West Coast of the United States." As the business of the Islands was principally conducted by Americans, Sumner, as a United States Senator, would "feel a deep interest in our prosperity."[32]

A formal declaration of the reciprocity policy was delayed due to the hesitancy of the Hawaiian Government to take any action that might possibly offend Great Britain and France. The representatives of both powers did not relish the idea of Hawaiian reciprocity with the United States, fearing that it would be likely to perpetuate the preponderance of American influence. Such an effect was highly probable, and Gregg thought this consideration alone should have an important weight in deciding upon the proposition.

On his way to Washington, Lee stopped for a few days in San Francisco where he interviewed Senators William M. Gwin and J. D. Stevenson as well as some other leading citizens and found them willing to support reciprocity with Hawaii. At the same time, they expressed fear that the project would be defeated by the most-favored-nation clauses embodied in existing treaties between the United States, Spain, Brazil, and other sugar-producing countries.[33] The California newspapers were almost entirely silent on reciprocity, as they were on filibustering to Hawaii and annexation of that country. In fact, the Envoy learned that the filibustering scare was mostly propaganda originating with the Hawaiian Steam Navigation Company, whose manager, G. W. Ryckman, and agents "created excitement in order to draw the Hawaiian Government into a connexion with the United States."[34]

This April stopover on the West coast resulted in letters from Gwin and Stevenson to Secretary Marcy on behalf of reciprocity. Gwin warmly recommended the project and was strongly of the opinion that reciprocity with Hawaii would be highly desirable and of great advantage to California and all U.S. possessions in the Pacific, without in the slightest degree injuring the Atlantic states. Louisiana could not suffer by such a treaty, for experience had shown that she could not send her sugar and molasses to the Pacific and sell it at a profit. In addition to the mutually satisfactory exchange of products, "this commercial intercourse," he indicated, "would produce an identity affecting an interest between the two countries, which would effectually Americanize that important group of islands, and smooth the way for their eventually becoming a possession of the United States. At least, it would prevent their ever falling into the hands of any other Power."[35] Stevenson wrote that a treaty that would give us the advantage of free ports at the Islands would "be of infinitely more importance" than two Pacific railroads. He claimed that since Lee's visit "our whole population have begun to feel a very deep interest in the negotiations."[36]

Actual negotiations were delayed by Lee's ill health. However, after his arrival in the capital on July 10, rapid progress was made on the reciprocity aspect of his mission. The Envoy was presented to President Franklin Pierce on July 11 and the following day was received by Marcy, at which time Lee rejected a general reciprocity treaty proposal. At the close of the interview the Secretary of State requested a list of articles which the Government of Hawaii would interchange with the Government of the United States duty free. On the thirteenth Lee submitted the proposal to admit "all flour, fish, coal, lumber, staves and heading, the produce of the U.S., into all the ports of the H. Is. free of duty, provided the Government of the U.S. will admit sugar, syrup of sugar, molasses, and coffee, the produce of the Hawaiian Islands into the ports of the U.S. on the same terms."[37] Although there was no duty imposed on coffee imported into the United States at that time, Lee had been instructed to request its insertion in the proposed treaty.

That same night Judge and Mrs. Lee spent the evening with President and Mrs. Pierce. In a frank and free conversation the President made clear that the United States did not desire to annex Hawaii. Rather, he was inclined *"to the opinion that the wisest policy for both countries is that of independence, and a free interchange of products."* He was pleased that Lee had been able to remove some of the objections to reciprocity which at first had suggested themselves to the Chief Executive and the Secretary of State, and he promised that the matter would receive prompt attention.[38]

In a meeting the next day Marcy attempted to add tobacco and rice to the free list to offset the possible opposition of sugar-producing countries and also to obviate any difficulty arising under the most-favored-nation clause. Lee objected on the grounds of the loss of revenue and the necessity of protecting Hawaiian tobacco interests and countered by requesting the omission of flour, stating that he considered the United States' free list too large. Marcy, in turn, wished to limit sugar importation to the unrefined products and thus meet the opposition from Louisiana, Texas, and Mississippi, which might endanger the ratification of the treaty in the Senate. He promised to bring the differences of points of view before his colleagues in the Cabinet on the following Monday and to do everything in his power to hasten the negotiations. The conversations continued on July 17 and 18, resulting in a final draft. Flour was placed on the free list, but tobacco and rice were omitted. Lee tried to get fish oil included and pressed for a revision of Article VII of the Jarves-Clayton Commercial Treaty of 1849. But Marcy would not entertain either of these propositions, arguing that the whaling interests of New England would oppose ratification of the treaty if they were included.

The treaty, signed by the negotiators on July 20, 1855, to "take effect as soon as the law required to carry it into operation," had been passed by Congress and approved by the King in Council. It was to remain in force for seven years and further, until the expiration of twelve months after either of the parties gave notice to the other of its wish to terminate the same. If possible, ratifications were required to be exchanged at Honolulu within eighteen months or earlier. The articles to be admitted duty free into the United States from Hawaii were unrefined sugars, syrups of sugar, molasses, coffee, and arrowroot. Those to be admitted duty free into Hawaii from the United States were wheat, flour, fish of all kinds, coal, timber and lumber of all kinds, staves and heading. Unmanufactured cotton and wool, pelts, furs, undressed skins, seeds, unpreserved vegetables, undried and unpreserved fruits, butter, poultry, eggs, and tallow were to be reciprocally received by both countries.[39]

The treaty reached Honolulu on September 16 and was approved and accepted by the King and Privy Council the following day. The public authorities of the Kingdom were highly pleased with the results of Judge Lee's mission. The King remarked to Gregg that nothing since the commencement of his reign had afforded him more gratification. On Gregg's delivery of President Pierce's letter to him, Liholiho took the occasion to reply to the Commissioner that the treaty "is but one link in the chain that binds the two countries in relations of the most happy kind." He considered "the convention of the greatest importance not only to those who are numbered among my subjects, but to every American citizen who has any interest upon these Islands. I do not doubt but that its effect will be to call hither more of your enterprising countrymen, and direct towards the now partially developed resources of the Archipelago, the attention of your judicious, but ever ready capitalists." Under this treaty he expected "to see American citizens raising the produce which American ships will carry to an American market. But their prosperity will

be ours. Indeed the mutual interests of the two countries are so interwoven in this regard, that it would be a difficult task to define a line
between them."[40]

Judge Lee's popularity soared to new heights. On his triumphant
return to Honolulu in the spring of 1856 he was repeatedly fêted,
and the Privy Council, having passed a resolution of thanks for his
services and success in November, proceeded to pass another resolution of gratitude to all who had made the treaty possible.

Robert C. Wyllie was especially overjoyed; he felt that not only
had his past policy been vindicated but a quietus had been placed
on what had been "virtually a premium on annexation." The advantages, in his opinion, were not all confined to the side of the Islands,
as some intimated; proof of his contention was the increasing Hawaiian
consumption of timber, lumber, shingles, and fish from Puget Sound.[41]

Commissioner Gregg was certain that the effects of the treaty
would be "to secure beyond question, the preponderance of American
influence in Hawaiian affairs." He sincerely hoped that there would
be no difficulty in the way of ratification, that the Senate would act
quickly in order to offset the opposition to the United States by the
British and French representatives in Honolulu. He had repeatedly
informed Marcy of the conflicting interests of the British and American residents of Hawaii and of the French efforts to obtain a new
commercial treaty. The Commissioner now warned that "failure to
ratify would be peculiarly unfortunate" at a time when France and
Great Britain, through their agents, were seizing every opportunity
to create prejudice against the United States.[42]

News of the conclusion of the proposed treaty caused annoyance
to the English and French residents in Honolulu who had predicted
that U.S. stipulations would be of such a character that the Hawaiian
Government's request for concessions could not be considered. Moreover, Great Britain had made a treaty with Hawaii in July, 1851,
which provided that "neither country should charge higher duties
upon articles from the other than upon the same articles from any
third power." Hawaii "was no longer free to extend to Great Britain
even the opportunity to purchase concessions." In fact, it appeared
that she might be obliged to break her promise to Great Britain and
to give the United States exclusive preferential treatment. The problem, however, was eliminated when Lord Clarendon, British Secretary
of State for Foreign Affairs, informed the Hawaiian Government that
"as the advantages conceded to the United States by the Sandwich

Islands are expressly stated to be given in consideration of and as an equivalent for certain reciprocal concessions on the part of the United States, Great Britain can not, as a matter of right, claim the same advantages for her trade under the strict letter of the [British-Hawaiian] treaty of 1851."[43] Clarendon had apparently yielded to the American interpretation, or the so-called conditional form of most-favored-nation treatment, as opposed to the European unconditional form.

In the meantime the United States Senate showed no inclination to hasten the ratification process. On December 27, 1855, President Pierce transmitted the treaty to that body for consideration with a view to ratification. It was received on January 3, 1856, read on the tenth, and referred to the Committee on Foreign Relations where it remained until July 7, when Senator James M. Mason reported it back to the Senate.[44] This long delay caused anxiety in Hawaii which led the Cabinet in April to request to Joel Turrill, former American Consul in Honolulu who had returned home, to lend his support to the treaty. He went to Washington but accomplished little. In May, Elisha H. Allen, Minister of Finance, who had arranged to visit the United States on private business, was named Envoy Extraordinary and Minister Plenipotentiary to the United States and instructed to attend to several issues, including the vexatious George Bailey case, an explanation of the treaty and an attempt to have it ratified.

Arriving in San Francisco, Allen became a lobbyist for reciprocity and enlisted the support of the press. In California he was led to believe that the treaty would be ratified, but when he reached New York and Washington he found a powerful opposition organized by Senator John Slidell of Louisiana and Senator Jacob Collamer of Vermont, who professed to fear that the wool interests of his state would suffer from the agreement. Congress was about to adjourn and several proponents of the treaty had left the capital. Senator William H. Seward of New York advised not to attempt to get a vote at that time. The treaty was read for the second time and considered in the Committee of the Whole on August 13, was debated again on August 22, and then tabled without opposition.[45]

After Congress had adjourned, Allen conferred with Secretary Marcy on August 25 and then inquired in writing whether it would be desirable for him to return at the next session and also if some modification of the treaty would render it more satisfactory. Marcy repeated that he had verbally communicated that there was considerable opposition to it in the Senate and that he believed that its fate was now doubtful. He was of the opinion that some opposition might be overcome by modifications which, however, would not impair the value of the treaty to the Hawaiian Government; in his judgment it was important to have someone in the capital who would understand the interest of that Government if slight revisions were made. The Secretary mentioned that if the Senate approved the treaty some action on the part of the House of Representatives would be required before the measure could go into effect, and Allen's presence might also be useful in removing differences which might arise in that quarter. Marcy closed his note with the statement that he regarded "the conclusion of the Treaty as a measure of great importance to both countries, and should be much pleased to have your aid in accomplishing that object."[46]

Allen left Washington for his old home in Bangor, Maine, with plans to return at the next session and consider possible revisions of the proposed treaty. After Congress opened, he and Marcy labored to overcome the opposition to the argument that under the most-favored-nation clause other sugar-producing states would demand equal privileges in the United States market. The treaty was considered in an executive session of the Senate on February 18, 1857, and an effort to bring it up again on February 20 failed.[47] Since this was the short session at the close of President Pierce's term, the influence of the outgoing administration was negligible.

Throughout this period, strong and active opposition came from senators who represented sugar and wool interests and from others who objected on constitutional principles. In addition to the argument based on the most-favored-nation clause, the question was raised concerning the right of the Senate alone to regulate duties. Since a tariff is a revenue measure which should be considered by the House of Representatives, some challenged the constitutional right of the upper house to modify rates by treaties. Moreover, it was predicted that if this treaty went into effect, sugar from the Philippines, China, and the East Indies would be fraudulently shipped into the United States through Hawaiian ports free of duty. Still another objection voiced was made by southern senators on the grounds that the Hawaiian Islands had free labor.[48]

In the special session called by President Buchanan after his inauguration, the treaty was again referred to the Committee on Foreign Relations, was adversely reported by that Committee, and was considered by the Senate on March 13. An attempt of Judah P. Benjamin of Louisiana to have it tabled failed by a vote of thirty to fourteen. Now the friends of the treaty were confident that it would be passed. But Senators Benjamin and Slidell threatened a filibuster to prevent the question of ratification from coming to a vote. The treaty failed to secure approval within the stipulated time for ratification, and no attempt was made to revive it.

One who worked to prevent ratification of the treaty was David L. Gregg, who, from the announcement of Judge Allen's mission, was determined that it should remain "entirely bootless." In a dispatch and in a private letter of June 5, 1856, the Commissioner informed Secretary Marcy of Allen's subservience to Minister of Foreign Affairs Wyllie, conduct which was "truly surprising" and so apparent that it had "become a subject of comment in every circle," of "his party malignity" which knew no bounds, and of his practice of ridiculing the Franklin Pierce administration on all convenient occasions. Gregg disclosed that Allen's popularity among Americans was "at the very lowest ebb." To yield to the views he "is sent to urge, will build up Mr. Wyllie and English influence to an immense extent. This Mr. Wyllie has distinctly in view. Mr. Allen may not see it but it is nevertheless true."[49] Moreover, the United States diplomatic representative in Hawaii who was acquainted with several influential people in and out of Congress, including Stephen A. Douglas, Lyman Trumball, John Forsyth, and T. L. Harris, sent disparaging letters to Harris and Trumball, explaining that success for Allen would bolster the British party and influence in Hawaii to the detriment of American interests there.[50]

A Million-Dollar Industry

In spite of the failure of the Senate to ratify the treaty, the Hawaiian sugar producers profited some from the United States Tariff Act of March 3, 1857, which lowered the duty on sugar from thirty to twenty-four per cent. Further, American interests more than held their own in the economic life of the Islands. During the twelve-year period from 1845 to 1856 inclusive, the Custom House statistics for imports into Hawaii illustrate the paramountcy of the United States in the commerce of the Islands. During this period the importations of merchandise from the United States were of the value of $6,935,748.21, while those from all other countries amounted only to $5,617,358.33. During the same period the value of merchandise imported from Great Britain and the British colonies was $2,110,523.43 —less than a third of that of the United States—and from France the value was $71,941.20. The statistics likewise made equally clear the immense predominance of American whaling and merchant ships over the vessels of all other nations frequenting Hawaiian ports.[51]

The Hawaiian sugar industry, that had been in the economic doldrums in 1857, was given a new impetus by the Civil War, during which Louisiana sugar was not available in the North and West. Using Chinese labor transported by the William E. Matson shipping interest, Hawaiian planters took advantage of the South's inability to produce raw cane sugar during the conflict. The aggregate yield of sugar grown in the Islands in 1857 was 700,556 pounds; this figure had risen to 2,567,498 pounds in 1861; five years later the aggregate yield was 27,050,000 pounds. This great increase in expansion from 1861 to 1866 reflected the influence of the war in the States upon Hawaiian economy. Sugar had become a million-dollar industry.

AGGREGATE YIELD OF SUGAR IN THE
SANDWICH ISLANDS, 1852–1866

YEAR	POUNDS	YEAR	POUNDS
1852	730,000	1861	2,567,498
1856	554,805	1862	3,005,603
1857	700,556	1863	5,292,121
1858	1,204,061	1864	10,414,441
1859	1,826,620	1865	15,318,097
1860	1,444,271	1866	27,050,000

Mark Twain, *Letters from Honolulu
Written for the Sacramento Union*, p. 36.

The Hawaiian planter enjoyed certain advantages over the Louisiana planter, including cheaper land, labor, and capital outlay, a surety of a crop on land favorably situated for irrigation, and a frost-free climate, which meant that the cane could be planted in some parts of the Islands in almost every month in the year and might stand for several months after ripening without deteriorating; consequently, the mills could take their time and grind comfortably along in all seasons. In contrast, since Louisiana had only five or six weeks in which to harvest her crop, the juice was generally green and the sugar necessarily inferior to that of the Islands.[52] This combination of advantages together with the availability of American capital stimulated sugar production. Therefore, it is highly probable that even without the artificial stimulus afforded by the abnormal demand due to the Civil War, the sugar industry would have advanced steadily, though not so rapidly.

It should be mentioned that while Hawaiian planters might be favored over those of Louisiana, the amount of land in the Islands suitable for the cultivation of sugar cane was very limited. Even in the 1880's, after several irrigation ditches had been completed, that area was variously estimated at about 100,000 acres, at the utmost 200 square miles, a large part of which constantly had to lie fallow. Louisiana, on the other hand, was rich in natural and acquired wealth and possessed over 40,000 square miles of rich alluvial soil unsurpassed for the production of sugar and other staples.[53]

Notwithstanding its rapid expansion, in 1866 the Hawaiian sugar industry's future was by no means bright. Competition of Far East low grade sugars (below number 12 Dutch standard in color)[54] and the increasing activities of the sugar refineries in San Francisco complicated the sugar industry for Hawaii. As long as prices remained high and the market was able to absorb readily all the sugar produced in the Islands, the industry continued to prosper and speculative investments were able to pay. But after the Civil War, prices dropped, the greater part of the price decline—about two cents a pound— occurring in 1866. The glutted state of the market was partly due to the steadily rising production of sugar in Hawaii and to the overstocked San Francisco refineries.

The Civil War and post bellum period witnessed the development of the sugar refining business in San Francisco. The first refinery in that area was opened in 1855. Eight years later Claus Spreckels and his brother-in-law established the Bay Sugar Refinery, which processed raw sugar from the Hawaiian Islands. Others refineries were started, and by 1867 three companies operated four refineries in the bay city. Whereas these companies manufactured some fine white sugar, the refining methods then used resulted in a large quantity of light yellow sugar commonly called "coffee sugar." In the retail trades the "grocery grades" (which could be consumed without having to be refined) of sugar produced in Hawaii competed directly with the yellow "coffee sugars" put out by the refineries. The raw material used by the refineries was low-grade sugar, some of which was obtained from Hawaii, but most of which came from the Philippines, China, and other Far Eastern countries. Competition between the refineries combined with the increased production of the better "grocery grades" of sugar in Hawaii overstocked the market and contributed to the decline in prices in 1866.

As a result, the Kingdom suffered a serious depression during the latter half of 1866 and most of 1867. The suggested remedies for the situation were: 1) a reciprocity treaty with the United States or annexation to that country; 2) a working agreement with the sugar refiners of San Francisco. The latter was achieved through contracts to buy more than half of the 1867 crop in "refinery grades." These contracts were renewed with an upward price adjustment for the crop of 1868, but at the end of that crop year the plan was abandoned. Prices had improved, consumption of sugar was increasing, and planters did not like their operations to be restricted by contracts with refiners. However, a tariff-free market in the United States was not realized at this time.

NOTES

1. Hawaiian Sugar Planters' Association, *Story of Sugar in Hawaii* (Honolulu, 1926), pp. 2, 3, 8; Lorrin A. Thurston, "Sugar: Its Status and Development," *Pacific Commercial Advertiser*, July 2, 1906, p. 31.
2. Missionary Letters, VI, 1569. A Transcript copy in the Hawaiian Mission Children's Society Library, Honolulu, contains letters and parts of letters from the Sandwich Islands missionaries to the corresponding secretaries of the American Board of Commissioners for Foreign Missions in Boston.
3. Hiram Bingham, *A Residence of Twenty-one Years in the Sandwich Islands* (Hartford and New York, 1848), p. 340; Thurston, p. 31.
4. Josephine Sullivan, *A History of C. Brewer & Company, Limited, One Hundred Years in the Hawaiian Islands 1826–1926* (Boston, 1926), p. 107.
5. Beechey to Don Mariano Guadelupe Vallejo, Feb. 18, 1827, Vallejo Documents, XXIX, No. 114, p. 186, postscript, Bancroft Library, University of California.
6. Sullivan, p. 106.
7. Sullivan, pp. 103–05.
8. *Polynesian*, Feb. 5, 1853; cf. *ibid.*, Sept. 21, 1850.
9. Royal Hawaiian Agricultural Society *Transactions*, Vol. I, No. 2, p. 53, and No. 4, pp. 49–50, Vol. II, No. 1, pp. 7–8, 17–18; Ethel Mosley Damon and Mary Dorothea Rice Isenberg, *A Story of Pioneers on Kauai and What They Built on That Island Garden* (2 vols., Honolulu, 1931), I, 405–08; Sullivan, p. 72.
10. Armstrong to Chapman, May 4, 1849, Armstrong-Chapman Papers.
11. Hawaiian Sugar Planters' Association, *Story*, p. 67; Sullivan, p. 110, 112.
12. H. A. Peirce to J. F. B. Marshall, Nov., 1852, Jan. 4, March 3, 1853, Hunnewell, MSS, Harvard College Library; *Polynesian*, March 19, Aug. 13, 20, Dec. 10, 1853, Jan. 14, Feb. 11, May 20, 27, 1854; "Honolulu Iron Works Company," *Honolulu Star Bulletin*, April 12, 1920, pp. 60–61; RHAS *Transactions*, Vol. I, No. 4, p. 4, Vol. II, No. 1, pp. 65, 95, 136.
13. RHAS *Transactions*, Vol. I, No. 2, p. 118, Vol. I, No. 4, pp. 66, 67. Burbank was manager of the Koloa Plantation 1851–57.
14. *Penal Code (and Laws of) 1850* (Honolulu, 1850), pp. 144–45; Theodore Morgan, *Hawaii: A Century of Economic Change, 1778–1876* (Cambridge, Mass., 1948), p. 184.
15. *Polynesian*, Oct. 23, 1852.
16. Sullivan, p. 112. C. Brewer and Co. invested its funds in sugar even earlier than Castle and Cooke.
17. Thurston, p. 31; Charles Nordhoff, *Northern California, Oregon, and the Sandwich Islands* (New York, 1874), p. 57.
18. Mark Twain (Samuel Langhorne Clemens), *Letters from Honolulu Written for the Sacramento Union*, pp. 34–35, published in *Sacramento Weekly Union*, Sept. 29, 1866; Nordhoff, p. 57.
19. Wyllie to Theodore Shillaber, H.H.M. Special Commissioner to His Excellency the Governor General of California, Sept. 28, 1848, AH, FO & Ex.; *Polynesian*, Oct. 7, 1848. Wyllie's action resulted in a long and heated correspondence between him and Ten Eyck, upon whom special powers for negotiating a commercial treaty had been conferred. See AH, FO & Ex. file from October 12, December 5, 1848, printed in a collection bearing

the title "Official Correspondence between Anthony Ten Eyck, Commissioner of the United States, and Robert Crichton Wyllie, Esquire, His Hawaiian Majesty's Minister of Foreign Relations, upon the subject of the Mission to the Governor of California of Theodore Shillaber, Esquire."

20. James J. Jarves, "Minutes of an Interview with Mr. Buchanan, Oct. 26/48 —at Dept. of State—Washington—D.C.," AH, FO & Ex., (published in Albert Pierce Taylor, "Secrets of the Hawaiian Archives," *Paradise of the Pacific, Hawaii's Illustrated Monthly Magazine*, XXXIX (1926), No. 7, pp. 13, 15).

21. *Polynesian*, Jan. 17, Feb. 14, 1852; cf. *ibid.*, Jan. 31, March 6, 1852.

22. Severance to Webster, No. 38, Jan., 1852, with encl. cutting from the *Polynesian* of Jan. 17, 1852, USDS, Dispatches, Hawaii, IV.

23. *Ibid.*, Nos. 39, 40, Feb. 14, March 2, 1852. The latter is misdated 1851 instead of 1852.

24. Memorial dated Feb. 28, 1852, encl. in Edwin O. Hall, secretary of the RHAS, to Severance, March 2, 1852, USDS, Hawaiian Legation Archives, Miscellaneous Letters Received, 1846–1852; *Polynesian*, March 6, 1852.

25. Severance to Webster, No. 47, March 8, 1852, USDS, Dispatches, Hawaii, IV.

26. Gregg to Marcy, No. 76, March 12, 1855, *ibid.*, VI.

27. Minutes of Cabinet Council, Cabinet Council Records, II, 23, 24, 41, 48; Cabinet Council Minute Book, Jan. 30, Feb. 14, March 10, 14, 15, 1855.

28. General Instructions to Mr. Lee, March 19, 1855, AH, Local Officials, Lee's Mission. In Privy Council there was a proposition to make the mission private and keep it from Gregg's knowledge. Reportedly, Judge Lee favored this on the alleged ground that the Commissioner would not be likely to approve the object. Others advocated openness and frankness, and their sentiments prevailed, the general opinion being that Gregg might be counted on to aid the project. Cf. David L. Gregg, Private and Official Interviews, II, interview with Wyllie, March 12, 1855.

29. Gregg to Marcy, Nos. 76, 77, March 12, 14, 1855, USDS, Dispatches, Hawaii, VI.

30. *Ibid.*, Nos. 77, 79, March 14, 17, 1855, with encl. D in former.

31. D. A. Ogden to Marcy, March 17, 1855, USDS, Consular Letters, Honolulu, VI.

32. Allen to Sumner, March 17, 1855, Charles Sumner Papers, XXVII, 71, MSS, Harvard College Library.

33. O. E. Hooley, "Hawaiian Negotiation for Reciprocity, 1855–1857," *Pacific Historical Review*, VII (1938), 131.

34. Gregg to Marcy, No. 93, April 20, 1855, No. 161, April 25, 1856, USDS, Dispatches, Hawaii, VI, VII.

35. Gwin to Marcy, April 20, 1855, Marcy Papers, LIX, Library of Congress.

36. Stevenson to Marcy, April 23, 1855, *ibid.*

37. Lee to Marcy, July 13, 1855, USDS, Hawaii, Notes from, II. The word "unrefined" was written in pencil before "sugar."

38. Lee to Wyllie, No. 5, July 14, 1855, AH, FO & Ex., 1855, Mission of W. L. Lee.

39. For the text of the treaty see *Sen. Docs.*, 56th Cong., 2nd sess., No. 231, Pt. 8, pp. 148–49; *Sen. Reps.*, 53rd Cong., 2nd sess., No. 227, pp. 45–46; USDS, Hawaii, Notes from, II; cf. Elisha H. Allen Papers, Library of Congress.

40. *Polynesian*, Sept. 22, 1855; encl. A in Gregg to Marcy, No. 118, USDS, Dispatches, Hawaii, VI.
41. Wyllie to Sir John Bowring, Oct. 5, 1855, AH, FO & Ex., Misc. For. Corresp.; Foreign Office Letter Book, 1854–1856, pp. 82–84.
42. Gregg to Marcy, No. 118, Sept. 18, 1855, USDS, Dispatches, Hawaii, VI.
43. United States Tariff Commission, *Reciprocity and Commercial Treaties* (Washington, 1919), pp. 110–11, 418; cf. pp. 418–20.
44. *Journal of the Executive Proceedings of the Senate of the United States, From December 3, 1855 to June 16, 1858* (Washington, 1887), X, 12, 13, 111. (Hereafter cited as *Sen. Ex. Journal*).
45. *Sen. Ex. Journal*, X, 147, 155.
46. Marcy to Allen, Aug. 30, 1856, USDS, Hawaii, Notes to, in one vol.
47. *Sen. Ex. Journal*, X, 197, 200.
48. *Washington Post*, Jan. 2, 1883.
49. Gregg to Marcy, No. 168, June 5, 1856, and private letter of the same date, USDS, Dispatches, Hawaii, VII.
50. Gregg to Harris, June 12, 1856, Gregg to Trumball, June 27, 1856, in Private Letters, Pt. 1.
51. Wyllie to Gregg, No. 12, Oct. 24, 1857, encl. B in Gregg to Cass, No. 244, Nov. 2, 1857, USDS, Dispatches, Hawaii, VIII.
52. Mark Twain, pp. 38–42. Even without a reciprocity treaty the products of the Islands constantly increased. In 1860 Hawaii exported 1,444,271 pounds of sugar, in 1864, 10,414,441, in 1868, 18,312,926, and in 1871, 21,760,733 pounds (Nordhoff, p. 57).
53. H. M. Whitney, "The Hawaiian Reciprocity Treaty," a report on the results of the Hawaiian Reciprocity Treaty read before the Planters' Labor and Supply Company, Oct. 19, 1882, published in the *Hawaiian Gazette*, Supplement, Oct. 25, 1882.
54. Number 12 Dutch standard was a standard of equality recognized by all nations. It meant a quality of sugar, crude, full of impurities, unfit for domestic consumption, and bearing the same relation to table sugar that raw cotton bears to a piece of muslin.

3

RENEWAL OF RECIPROCITY
NEGOTIATIONS

Efforts of McBride and McCook

ALTHOUGH the Civil War brought unprecedented prosperity to the Hawaiian sugar industry, all concerned realized that a cessation of hostilities would lead to a drop in prices. Moreover, there was a desire on the part of Secretary of State William H. Seward not to allow relations with Hawaii to deteriorate too seriously because of preoccupation with internal difficulties or Kamehameha V's British penchant. In 1863, in an effort to restore American political dominance and to promote American interests in Hawaii, the United States Government raised the rank of its diplomatic representative in the Islands from Commissioner to Minister Resident, an act greatly appreciated by the Hawaiian Kingdom.

The newly appointed Minister, James McBride, in a dispatch of December 10, 1863, submitted to Seward various reasons why a reciprocity treaty should be made, arguing that such a treaty would work to the economic advantage of both countries, "would be singularly beneficial to the States and Territories bordering on the Pacific Ocean," and would tend to secure for the United States the friendship of the Hawaiian Government and people. He maintained it "would place these islands, in their social and commercial relations with the United States," very much in "the attitude of a State in the Union, which, I presume would not be considered in any sense of the word injurious to us."[1]

Nine months later the Minister recommended that, if a reciprocity treaty should at any time be negotiated with the Hawaiian Government, a fee simple to a piece of land at the port of Honolulu, "sufficient for a wharf and buildings for a Naval Depot, and also for a dry dock, should be made one of the conditions of said treaty."[2] He reasoned that because of the necessity of defending our new states and territories on the Pacific slope and the augmented commercial relations with the Islands, China, and Japan, a permanent installation would be increasingly important in the future.

McBride apparently was acting upon his own initiative, motivated, no doubt, by anxiety over growing British interest in Hawaii. His dispatch, urging the acceptance of the act of 1855 for mutual reciprocity, was received at the State Department on February 2, 1864. Evidently his son, J. R. McBride, who was then a congressman from Oregon, informed Charles Sumner of the communication, for only two days later the Senate adopted a resolution introduced by that member requesting the President, "if not incompatible with the public interest, to communicate to the senate any recent correspondence at the Department of State relating to a proposed reciprocity treaty between the United States and the Sandwich Islands." In response to the resolution, the Secretary of State replied immediately that an application had been received to revive the uncompleted reciprocity treaty of 1855. "After due consideration, however, especially in connection with the probable effect of such a measure on the public revenue at this juncture, it has not been deemed advisable further to entertain the subject."[3] Seward immediately informed McBride that it was inexpedient to adopt the policy of reciprocity at that time but that the subject would receive "earnest consideration."

Before this reply reached Honolulu, Hawaiian authorities, aware of the intimate economic and cultural relations of their country with the United States and alive to the value of reciprocity, decided to renew negotiations on the subject. Chief Justice Elisha Hull Allen was, in March, 1864, appointed Envoy Extraordinary and Minister Plenipotentiary to Washington on a mission of several purposes, the main one being to obtain the ratification of the uncompleted reciprocity treaty of 1855 or to negotiate a new one.[4] Allen was received by President Lincoln, who discussed the subject with him, and without committing himself on reciprocity, assured him of the profound interest of the United States in the Islands. The Chief Executive wrote: "In every light in which the state of the Hawaiian Islands can be contemplated it is an object of profound interest for the United States. Virtually it was once a colony; it is now a near and intimate neighbor. It is a haven of shelter and refreshment for our merchants, fishermen, seamen, and other citizens when on the lawful occasions

they are navigating the Eastern seas and Oceans. Its People are free
and its laws, language and religion are largely the fruits of our
teaching and example."[5]

In long interviews with Secretary Seward, Chief Justice Allen
advanced strong economic arguments in favor of reciprocity, emphasized the strategic importance of the Islands, and indicated his willingness to offer the most favorable terms possible in order to satisfy
Americans whose objections to reciprocity might have prevented the
ratification of earlier treaties. The Chief Justice talked with a number
of senators and representatives, some of whom, including the Oregon
members who had been instructed by their state legislature to work
for such a treaty, promised their support. On the recommendation
of Seward, Allen conferred with Secretary of the Treasury Salmon P.
Chase and his old friend and Chase's successor, W. P. Fessenden,
who was in general opposed to all reciprocity treaties and offered
little encouragement.

During this 1864 attempt to secure reciprocity, the West coast,
particularly the state of Oregon, indicated special interest in the
outcome, and joint resolutions were passed by both houses of its
legislature on October 14 and forwarded to Secretary Seward by
J. R. McBride *et al.* In an accompanying letter the men observed
that the enumerated products to be exported by both countries in
no way conflicted with each other, as was the case with the Canadian
provinces. A treaty to facilitate a mutual exchange between the United
States and the Hawaiian Kingdom would, on the contrary, be a great
advantage to both. To the objection that the proposed treaty would
affect the revenue derived from importation, the opinion was advanced
that the amount of income flowing into the national treasury from
Hawaiian imports was so trifling that it would not seriously embarrass
the negotiations. The advantages of the treaty in furnishing a market
free of duty for some of the leading staples of the Northwest coast
and the profit arising from the employment of additional capital and
labor in the trade, it was believed, would more than compensate the
Government for the loss of revenue.[6]

Chief Justice Allen advanced similar arguments and produced
numerous statistics to prove the paramountcy of American interest
in the Islands, but to no avail. The Envoy persisted in his efforts,
reiterating his arguments to the Secretary of State in a lengthy communication at the close of the year.[7] Finally, Seward informed him
that his dispatch had been submitted to the President, who, after

due consideration of the matter, "is of opinion that the present temporary state of civil war renders such a negotiation inconvenient and inexpedient. We hope for a change at no very distant period, and, then the subject will be resumed with pleasure."[8]

In addition to the internal conflict, another adverse effect on Hawaii's proposal was the increasing hostile attitude in Congress toward the Marcy-Elgin Treaty of 1854 which provided for free trade between Canada and the United States in enumerated products. The expansionist members were determined to abrogate the agreement, a determination which they carried out two years later, believing—and the thought may have been shared by Secretary Seward—that the resulting dislocation of Canadian commerce might quicken natural impulses for voluntary annexation.

Two factors combined to raise again the question of a reciprocity treaty during the year 1866. The most important was an acute post-Civil War depression in the Hawaiian sugar industry which caused some businessmen and planters in the Islands to feel that the whole plantation interest would be ruined if a reciprocity treaty were not obtained. The other factor was the appointment of General Edward M. McCook, a personal friend of President Johnson, as Minister Resident —the first of a group of Civil War generals and colonels who exchanged military commands for diplomatic and consular posts.

Before leaving for Hawaii, the General invited James B. Williams, a sugar manufacturer later associated with Claus Spreckels, to visit him in his Fifth Avenue hotel. Williams spoke of the importance of the Hawaiian Islands to the United States and of the need for a reciprocity treaty; he hoped he had started the Minister "right," and that he would "keep right."[9]

Edward M. McCook, although a general, was only thirty-two years of age, "good looking, bright and intelligent," with "a decided military bearing." He was well-received in the Islands, for the King had a fondness for the military. The new Minister decided to spend his salary by "conspicuous consumption," and through his ostentation —he owned a thousand-dollar span of American horses—he made his presence felt in Honolulu. This display of wealth was in decided contrast to the behavior of some of his predecessors.

McCook, who had "a large pecuniary interest" in a treaty, advocated reciprocity as the best means of cementing Hawaiian-American ties and of preparing the way for peaceful annexation; he consorted with planters, influential businessmen, and others, in an effort to initiate a new drive for a reciprocity treaty. He visited the United States three successive winters to secure the administration's favorable consideration of the treaty and to exert influence upon sugar refiners, chambers of commerce, and senators. The Honolulu Chamber of Commerce's assignment was to induce the Hawaiian Government to take appropriate action. H. A. P. Carter and Captain James Makee called on the Ministry on November 20, and persuaded them to hold a Cabinet meeting the following day. The officials studied the problem intermittently for more than three months before reaching a decision to reopen negotiations. From the record of previous efforts, some members doubted the success of the negotiations. Also, to be considered was the means of making up the loss of revenue resulting from the remission of duties.[10]

The new Minister of Foreign Affairs, Charles de Varigny, like his illustrious predecessor, Robert C. Wyllie, wished to preserve the sovereignty of the Hawaiian King and was anxious to find a policy that would diminish the demands for annexation. But he was confronted with a dilemma. A reciprocity treaty, he realized, would be of tremendous advantage to the agricultural and business interests of Hawaii and would assure prosperity for the stipulated term of seven years; but if after that period of time the American Government declined to renew the treaty, the Islands would face a terrible commercial crisis. "Menaced by imminent ruin, would not our planters rally to the idea of annexation to the United States, which, by permanently taking off the tariff duties, would remove all fears for the future." Reasoning further, Varigny believed that "seven years would give us time to establish our production on a solid basis, and would especially open to us, by similar negotiations, other markets which would compensate for the loss of the California market, in case our most pessimistic previsions should be realized."[11] Since some other members of the Cabinet and the business interests favored the project, he decided to take the calculated risk; on March 7, 1867, the Cabinet empowered Charles C. Harris, Minister of Finance, to go to Washington on the special mission.[12]

Meanwhile, in the previous November, Minister McCook and his wife had journeyed to California on the U.S.S. *Vanderbilt* with Admiral H. R. Thatcher, ostensibly for Mrs. McCook's health, but with an ulterior purpose well known in Honolulu—in fact part of the cost of his trip was defrayed by Honolulu businessmen.[13] In San Francisco he conferred with the sugar refining interests and obtained their point of view. From the coast he requested and received permission from the Secretary of State to proceed to Washington. Once in the capital he was successful in interesting President Andrew Johnson, Secretary of State Seward, and several members of Congress in the proposal. Seward, however, was cautious and sought the advice of Secretary of the Treasury Hugh McCulloch, to whom he submitted a copy of the proposed treaty of 1855, pointed out its desirability, mentioned "an important political consideration," and expressed the opinion that the possible increase in sugar importation would not prove injurious to Louisiana.

McCulloch prepared a detailed study of Hawaiian trade in which he concluded that the projected treaty of 1855 had not provided sufficient advantages to the United States by failing to admit free such important exports as hardware, cotton, manufactures, clothing, boots and shoes, furniture, drugs, and similar commodities. A treaty based on the schedules of 1855, if operating in 1866, would have resulted in the admission into Hawaii duty-free American products worth less than $100,000 out of a total trade of $1,051,639. But the political considerations appeared to Secretary McCulloch "to be of such importance as to entirely overshadow the comparatively trifling interests involved in the commerce of these islands." Although McCulloch was inclined to regard the treaty with favor, he recommended that the schedules of the unratified treaty of 1855 be revised in order to provide a "fair equivalent in trade" to the commerce of the two countries.[14] In answer to a Senate resolution of January 31, 1867, inquiring "whether, in his opinion, American interests would not be subserved by a treaty of commercial reciprocity with the Hawaiian Islands," he replied that such a treaty "would have the immediate effect to reduce in some degree the revenue derived from customs, while it would, on the other hand, undoubtedly tend ultimately to an enlargement of national commerce."[15] The project received the approval of the administration, and on February 1, 1867, President Johnson affixed his signature to the formal document authorizing McCook to negotiate and sign a treaty of reciprocity with the Hawaiian Kingdom.

The newly organized Hawaiian Club of Boston, "an association of gentlemen interested in the prosperity of the Hawaiian Islands, and the promotion of American interests there," naturally espoused reciprocity, and even before McCook was authorized to negotiate, the Club's president, James Hunnewell, called the attention of the president of the Boston Board of Trade to the reported progress to secure a treaty and requested that the board "use their influence to secure its adoption."[16]

Moreover, the Hawaiian Club learned in February that the Ways and Means Committee of the House of Representatives proposed an amendment to the tariff that would add a half cent per pound duty on raw sugars above number 12 Dutch standard, which in the process of manufacture had been "boiled in vacuum pan or purged in a centrifugal machine." This information disturbed the members of the Club, who were convinced that it would discriminate "fatally against Hawaiian planters, mostly Americans, and favor California refiners, mostly foreigners." The San Francisco refiners, by taking the poor sugars of China and Manila and making an article that drove out everything refined on the Atlantic coast, monopolized the white sugar market of California and Oregon. But one-third of their product had to be in yellow sugars, and with these the Hawaiian sugars made by centrifugal process had been able to compete, though the high duty left but a small margin of profit. The proposed additional half cent would either drive the Island sugars, which meant virtually the Island trade, to British Columbia and other foreign ports, or ruin the planting interests of the Islands already much depressed, or compel the planters to forego their valuable apparatus and to make low grades of sugar in the vain hope of competing with China and Manila for the supply of the refiners. Consequently, the Club opposed the adoption of the amendment. Its secretary wrote to two members of the Ways and Means Committee: "Indeed, the failure of the tariff bill in toto would generally be very acceptable to our business men, manufacturers as well as importers."[17] Even more agreeable to the Hawaiian Club was the prospect of a reciprocity treaty.

Treaty of 1867

In San Francisco, General McCook, who was returning to Honolulu via Panama, met Charles C. Harris who was traveling to Washington. The two men proceeded forthwith to draft a treaty. While so engaged they visited the San Francisco and Pacific Sugar Company to collect data regarding the refining industry in the bay city. This information was furnished by R. Feuerstein, an agent who had returned only a few weeks before from Honolulu, where he had concluded contracts between the Company and many of the large planters. Therefore, it was not a coincidence that the treaty as drafted and signed the week of May 21, 1867, was well suited to the needs of the refiners and was in line with the agreements arrived at previously by Feuerstein in Honolulu.

This treaty provided for the admission of specified Hawaiian products into the United States free of duty; included were arrowroot, coffee, fruits and vegetables, rice, furs and skins, ornamental woods, tallow, unmanufactured cotton, and sugar not above number 12 Dutch standard of color. This latter provision was inserted to protect the Pacific coast refiners against competition from high grade Hawaiian sugar. McCook and Harris, anxious to meet the recommendations of the United States Treasurer and determined to ensure the passage of their treaty, broadened the free list of exports to Hawaii over that of 1855. Included were agricultural implements, building materials, boots and shoes, meats, fish, bread, cotton manufactures not over one hundred sixty threads to the square inch, woolens other than ready-mades, hardware, ice, iron, lumber, and petroleum.

The value of goods to be admitted duty free from the Hawaiian Kingdom into the United States was estimated to be $629,385, whereas the amount of exports from the United States to be admitted free of duty into Hawaii would be $813,747, making the reciprocity, as concerned the gross value of the products involved, nearly equal. The balance was actually in favor of the United States, but because the rate of import duties levied by Washington was much larger than the rates levied by the Hawaiian Government, the sum of the revenue remitted by the United States would be greater. Actually the difference was unimportant, but it was later used as an effective argument by the opponents of the treaty. General McCook considered the treaty more equitable in its reciprocity than our Canadian treaty.

Minister McCook was pleased with his labors and anticipated significant economic and political advantages for the United States. Reporting from San Francisco to Secretary Seward he wrote: "I think the consummation of this treaty, will largely benefit the commercial and manufacturing interests of this Coast, and of the Country; and prove the initial step towards the acquisition of the islands, should this country ever want them." In June he averred: "When the Pacific Rail Road is completed, and the commerce of Asia directed to our Pacific Ports, then these islands will be needed as a rendezvous for our Pacific Navy, and a resort for merchant ships, and this treaty will have prepared the way for their quiet absorption." Its ratification would "result in securing for us the entire political and commercial control of these Islands which are far richer in agricultural resources than Cuba or any other of the West Indies Islands."[18]

In a private letter to the Secretary of State, the Minister discussed the purchase of the sovereignty of the Islands and expressed his desire to be in Washington at the time the treaty would come before the Senate for ratification. Seward granted McCook leave to come to the capital at the next meeting of Congress and authorized him to approach the "proper authority" on the subject of annexation, to "receive overtures," and to report the same to the State Department.

After the treaty was signed, the roles of the two negotiators were reversed. McCook returned to his post in Honolulu to explain the treaty to the Hawaiian Government and to exert whatever influence might be required to ensure its ratification; Harris performed a similar mission in Washington. The former's role proved easier.

Not only formal ratification by the King of Hawaii but also an act of the Legislature were required to carry the treaty into effect. One obstacle in the way of legislative action in Hawaii was the presence in Honolulu harbor of the U.S.S. *Lackawanna* under the command of Captain William Reynolds. He was a resident of the Islands during much of the period 1852–61 but returned home to serve in the Civil War. Reynolds was unpopular in royal circles because of his advocacy in 1854 of the annexation of Hawaii to the United States. In the spring of 1866, the Pacific squadron was divided by the establishment of South and North Pacific squadrons; the *Lackawanna*, while still forming part of the latter squadron, was assigned for an indefinite period to Hawaiian waters. Once there, her captain proceeded to dispatch communications to the Secretary of the Navy in which he emphasized the strategic importance of the Islands and described their political conditions.

The King and Ministry objected to the permanent stationing of any foreign vessel in the ports of the Kingdom. Moreover, in official circles there was the belief that Reynolds, in the absence of the United States Minister Resident, was charged with a mission of surveillance for a government desirous of assuring itself as to what extent the treaty would be advantageous to the Islands and popular with the people. This conviction, together with Reynold's alleged interference in political affairs, made him *persona non grata* in royal circles.

Finally, Kamehameha V and Minister of Foreign Affairs Charles de Varigny informed McCook that before entering into consideration of the treaty of reciprocity the Government desired the departure of the *Lackawanna*[19] from the Kingdom.

In a private and confidential dispatch the Minister Resident informed Secretary Seward that the presence of the *Lackawanna* in Hawaiian waters was straining relations between the two countries; he charged Captain Reynolds with interfering, or having intentions of interfering, in internal political affairs in Hawaii, showing disrespect to the King, and otherwise acting in capacities unwarranted by his orders.[20] By a fortunate coincidence, Reynolds in July received orders to survey and take possession of the uninhabited Brooks Island, now known as Midway;[21] he sailed to that assignment on July 30, 1867.

On the same day that the *Lackawanna* lifted anchor, the King issued a call for a special session of the Legislature to meet on September 2, and McCook was invited to confer with the Cabinet about the terms and provisions of the treaty. There was some opposition from three different groups. One wanted all grades of sugar—not just those below number 12 Dutch standard of color—admitted free of duty to the United States; a second disliked the further growth of American influence and interest which would result from the treaty; a third group wanted annexation rather than reciprocity and felt that the latter would delay the former. The official organ of the Government, the *Hawaiian Gazette*, was unenthusiastic in its reception of the treaty, whereas the Hawaiian-language newspaper, *Au Okoa*, which was sponsored by the Government, more directly opposed the agreement.[22] However, the Cabinet, anxious to quiet the talk of annexation, gave the measure strong support, and since most members of the Legislative Assembly considered reciprocity desirable, on September 10 an act implementing the treaty was passed by a vote of thirty-three to four. The treaty was ratified by Kamehameha V on the thirtieth. Only two days later, the *Lackawanna* returned to Honolulu after her cruise to the northwestern chain, and for seven months, until she sailed on May 6, 1868 for San Francisco, her presence was disturbing.[23]

Captain Reynolds continued his epistolary diplomacy, which was not confined to the Navy Department, but was also directed to members of Congress, to the Hawaiian Club of Boston, and to the *San Francisco Evening Bulletin*. One communication of January 20, 1868 to Secretary Welles emphasized the United States' need for the Islands from a military point of view and concluded: "if necessity requires the Hawaiian Islands as a naval station for the United States, we need them now!"[24] An unsigned letter to the *San Francisco Evening Bulletin* generally attributed to Reynolds stated that during the past ten years there had been a gradual growth of American sentiment in the Islands, which reached a point of enthusiasm and high expectation in July, 1868, "when the reciprocity treaty checked the desire for annexation and from that time to the present a positive anti-American feeling has gained strength and found utterance, especially among those not interested in securing the treaty." The attitude of the Hawaiian Government was more adverse to the United States than at any former period. The writer of the letter expressed the honest conviction that should the treaty pass, it would be far more difficult and more costly to obtain the Islands at the end of seven years, for they "so enriched could better afford to remain independent, and as in the case of Canada, reciprocity in trade would accomplish nothing in securing political friendship."[25]

The second irritant in the relations between the United States and Hawaii while the treaty was under consideration was the "secret" mission to Hawaii of Colonel Zephaniah S. Spalding, who had served in the forces of the Union Army and had come out of the Civil War with the rank of lieutenant-colonel. In September he was appointed by Secretary Seward, who wanted to have all possible information on the subject, ostensibly as a bearer of dispatches to Minister McCook, but actually as a confidential agent paid from Secret Service funds to report to the Secretary[26]—not to the Department of State—what the feelings of the country were and "what effect the reciprocity treaty would have on the future relations of the United States and Hawaii."[27] The assignment reportedly was known only to William H. Seward, the Colonel's father, Congressman R. P. Spalding of Ohio, and Senator James W. Grimes of Iowa. While on his way to the Islands, Colonel Spalding met in San Francisco General McCook, who was traveling to the East and Washington to lobby for his treaty.

Spalding arrived in Honolulu in December, 1867. Posing as a prospective cotton planter, he observed the situation and, between December 10 and April 14, wrote long monthly letters to his father who delivered them to Seward. On his arrival he wrote that he found " 'Treaty or a————n' the cry with a good many who are dependent on the sugar plantations and to whom the duty is quite an item." After a month's observation he analyzed the attitude toward the treaty as being either friendly, inimical, or neutral. The King and Ministers favored it because it would bring capital to the Islands; so did planters and others interested in the sugar industry for the increased prices they expected to receive. Merchants were divided, with some maintaining that it would benefit the country and themselves by enabling them to import American goods free of duty, while others felt that England would continue to furnish goods cheaper than the United States, so that trade would not be diverted. Opposing reciprocity, Spalding found "nearly every man *not* interested in sugar, and in favor of annexation!" The only argument he heard in favor of the treaty was "that it will make these Islands dependent upon the United States, and that on the expiration of the treaty (in 7 years) the people will demand a renewal of annexation." The secret agent reported that there could "be no doubt as to the future of the country," that "it is considered only a question of time when the Eagle will gather these little Islands under his wing. The 'pear may be hardly ripe!' but I think it will fall into the right basket when it does fall, and although its maturity may be hastened by a little diplomacy and perhaps the expenditure of a few dollars, I think it would be worse than foolish to pluck the fruit by force."

In March Spalding observed that the San Francisco refiners were "the 'head and front' in this treaty. The Islands wanted it differently but the Sugar Refiners would not consent! They furnished the largest proportion of the 'material aid' required to get it through, and demanded the largest share of the profits." He was told by an American merchant of Honolulu and one of the best friends of the treaty that he (the merchant) preferred annexation, but Spalding said "we could not get annexation, and therefore tried for the Treaty in the hope of its leading to annexation . . . by bringing in a larger American element, and enabling American interests to some day control the government."

In this fourth and last letter to his father, Spalding reaffirmed his earlier opinion that there would be "no hope for annexation while there was a chance for 'Reciprocity.'" Events had not changed his mind. On the contrary, he felt that the desire for annexation was stronger in mid-April than it had been at any time since his arrival "simply because the prospects for the treaty are felt to be almost hopeless, and the Planters *must* have relief by annexation!" After discussing the attitude of the missionaries toward annexation and dis-

missing their passive opposition as not insuperable, Spalding concluded: "It is time to decide upon the plan of action—If we want
these Islands immediately, I have no doubt the Lackawanna imbroglio
will furnish the pretext for taking them à la England or France."[28]

During the spring and summer of 1868, Spalding directed the
United States consulate under a temporary appointment as vice-consul
and for a part of the period served as chargé d'affaires at the United
States Legation. Since the fact of his secret mission, along with cer-
tain of his other activities, had become known to Hawaiian officials,
Stephen H. Phillips, Attorney General, Acting Minister of Foreign
Affairs, and at that time a supporter of the King, became antagonistic
and refused to continue to recognize Spalding as vice-consul. In the
autumn of 1868, Spalding was given a regular commission as United
States consul for the port of Honolulu, and the following January the
Hawaiian Government acknowledged him in that official capacity.
He remained in the position until fall when he was superseded by
an appointee of the new Grant administration. The attitude of the
Hawaiian Government toward Reynolds and Spalding, justifiable as
it was, did not in any way improve the chances of the reciprocity
treaty in the United States Senate.

The most active and best organized support of the treaty in the
United States came from the Hawaiian Club of Boston, some of whose
officers were also influential members of the Boston Board of Trade.
Throughout the period the treaty was under consideration in the
Senate, the Club supported reciprocity—though with diminishing
enthusiasm—as well as the retention of Captain William Reynolds
at the Islands, and waged an active and expensive propaganda campaign in favor of both. On learning that Minister Harris was en route
to Washington, a committee of three—James F. B. Marshall, Edward
P. Bond and William J. Bingham—was appointed "to tender to him
the cooperation and courtesies of the Club."[29]

The vice-president, General Marshall, went to Washington to
lobby actively for reciprocity. Immediately after the submission of
the treaty to the Senate on July 13, he tried to remove the impression created by his friend, Captain Reynolds, "that without a reciprocity treaty, the Islands would fall into our hands from their own
inability to stand alone, while the Treaty would galvanize them into
new life." In fact, Marshall took the opposite view, believing "that
if annexation were desirable this treaty will be the surest way to bring
it about." He soon discovered a strong feeling in favor of annexation

and a belief among its advocates that the confirmation of the treaty, by giving the Islands the substantial benefits of annexation, would prevent or delay the accomplishment of that event. He argued, however, that the "measure would hasten, not hinder annexation, by uniting in the closest ties of interest the two nations, and giving us the 'inside track' for the future." But there were those who were impatient and did not care to wait for future developments, such as, Senator James W. Grimes of Iowa, who was strongly opposed to the treaty and favored "our friend's remedy of summary occupation."

Although Marshall felt that the Hawaiian Club's advocacy of the treaty "would have great weight" with some who opposed or were lukewarm about it, the summer brought no success. In fact, only six days after the submission of the treaty to the Senate, Harris began to get nervous and Marshall thought the Minister would "be voted an intolerable bore by those officials—legislative or executive—with whom he is brought in contact. What fools people can make of themselves when they try. He is indefatigable & persevering however, and will not fail of his object for want of following it up."[30] Harris labored diligently to satisfy congressmen and others that the Hawaiian Government in general and C. C. Harris in particular had been true friends to American interests and that they favored the Union cause in the rebellion. Marshall was convinced that the Envoy would hardly succeed, and should admit this fact. Actually, though industrious, the so-called "renegade American" carried no prestige or personal influence. He was looked upon by Secretary Seward, Charles Sumner and "many other senators with suspicion and as lacking high character." In fact, Sumner, who favored the treaty and was chairman of the influential Committee on Foreign Relations, turned from the commissioned Envoy to the Hawaiian Club for facts and opinions on the subject of reciprocity. During the recess of Congress the organization lost no time in soliciting information for the Senator and in informing him and others of its views.

In July or early August Edward P. Bond received Henry A. P. Carter's letter of May 16, 1867, in which the possibility of annexation was discussed at length. "Harris," Carter wrote, "doubtless thinks that he can do as well under the U.S. rule as he will here when the King is gone and the Government be ruled by the people." The Finance Minister believed that if reciprocity were not gained, annexation would be sought; he considered reciprocity better than annexation for both countries. The letter continued: "Some oppose Reciprocity because they prefer annexation and think the former would help to postpone the latter but I do not think annexation would be acceptable to the U.S. Government now but after a few years of Reciprocity I think it might be more so."[31]

This communication apparently did not affect the avowed policy of the Club whose members were convinced that under the existing attitude of the Hawaiian Government "there could be no annexation except by force; and there seems to be nothing in the situation which could authorize or excuse such a procedure."[32] In Washington, Harris, though not averse to discussing annexation, had told Marshall that the King was exceedingly sensitive on that point and that there was no prospect of his being brought to entertain the question. On his return to Boston, the vice-president of the Hawaiian Club prepared a letter to Senator Sumner setting forth the position of the Club, recommending positive action on the treaty, and enclosing a copy of a resolution which called for the constant presence of an American vessel of war at the Hawaiian Island. He stated that Captain William Reynolds of the U.S.S. *Lackawanna,* "by his previous residence at the Islands, his intimate knowledge of Hawaiian affairs, and his high character for intelligence and patriotism, is eminently qualified to watch over and protect our interests in that quarter."[33]

With, no doubt, Carter and Harris' words in mind, Marshall wrote Captain Reynolds to ascertain the "exact condition of affairs at the Islands, and what the feeling is among natives and foreigners toward the U.S. before the next meeting of Congress," when the Senate would act upon the treaty. General Marshall stated at length the position of the Club, which was that they did not favor annexation of the Islands to the United States if American interests could be otherwise fully secured and a predominant American influence in the Government established. It seemed to the members that through the ratification of the reciprocity treaty the predominance of American interests would be secured and "the predominance of American influence in Hawaiian councils would naturally follow. That if annexation was desirable, the adoption of this treaty would be the best initial step towards such a result; and if it was not desirable, that its substantial advantages without its embarrassments would be secured by its operation." Marshall believed that the sugar interests which this treaty would foster would become the controlling influence in the Hawaiian Government and that if the United States wished to annex the group at the expiration of the seven-year term of the treaty, "a notice of termination would at once bring unconditional proposals for annexation from the Island, as the only means of averting the general ruin which a return to our onerous sugar duties would involve." These were the chief reasons which, to the Club, seemed to favor the adoption of the proposed treaty. Annexation in 1867 would meet the approval of only "a part of our people, under any circumstances, and forcible annexation would be still less favorably regarded."[34]

Edward P. Bond, in answering Carter's letter, disclosed that reciprocity did not find such general favor as Harris and Seward had anticipated and that the best efforts of its friends would be required to secure the ratification of the treaty in December. He observed:

> Some oppose all reciprocity treaties as an infringement of the right of the Representatives to the first voice on all revenue measures. Others—and these are the most formidable opponents, favor speedy annexation, be it treaty or otherwise, and think that reciprocity, by giving the leading interests at the Islands all that they want without the burden of our war taxes, will indefinitely postpone this step.
>
> I favor, and I believe all our Club do, reciprocity as better than annexation now, for all parties, and as a step to peaceful absorption of the Islands, whenever, through the failure of the native race, or other cause, it shall become desirable.[35]

Bond requested Carter to send the Club all the facts and figures bearing upon the political and commercial aspects of reciprocity, including those concerning degrees of sentiment among Americans, other foreigners, and natives at the Islands. The more material the better, for the Club had a triangular battle to fight. It intended to work with Harris in good faith for his treaty, "but," the Secretary wrote, "if he opens new issues—tries to get rid of the *Lackawanna*, or to get an indorsement of the *coup d'état* and other anti-American measures, we have given him to understand we shall oppose him."[36]

In September Bond communicated with the secretary of the New York Chamber of Commerce. He and Marshall visited other members to bring to their attention the importance of the Government's keeping a vessel at the Sandwich Islands, and to explain those "considerations arising out of the present state of affairs at the Islands" which really had the most force in Bond's mind, but which he could not state in writing. The two officers of the Hawaiian Club also talked with Captain Edgar Wakeman, a surveyor, who took a lively interest in Hawaiian affairs and expressed his willingness to confer with Secretary Seward and to attend the meeting of the Chamber of Commerce, of which he was a member, when the topic should be discussed.[37] The subject of a national warship remaining in Hawaiian waters was called to the attention of the Secretary of the Navy by the New York organization and also by petitions from the merchants of Boston and New Bedford. At a special meeting of the Hawaiian Club on October 31, Marshall briefly reported what action the Club had taken to further the adoption of the treaty, and Charles C. Harris, as a guest of the Club, reviewed the reciprocity negotiations which had taken place and asked the members to use their influence to secure the ratification of the treaty, which was in the hands of the Senate Committee on Foreign Relations.[38]

The following month General McCook returned to the States and, in a conversation with Henry A. Peirce, indicated that a petition or memorial from the Boston Board of Trade in favor of reciprocity addressed to Congress or the President would greatly assist in the ratification of the treaty. Although the General could give no reason or proof, he claimed that the impression existed at Washington that the only opposition to the treaty would come from Boston.

Meanwhile, on November 2, Senator Cornelius Cole of California had requested the president of the San Francisco Chamber of Commerce, R. G. Sneuth, to give his opinion as to whether the reciprocity treaty should be ratified or not, "whether it would be advantageous to our interests or otherwise." While there was general agreement within the Chamber that the measure "would be an eminent benefit to the state" and to the West coast, there was considerable division of opinion in California on the most efficacious action to be taken toward reciprocity. Governor Frederick F. Low favored the treaty, and because he expected Senate objection to its ratification, he requested the San Francisco Chamber of Commerce to take immediate measures to have the commercial aspects of the agreement properly presented. At a meeting of the Chamber in the evening of November 22, George Gordon, president of the San Francisco and Pacific Sugar Refinery, stated that the Hawaiian Islands' situation gave them a bonus of a cent and a half per pound in supplying the people of California. "All the advantages of the treaty would inure to the people of California," and for this reason it would be strongly opposed by the sugar men of the East who had sought for years to rule the market. The trade for manufactured goods would rapidly increase with the improved conditions of the plantations. He viewed the treaty as a measure in which the commercial consideration was secondary and the political paramount. Although it was generally supposed that the treaty would be a great benefit to the refineries, the sugar contracted for during all the period of the treaty would not equal more than twelve or thirteen ordinary Manila cargoes. He was of the opinion that it made little difference what the Chamber of Commerce said or did; its recommendation would have no weight at Washington, except weight operating against the treaty. In short, the recommendation of the Chamber would prevent the adoption of the treaty and the members would assist its passage most by reporting themselves indifferent to its fate.

Mr. Feuerstein, an agent of the San Francisco and Pacific Sugar Refinery, who, like its president, had pointed out that sugar was only about five-eighths of the trade affected by the treaty, indicated that other articles, for example coffee, were embraced in its provisions; hence, the treaty would benefit the inhabitants of the Pacific coast. For these reasons he supported the treaty but considered its life of seven years too short. A treaty at best was ephemeral, and capital was too sensitive to emigrate with only a seven-year security. Since three years were required to cultivate a plantation, one that was started when the treaty was ratified could have four profitable years during the treaty's continuance but would have no prospect beyond that time. He considered it highly improbable that under these circumstances capital would go largely into sugar cultivation. This view was also held by George B. Merrill, a confirmed opponent of the treaty.[39]

Washington Bartlett brought up the most-favored-nation clause of treaties as an objection, whereas a Mr. Wise, who did not see how the treaty would benefit the people in general, thought it should be rejected. Two or three refineries would sell all the sugar they could manufacture at a trifle of a pound less than the cost of duty-paid sugar and would pocket the difference, while the United States would lose half a million of revenue. To take off the external duties and not replace them by internal duties was a certain way to prevent annexation.[40] The views that there was no reciprocity in the agreement, no public gain commensurable to the Government's loss and to the emolument of a few manufacturers, and that the terms of the treaty were dictated by the California refiners who did not permit free entry of higher grades of sugar became powerful arguments against the measure. It was denounced as a "stock-jobbing operation," which would give the refiners a "complete monopoly and absolute dominion over the Hawaiian planters."[41]

As a result of its meeting of November 22, the San Francisco Chamber of Commerce appointed a committee of four, of which George Gordon was chairman, to prepare a report. This, in the form of a twenty-eight-page Western Union telegram, was dispatched to the State Department on December 14. The four main conclusions of the committee were: 1) That the location of the Sandwich Islands is such that any strong naval power fortified thereon would hold the key to the commerce of the Pacific so that it could not prosper, or even exist, without that power's permission. 2) That France, England and the United States are striving for that possession. 3) That this reciprocity treaty appears to be the best, if not the only way of preventing an unfriendly or hostile power from obtaining them, and it will ultimately secure their possession for the United States. 4) That the commerce of the Pacific coast of the United States will be immediately and largely benefited by the treaty. McCook pointed out to Seward the fact that a document of such great length telegraphed from the other side of the continent showed that the merchants of San Francisco regarded the ratification of the treaty as of vital importance to the interests of their region.[42]

In the East, friends of reciprocity directed their efforts toward securing the support of Boston, New York, and Philadelphia businessmen. Peirce requested Edward P. Bond, one of the most esteemed of Hawaii's former residents, to do what was necessary to enlist the Boston Board of Trade, of which he (Bond) was assistant secretary.[43] Having gone to the Islands for his health in 1851, Bond was soon appointed Circuit Judge of Kauai and, from 1856 to 1861, District Attorney on Maui; subsequently, he returned to West Newton to become the founder of the Union Safe Deposit Company of Boston, in which he served until his death in 1893. McCook also wrote Bond suggesting that the memorial be addressed to Senator Charles Sumner "and be made *strong*." The Minister referred to the action of the San Francisco Chamber of Commerce in placing on record its approval of the treaty and indicated that this statement embodied some of the best reasons for ratification and that he could suggest nothing further. He mentioned that the case of reciprocity with Hawaii was quite different from that with Canada—"practically they are as dissimilar as possible." General McCook reported that the principal objection urged in Washington "is that the treaty will postpone annexation, and if defeated the planters through their poverty will be forced to do *something* which will lead to the acquisition of the islands." He met this argument by suggesting that impoverishing the Islands would result in an exodus of the larger part of the American population, and with them would go American influence and all hope of peaceable acquisition. On the other hand, the treaty would "stimulate American Emigration, and fix American influence so that upon the death of the present King the Government will quietly pass into our hands." Bond was informed that the Philadelphia Board of Trade would follow the lead of Boston as soon as the former was furnished with the facts.[44]

The Boston Board of Trade forwarded to the Senate a memorial which first emphasized the economic reasons for supporting reciprocity, the "needed relief and protection to our citizens resident at the Sandwich Islands," who had "furnished the capital there employed in agriculture and commerce," an investment which "is now in jeopardy, and . . . unless trade is revived through the action of this treaty, much of it must be hopelessly lost." Further, the Sandwich Islands were a rendezvous for our ships engaged in the whale fisheries in the North Pacific and in the guano trade of the central Pacific, and doubtless would become the coaling station and entrepôt of the lines of American ocean steamers which would soon be traversing the Pacific. There were considerations other than these purely commercial ones that had a bearing on our interests. From their geographic position the Sandwich Islands must be of great strategic importance. The memorial concluded: "They are the Bermuda and the Nassau and the St. Thomas of our Pacific Coast. We cannot afford to have them in the hands of an enemy or of a doubtful friend. We must bind their government and people to us by ties of mutual interest and good feeling so strong that, from this time forth, American influence shall be paramount in their councils, and that, should circumstances hereafter occur to change their sovereignty, they shall naturally, peacefully and surely gravitate to our Union. The negotiation of this treaty which has already been ratified . . . by the Hawaiian Assembly, furnishes an admirable opportunity to cement these ties."[45]

Peirce joined McCook and Wood in Washington in December and remained there until Congress adjourned on the twentieth, to reconvene January 6. This active and keenly interested member of the Hawaiian Club interviewed a large number of senators and attempted to impress them with his views on the importance of the Hawaiian Islands to this country, insisting that the ratification of the treaty "would be the surest, safest, and most proper way in the end to acquire their possession." Senator Grimes, chairman of the Committee on Naval Affairs, and others with him, would not listen to arguments for a reciprocity treaty and believed "that we should take possession *at once*." Peirce reported to Bond: "It appears, our friend Reynolds has written to him in that vein." Another point raised against a reciprocity treaty was that a loss of revenue to the United States amounting to some $400,000 to $600,000 per annum would not be permitted by some members. Justin S. Morrill of Vermont and a few others would "throw in their peculiar views as to the constitutionality of *all* Reciprocity *Treaties*." Although the Committee on Foreign Relations would favor it, Peirce doubted whether the treaty would be ratified by the Senate. He concluded: "It is only in view of *annexation* that the treaty has a ghost of a chance. *Annexation—annexation*, seems to be the cry and object of all. If we can prevail with Senators to believe that the treaty will increase the chances of success of that great object, it will be ratified; and on no other ground."[46]

Securing treaty ratification was an insuperable task. Before Congress adjourned in December, the opposition had become very strong, contending that the sugar planters already got so much that they were disinclined to annexation and giving them more would not further the cause. The only "hearty working friends" the treaty had among the senators were those from California, Oregon, and Nevada, adjudged to be aligned with the refiners. The strongest supporters of the treaty in the East, the Hawaiian Club members, accordingly had to elect to continue their work for the measure, or to oppose it. Notwithstanding its defects and the members' disappointment with its terms, they decided that they ought to support it for three reasons: 1) It was the best treaty they could get. When completed and signed at San Francisco, it was subject only to ratification or rejection by the Government. When Hawaiian officials had wished to make some changes, they were told that the measure must stand or fall as a whole; therefore, amendments were out of the question. The Club felt that if this treaty were rejected, there would be no hope of another for years. 2) Nearly all the Americans at the Islands favored it; the Club could hardly oppose a measure which the resident Americans had at heart simply because it did not give them as much as they wanted. 3) It was the deliberate judgment of the members "that *on the whole* it will benefit the Islands and bind them to the United States." Therefore, remembering the old adage that "half a loaf is better than none," the Club continued to support the treaty as the best means of saving their countrymen at the Islands from bankruptcy and of restoring and strengthening American influence there. Moreover, Bond was not convinced that the San Francisco refiners had secured a monopoly. They might have a monopoly for the year or two that they had a contract with the planters, but after that time they would have to pay remunerative prices for the sugar crop, or it would go around the Horn.[47]

In Washington the treaty was considered intermittently over a period of three years—July, 1867 to June 1, 1870—in five sessions of Congress. During this time Charles C. Harris, Dr. John Mott Smith, chargé d'affaires, and finally Chief Justice Elisha H. Allen successively exerted their influence and lobbied for ratification. Harris and Smith's efforts were supplemented by those of Minister McCook who returned to Washington in the autumn of 1867, bringing with him Dr. Wood, who proved to be of aid to the treaty's cause.

Harris journeyed to Portland, Maine, and to Burlington, Iowa, in an effort to convert Senators W. P. Fessenden and J. W. Grimes to reciprocity. Although he was cordially received, he did not succeed in changing the minds of the two staunchest opponents of the treaty. The Minister remained in the States lobbying for the treaty until July, 1868. The Hawaiian Government decided not to have him return to Washington for the winter of 1868–69, but sent in his place Dr. Mott Smith. Knowing that the latter was not only unacquainted with the nation's capital, but also inexperienced in lobbying there, General McCook again requested and received permission to visit Washington to render assistance. Just before his departure from Honolulu, the Minister sent five hundred dollars to the chargé d'affaires to be used in the best way possible to influence native votes in the Legislature in favor of the ratification of the treaty. Later, when questioned by the Secretary of State on the procedure, the General explained that the payment was purely a personal matter and in no way represented United States policy.

Treaty Rejected

OMITTING the tedious details of the progress—or rather lack of progress—of the treaty in the upper chamber, a bare outline of its history is here presented. It was received by the Senate on July 13,

1867, and referred to the Committee on Foreign Relations. Six months later, on January 28, 1868, it was favorably reported out in a vote of four to three. On July 20, Charles Sumner, chairman of the Committee, presented and warmly defended the measure in executive session. He was followed by William P. Fessenden of Maine, a member of the Finance Committee and a former Secretary of the Treasury, who spoke in opposition. Although it was intended to have a second executive session on the following day, the amount of regular business to be transacted in open session prevented this. On July 24, the Sandwich Islands treaty was again discussed in executive session, with Senator Fessenden making the principal speech. After this attack there was a general belief that the Hawaiian measure would be immediately defeated. Sumner, however, came to its support in a long address which again raised doubts as to outcome. The two-to-three-hour debate was unusually animated and plainly indicated that the treaty would not receive the two-thirds vote needed for ratification, whereupon its friends, apprehensive of its defeat, moved to lay it on the table, a motion passed by a vote of thirty to twenty-one.[48]

McCook, returning to Honolulu, wrote to Senator Sumner from San Francisco, suggesting that the time for the exchange of ratification be extended and the whole matter postponed until the next session of Congress. Since the Minister had revisited the bay city, he had been more than ever impressed with the important influence the treaty would exert on the commercial and political interests of the Pacific coast, and he was "convinced that should the Senate ratify the treaty the future would vindicate the wisdom of the act." He hoped that the matter would be pressed to a conclusion before Congress adjourned.[49]

Failure to act on the treaty before the end of the session necessitated an extension of the ratification clause. Such an agreement was signed July 28 and submitted to the Senate on January 5, 1869. Meanwhile, in his message of December 9, 1868, President Andrew Johnson, who looked upon reciprocity as paving the way for eventual annexation, recommended approval of the treaty and accompanied his endorsement with the comment that the prosperity of the Hawaiian Islands "is continually disturbed by expectations and alarms of unfriendly political proceedings, as well from the United States as from other foreign powers. A reciprocity treaty, while it could not materially diminish the revenues of the United States, would be a guaranty of the good will and forbearance of all nations until the people of the islands shall of themselves, at no distant day, voluntarily apply for admission into the Union."[50]

At the opening of the first session of the Forty-first Congress, in March, 1869, the reciprocity measure was again referred to the Committee on Foreign Relations and was once more reported favorably to the Senate on April 7. The treaty again failed to receive active support; an effort was made on April 21 to bring it up for consideration, but the attempt failed by a vote of twenty-four to twenty-two. The Grant administration, which had come into office in 1869, officially favored the reciprocity treaty, but because Secretary of State Hamilton Fish was then more interested in Anglo-American relations, particularly in the settlement of the *Alabama* and other claims, and because of the North Atlantic fisheries dispute, and of President Grant's absorbing interest in Santo Domingo, little more than polite support was given to the treaty.

Chief Justice Elisha H. Allen arrived in Washington in January, 1870, was received "with great cordiality" by Secretary of State Hamilton Fish, and was presented to President Grant on January 15. Throughout the remainder of January and all of February, the Envoy labored tirelessly, interviewing senators, visiting the chambers of both houses and the speaker's room, attending to treaty business at parties and state dinners, and conferring with Secretary Fish and Secretary of the Treasury George S. Boutwell. To the former he reiterated his arguments in favor of commercial reciprocity with Hawaii and promised to prepare a résumé showing the existing treaties with countries producing the articles proposed to be admitted under the treaty.[51] On February 12 he received a favorable report from the Committee on Foreign Relations, but anticipated a tug of war in the Senate for the two-thirds vote. Allen conferred with Senators John Sherman, Morrill, and William Alfred Buckingham, all opponents of the treaty, who, without reversing their position, treated him "with great courtesy." Nevertheless, his "delicate self-respect" made this sort of address distasteful.[52]

The treaty was brought up for consideration and debated on April 21, but a delay of nearly six weeks ensued before it was again discussed on the floor of the Senate. Throughout the month of May Justice Allen "worked like a Roman," with all the industry and tact that he possessed, only to be disappointed by delays in bringing the treaty to a vote, by having it postponed because of the pressure of other business or the absence of some of its friends, as was the case on May 10 when the opposition was too strong for its proponents to press the measure. Convinced that he had done all that he could for the treaty, weary of the apparently interminable waiting, and anxious to see his wife, Allen contemplated leaving the city, but Senator Lot Myrick Morrill of Maine, who believed that the treaty would be received otherwise, urged him to remain. He argued that the opponents would say "the Hawaiian Minister had given up and gone home."

Although tired of Washington and exhausted by his duties, Justice Allen was always hopeful of a vote "next week." He was disappointed when, on May 17, the fifteenth Amendment intervened. In fact, there was so much legislation relating to Reconstruction that the regular business was retarded, but Sumner encouraged him by saying "a good mariner will not throw over the cargo in order to get into port sooner." By May 22 Allen was convinced that he would never advocate another treaty; the work involved was far too arduous and trying.[53] Finally, the treaty was debated on May 31 and again on June 1, when the vote was taken.[54] Even with an amendment reducing the term of duration from seven to five years, the Senate divided twenty for, nineteen against the treaty, which lacking a two-thirds majority, was defeated.

In the Senate the leader of the campaign for the treaty was Charles Sumner, who was sympathetic to the appeals of his Boston acquaintances. The stiffest opposition to reciprocity in this post bellum period came not from the sugar planters of Louisiana whose industry had been ruined by war and whose interests were not actually represented in Congress, but from New England and mid-western Senators, Fessenden of Maine and Grimes of Iowa,[55] and later from Justin S. Morrill of Vermont, the tariff expert and leader in Congress, and John Sherman of Ohio. Neither Fessenden nor Grimes, the two most influential opponents of the treaty, was in the Senate when the treaty was finally rejected, but most realistic men had concluded that passage was out of the question as early as April, 1868, when both senators were active and powerful.

One of the most potent objections to the treaty was the charge that there was no reciprocity in it, that Hawaii would be greatly benefited by the remission of duties, whereas the United States would lose revenue. This was an appealing argument, but it disregarded the political significance of cementing Hawaiian-American relations, and of supporting and protecting American capital invested in the

Islands which was supposed to make the treaty valuable to the United States. The importance of this political consideration was denied by some opponents. Senator Fessenden, for one, argued that "it is folly to pay for a thing which we already have in possession, that the power and prestige of the United States is sufficient to assure the concession of whatever naval and commercial privileges are needed in the islands, to extend or protect American commerce in the Pacific, and that American capital and citizens are needed at home, where there is ample field for their employment."[56]

Some opponents, like Colonel Z. S. Spalding and George B. Merrill, contended that the treaty would benefit primarily the California sugar refiners and, some added, the sugar planters of Hawaii. Professor Ralph S. Kuykendall states that this was "uncomfortably close to the truth, and frequent repetition of the charge undoubtedly had a very damaging effect."[57] Senator John Sherman employed this argument preceding the final vote on June 1, 1870. Justice Allen regarded the connection of the California refiners with the treaty as a misfortune which provided no strength "and made a coolness, if not an opposition to it in some quarters." He was inclined to the opinion that if the "treaty had been made, admitting all grades of sugar free of duty, it would have had more favor than limiting it to the lower grades."[58]

One of the most troublesome and persistent objections to the reciprocity treaty came from those who desired to see Hawaii annexed to the United States. They argued that the prosperity attendant upon reciprocity would destroy all prospect of annexation or would at least postpone it for a long time, emphasizing that passage of the treaty would most effectually quiet all desire and demand for annexation by giving Hawaii all the advantages of remitted duties and open ports without heavy taxation and without disturbance of her labor system.

These were the arguments broadcast by Captain William Reynolds, who in 1867 and 1868 addressed reckless and damaging letters to senators and to the Cincinnati *Commercial Advertiser*[59] and the *San Francisco Evening Bulletin*[60] to the effect that the American residents in the Islands did not approve of reciprocity. Both Marshall and Harris were aware of the impression that Captain Reynolds made on Senator Grimes, and the Minister noted that the article from the *San Francisco Evening Bulletin* had been "sown pretty broad-cast among Senators." Even before the treaty was reported out of com-

mittee, the damage had been done. Later General McCook attempted
to correct this impression by stating that there "is nothing in the
present aspect of political affairs at the islands, which will justify
Messrs. Grimes and Fessenden in their hypothesis that 'Reciprocity
will postpone annexation.' There is no possibility of either annexation or acquisition at present, except by force, and the agitation
of the question *now*, only postpones the event, and renders it
more difficult of peaceful accomplishment should one ever want the
islands."[61]

Charles C. Harris, reporting to the Hawaiian Minister of Foreign
Relations, complained of Reynold's influence, which he believed might
well have the effect of defeating the treaty: "We should have had
a comparatively easy time of it if it had been not for Reynolds' letter,
which one of the Senators has become much impressed with and
shows about with commendable assiduity. The tenor of the letter is
that our Treaty will have the tendency to defeat or postpone indefinitely annexation which he regards as more probable if we are driven
to poverty."[62]

The press reactions to the treaty, both in the United States and
in Hawaii, were varied and were by no means all favorable. Even in
California a section of the press, including the *San Francisco Evening
Bulletin*,[63] indicated that reciprocity would enrich only a few West
coast refiners and also delay annexation. The *Daily Alta California*
was favorably inclined toward reciprocity. Considering the relative
value of the imports into the two countries concerned, the *Alta* reported that the duties that would be lost to the United States Treasury
would be more than eight times the amount that would be lost to
the Hawaiian Treasury, but stated that financial considerations might
not be conclusive; there were "weightier reasons of a diplomatic and
political character . . . . Reciprocity with the Hawaiian Islands would
be the first step toward an eventual peaceable acquisition of that territory, now regarded with covetous eyes by France and Great Britain."[64]
The *San Francisco Times* urged the adoption of the treaty. Likewise
in the East, the *New London Democrat*, the New York *Evening Post*,
the *Washington Post*, and the *Washington Chronicle* were favorable.

While the reciprocity treaty was under consideration in the Senate,
the *New York Times* frequently published articles and editorials on
the growing importance of our interests in the Pacific, which had
"gained enormously by California." Numerous references were made
to the new steamship line between San Francisco, Japan, and China

which had "attracted our attention to a quarter of the globe whose commercial relations with this country ought to be of the closest and largest and most profitable kind." In the reciprocity treaty the King of the Sandwich Islands expected to find the greatest advantage for himself by opening up a market for all the sugar his subjects could raise.[65] That same newspaper, however, reported on November 9, 1867, that the treaty would

> be earnestly opposed by the American residents at Honolulu, who denounce it as a British scheme to prevent the annexation of the Islands to the United States. They say it was prepared by British subjects for that purpose, and that its ratification will kill the annexation movement, as it will relieve the Hawaiians of the payment of several millions of taxes and give them all the privileges of commercial intercourse with our Pacific Coast that they would have if our Government extended over them. They also state that the ratification of the treaty will result in the loss of a similar amount to our customs revenue without an adequate return, and will demand a thorough investigation with charges against one of our diplomatic officers, against whom it is alleged that he received a consideration to use the influence of his position to bring the negotiations to a successful issue.

The *Pacific Commercial Advertiser* hastened to correct this apprehension, but similar statements were made elsewhere, particularly by a California opponent of the measure, George B. Merrill, who asserted that only the King's advisers, "Englishmen, Frenchmen, and apostate Americans," favored the treaty "in opposition to real American interests, knowing that no idea of annexation to the republic could outlive the ordeal of prosperity which they think would obtain under the treaty. With all the commercial advantages of intercourse which exists between the states, why should anyone there think of annexation?" With reciprocity, Merrill contended, all hope of acquisition of those lands would fail, and the result would be "a firmer establishment of a monarchical government as a neighbor, whose acts will not tend to the benefit of the republic." Merrill was convinced that "Union with these states . . . is the only treaty concerning which, as merchants, diplomatists and civilizers, we should hold any argument."[66] The Honolulu *Bulletin*, for the same reasons, also looked with disfavor on the reciprocity treaty, but was friendly to annexation.

In addition to letters from Honolulu and some adverse articles in the American press, there were other causes that contributed to the defeat of reciprocity. The United States had what at that time was considered an enormous debt and needed all the revenue that could be obtained from any source. In addition to the loss incurred from the remission of duties on Hawaiian products, some senators feared indirect consequences of a reciprocity treaty with Hawaii that might lead the neighbors of the United States to desire a similar treaty. Senator Hannibal Hamlin believed that the United States Government could not afford to relinquish the seven or eight million dollars a year that it received from these neighbors; and therefore, any movement toward reciprocity anywhere would be opposed.[67] Moreover, the Marcy-Elgin Treaty, without in the least drawing Canada closer to us politically, had only recently been terminated, and Canadian ties with the mother country were strengthened by the creation of a dominion. Apathy and delay in the United States due to the pressure of more important business caused postponement of the question of approval—a deferment that allowed the opposition time to marshal its forces. The treaty came before the Senate at a time when Congress was preoccupied with problems of Reconstruction and with the quarrel between President Johnson and the radical leaders of Congress, culminating in his impeachment trial in 1868, and was denied adequate attention. While the treaty was, in a sense, an administration measure, Secretary Seward was the only member of the Cabinet especially interested in it. However, it did not become a narrow political issue, for the strongest advocate of the treaty in the Senate, Charles Sumner, was the President's bitterest enemy.

In Honolulu, the *Pacific Commercial Advertiser* persistently maintained that the treaty was rejected because the United States Government resented the unfriendly attitude of the Hawaiian Government toward Captain Reynolds of the *Lackawanna*.[68] The irritation and sharp diplomatic exchanges in Honolulu over the prolonged sojourn of this warship in Hawaiian waters certainly did not improve the chances for ratification in the Senate. On September 14, 1867, McCook conferred with M. de Varigny concerning the reciprocity treaty and was asked when the vessel would return to Honolulu harbor. The Frenchman said that he did not wish to see her, and hoped that when she did return she would have orders to leave immediately. When questioned as to his reasons, he replied that the commander of the ship, Captain Reynolds, was personally obnoxious to the Hawaiian Government: "when a resident at the islands his political sentiments were displeasing to His Majesty, and his Ministers." McCook inquired if Varigny wished "to establish the principle that before any American man of war can touch at these islands, you have the right to designate who *shall* command her and what his political principles shall be." The Minister replied: "We have the same right with regard to a man of war which we would have in relation to a diplomatic agent —the principle is precisely the same, and we have the right to refuse to receive the one or permit the other to remain in our port; and if the *Lackawanna* returns to stop here, we will order her preemptorily to leave; . . . this is our right and we are determined to exercise it." Since the Foreign Minister appeared adamant, McCook declined to discuss the matter further, except to suggest that if His Majesty's Government really desired the ratification of the reciprocity treaty, "it would probably be highly impolitic and imprudent to order away from your waters any man of war belonging to the United States, just at the time when my Government is endeavoring by the most substantial proof in their power to show their friendship for the Hawaiian Government."

Later in a conversation with the King, McCook remarked that he was leaving soon, and on his arrival in Washington he would lay the whole matter before the Secretary of State and call his attention to the objections of the Hawaiian Government to the presence of the *Lackawanna*. His Majesty replied that this had better be understood before the Minister left.[69]

There is no positive proof or even indication that the efforts of 1867–70 to reach a reciprocity agreement with the Hawaiian Kingdom, like those of the preceding decade, were defeated by the opposition of American sugar growers. Actually, there is some evidence —though inconclusive—which indicates that neither the southern planters nor the eastern refiners were responsible for the defeat of the treaty. The senators of Louisiana did not participate in the debates in 1868 and 1869; and while in 1870 they protested vigorously against proposed reductions in sugar duties in the pending tariff bill,[70] they apparently raised no strong opposition to the proposal to admit Hawaiian sugar free. It is, of course, true that in this period Hawaiian sugar, refined and sold on the Pacific slope, did not, for geographic reasons, compete with Louisiana sugar marketed in the East. Neither of the Louisiana senators was recorded against the treaty in 1870, although this is no proof that they would not have voted to defeat it had the margin been closer. Similarly, the refining interests of

New York, New Jersey, and Pennsylvania exerted no vigorous and concerted efforts against the treaty. The opponents of reciprocity represented Vermont, Iowa, and Ohio, not the Gulf and Atlantic seaboard states, as was the case two decades later. Yet we cannot assert that without this effective opposition the supporters of the treaty would have successfully overcome public apathy.

Certainly one of the most insidious forces working against the treaty was the idea that reciprocity in trade would tend to thwart or delay annexation.[71] There was general agreement among both friends and foes of the treaty that so far as the United States was concerned it was a political measure, and its champions outside the West coast supported reciprocity *now* as the best means of securing annexation *later*, while some of the most vigorous opponents of the measure feared it would postpone, not hasten, annexation. Thus, both those who favored and those who opposed the treaty had the same ultimate objective in view—annexation of the archipelago; they differed only in the method that they thought would best achieve it.

The treaty of 1867, like the one negotiated in 1855, offered no assurance that the Hawaiian Kingdom, after development by American capital and know-how and at the expense of American interest, efforts, and favor, would not at some future time come under the control of another maritime power. In short, there was no certainty that commercial reciprocity would inevitably lead to annexation.

Meanwhile, in the summer of 1869 Henry A. Peirce succeeded General McCook as American Minister in Honolulu and proceeded to advocate closer ties with or annexation of Hawaii to the United States. Always discreet and cordial with Hawaiian Government officials and his diplomatic colleagues, he nevertheless emphasized the importance of the Hawaiian Islands to the United States, and urged the establishment of a naval station and, in anticipation of Kamehameha V's death, the stationing of an American warship in Hawaiian waters to "exert a powerful interest in the settlement of political affairs, favorable to the United States." Peirce keenly observed the developing commercial rivalry in the Pacific and warned his government of the possibility of Hawaiian trade being diverted to Australasia and British Columbia. He predicted that the Hawaiian Islands would become the center of a web of transpacific steamship lines; therefore, the United States should act to preserve its supremacy in the archipelago.[72]

Official Washington was not at first agitated by these exhortations. The Minister's dispatch of September 20, 1870, again warning about the crisis that would follow the demise of the ailing sovereign, was read to the Cabinet by Secretary Fish on October 18, but aroused no interest other than the jocular remark by President Grant that "Sumner had better be consulted whether Annexation is desirable. Let him think that he originates it, and all will be well." Two months later, the Secretary read Peirce's dispatch of November 21, enclosing and commenting upon a long editorial by William L. Green entitled "Reciprocity Treaties, Annexation and Federation," which appeared in the November 19 issue of the *Pacific Commercial Advertiser*. The new editor, an English businessman of considerable residence in the Islands, declared: "We believe that this hankering after something that we have not been able to get, has had a most injurious effect on this country. . . . It is time the idea of either reciprocity or annexation be dropped once for all. Let us depend upon our own resources, and upon the markets of the world, and make the most of opportunities which we have, and of which no one can deprive us." Fish invited the attention of his colleagues to the matter, but no one responded and the subject was dropped. Later he recorded in his diary: "The indisposition to consider important questions of the future in the Cabinet is wonderful. A matter must be imminent to engage attention; . . . Alas."[73]

NOTES

1. McBride to Seward, No. 16, Dec. 10, 1863, USDS, Dispatches, Hawaii, X, printed in *Sen. Docs.*, 56th Cong., 2nd sess., No. 231, Pt. 8, p. 147.
2. McBride to Seward, No. 37, Sept. 16, 1864, USDS, Dispatches, Hawaii, XI, printed in *Sen. Ex. Docs.*, 52nd Cong., 2nd sess., No. 77, p. 133; cf. No. 36, Sept. 15, 1864, *ibid.* The Hawaiian Government had offered just such a lot to the United States in October, 1857: Wyllie to Gregg, No. 12, Oct. 24, 1857, encl. in Gregg to Lewis Cass, No. 244, Nov. 2, 1857, USDS, Dispatches, Hawaii, VIII.
3. *Cong. Globe*, 38th Cong., 1st sess., p. 481; *Sen. Ex. Docs.*, 38th Cong., 1st sess., No. 16, p. 1.
4. Wyllie's instructions of March 10, 1864, presented by Allen, June 9, 1864, USDS, Hawaii, Notes from, II; cf. AH, FO & Ex., file box 49, "1864–1865 Mission of E. H. Allen to Washington."
5. Reply by the President, June 9, 1864, *ibid.*; Elisha H. Allen Papers.
6. J. R. McBride *et al.* to Seward, Dec. 15, 1864, USDS, Misc. Letters, Dec. 1864, Pt. 2.
7. Allen to Seward, Dec. 31, 1864, USDS, Hawaii, Notes from, II.
8. Seward to Allen, Jan. 11, 1865, USDS, Hawaii, Notes to, I.
9. Williams to Bond, March 27, 1866, Correspondence of Edward P. Bond, MSS, Harvard College Library.
10. Cabinet Council Minute Book, Nov. 21, 1866, Jan. 14, 28, Feb. 19, March 7, 25, 29, 1867; Carter to Bond, Nov. 21, 1866, Bond Correspondence.
11. Charles de Varigny, *Quatorze Ans aux Iles Sandwich* (Paris, 1874), pp. 272, 278–79.
12. Cabinet Council Minute Book, March 7, 1867; cf. AH, FO & Ex., file box 58, folder labeled "C. C. Harris Mission to Washington." The following Harris-Varigny correspondence is in this folder.
13. Carter to Bond, Nov. 21, 1866, Bond Correspondence. Before McCook's departure the businessmen had raised $8,000 toward the expenses of the mission and hoped to get $15,000.
14. *Sen. Docs.*, 56th Cong., 2nd sess., No. 231, Pt. 8, pp. 147–52.
15. *Cong. Globe*, 39th Cong., 2nd sess., pp. 866, 903–04.
16. Hunnewell to the president of the Boston Board of Trade, Jan. 16, 1867, Hawaiian Club of Boston Letter Book, Harvard College Library, p. 82.
17. Bond to T. D. Elliot and to Alexander P. Rice, Feb. 27, 1867, *ibid.*, pp. 87–91.
18. McCook to Seward, No. 24, May 29, 1867, unnumbered and dated simply June, 1867, USDS, Dispatches, Hawaii, XII. All of McCook's dispatches are contained in this volume. Printed in *Sen. Docs.*, 56th Cong., 2nd sess., No. 231, Pt. 8, pp. 153–60.
19. McCook to Seward, Nos. 20, 31, July 23, Aug. 5, 1867. No. 31 is printed in *Sen. Ex. Docs.*, 52nd Cong., 2nd sess., No. 77, pp. 135–36; *For. Rels.* (1894), App. II, 141; cf. *Pacific Commercial Advertiser*, April 23, 25, Sept. 5, Oct. 10, 1868, June 19, 1869.
20. McCook to Seward, June 7, 1867, printed in *Sen. Ex. Docs.*, 52nd Cong., 2nd sess., No. 77, pp. 10–11.
21. The island, lying three thousand miles west of San Francisco, in position

177° W., 28° N., was discovered by Captain N. C. Brooks, commander of the Hawaiian bark *Gambia*, in July, 1857.

22. See *Pacific Commercial Advertiser*, March 14, 1868.

23. Some officials claimed that they did not want the *Lackawanna* to attract the attention of other powers and have them send ships of their own, but those intimate with the King said that it was only his personal enmity to Reynolds as a known associate of the annexationists that caused hostility to the presence of the vessel (Carter to Bond, May 16, 1867, Bond Correspondence).

24. Reynolds to Welles, Jan. 20, 1868, U.S. Navy Dept., Letters, No. 3, File No. 1128–36.

25. "The Hawaiian Islands and the Treaty," *San Francisco Evening Bulletin*, Sept. 21, 1868.

26. Some excitement was occasioned when Spalding's name appeared on the published account of the letter from the Secretary of State to the Senate listing the secret agents appointed by him.

27. *Sen. Docs.*, 56th Cong., 2nd sess., No. 231, Pt. 6, p. 593.

28. Spalding to his father, Dec. 10, 1867, Jan. 15, March 29, April 14, 1868, USDS, Dispatches, Hawaii, XII. The last one, misdated 1869 in printing, appears in *Sen. Ex. Docs.*, 52nd Cong., 2nd sess., No. 77, pp. 142–45.

29. Minutes of the meeting of June 20, 1867, Hawaiian Club Papers, MSS, Harvard College Library.

30. Marshall to Bond, July 15, 18, 19, 1867, Bond Correspondence.

31. Carter to Bond, May 16, 1867, Bond Correspondence.

32. *Hawaiian Club Papers*, edited by a committee of the Club (Boston, 1868), p. 53.

33. Bond to Sumner, Sept. 18, 1867, Hawaiian Club Letter Book, pp. 98–99, with Marshall to Sumner, Sept. 1, 1867, encl.

34. Marshall to Reynolds, Aug. 14, 1867, *ibid.*, p. 94, and Bond Correspondence. His letters to Sumner and Reynolds were adopted by the Hawaiian Club at its meeting of Aug. 28, 1867. Cf. Minutes of that date and of Oct. 28, 1867, Hawaiian Club Papers, MSS.

35. Bond to Carter, Aug. 19, 1867, Hawaiian Club Letter Book, pp. 95–96.

36. *Ibid.*

37. Bond to W. E. Dodge, Sept. 27, 1867, *ibid.*, pp. 100–01. Captain Wakeman, as an agent of William H. Webb of New York, promoter of steam navigation, later reported on the harbor of Pago Pago, Tutuila, in the Samoan Islands. See *Report of Capt. E. Wakeman to W. H. Webb, on the Islands of the Samoan Group . . . September 20, 1871* (New York, 1872), pp. 7, 14–15, 16.

38. Minutes of the meetings of Sept. 25, Oct. 28, and 31, 1867, Hawaiian Club Papers, MSS.

39. *San Francisco Evening Bulletin*, Nov. 22, 1867; George B. Merrill, "Hawaiian Civilization," *Overland Monthly*, I, (1868) 80.

40. *San Francisco Evening Bulletin*, Nov. 22, 1867.

41. Merrill, p. 80; Merrill to Bond, Oct. 29, Nov. 28, 1867, Bond Correspondence.

42. McCook to Seward, Dec. 20, 1867, USDS, Dispatches, Hawaii, XII. A copy of the telegram is included and also encl. in McCook to Bond, Jan. 5, 1868, Bond Correspondence.

43. Peirce to Bond, Nov. 25, 1867, *ibid.* In the early 1890's his son Lawrence served as Hawaiian consul for Boston and Portsmouth.

44. McCook to Bond, Dec. 14, 1867, *ibid.*
45. Memorial of Boston Board of Trade, Dec., 1867, in folder VI, *ibid.*
46. Peirce to Bond, Dec. 14, 1867, *ibid.* Marshall returned to the capital in the new year to assist in the labors.
47. Bond to John C. Merrill, Dec. 20, 1867, *ibid.* On Feb. 27, 1867, in letters to T. D. Elliot and A. P. Rice, Bond maintained that the "San F. refiners have now the monopoly of the white sugar market of California and Oregon."
48. *Sen. Ex. Journal*, XV, 792, 793, XVI, 158, 334, 354–55; cf. *New York Times*, *New York Tribune*, June 25, 26, 1868.
49. McCook to Sumner, May 29, 1868, Charles Sumner Correspondence, LXXXV, MSS, Harvard College Library.
50. James B. Richardson, ed., *A Compilation of the Messages and Papers of the Presidents* (10 vols., Washington, 1896–99?), VI, 689; *For. Rels.* (1894), App. II, p. 146.
51. Hamilton Fish Diary, Jan. 14, 15, Feb. 10, 1870, I, Pt. 3 typed copy, pp. 320–21, 364, Library of Congress; Allen to Mrs. Allen, Jan. 13, 15, 21, 23, 28, 1870, Allen Papers.
52. Allen to Mrs. Allen, Feb. 12, 17, 1870; cf. *ibid.*, Feb. 5, 9, 10, 14, 16, 1870.
53. *Ibid.*, May 17, 21, 22, 1870.
54. *Sen. Ex. Journal*, XVII, 463–66.
55. Grimes fell ill in the summer of 1868 and Fessenden died in the autumn of 1869.
56. Mott Smith to S. H. Phillips, No. 5, April 7, 1869, AH, Treaty Docs.
57. Ralph S. Kuykendall, *The Hawaiian Kingdom 1854–1874: Twenty Critical Years* (Honolulu, 1953), p. 220.
58. Allen to Harris, June 2, July 10, 1870, AH Treaty Docs.
59. Harris to Varigny, unofficial, Nov. 26, 1867.
60. *San Francisco Evening Bulletin*, Sept. 21, 1868, reprinted in *Hawaiian Gazette*, Oct. 21, 1868, and in *Pacific Commercial Advertiser*, Oct. 24, 1868. Similarly, the British Consul General in Honolulu reported that little interest seemed to be taken by American residents there in the Reciprocity Treaty, a fact which possibly indicated that if the treaty failed, the annexation project would "come up again stronger than ever." Wodehouse to FO, No. 10, April 29, 1867, FO 58/112.
61. McCook to Sumner, May 29, 1868, Charles Sumner Correspondence, LXXXV, 67.
62. Harris to Varigny, Dec. 20, 1867.
63. *San Francisco Evening Bulletin*, Nov. 22, Dec. 14, 1867.
64. *Daily Alta California* (San Francisco), Nov. 20, 1867; cf. *ibid.*, Jan. 25, Feb. 15, 1868.
65. See "Our Flag in the Pacific," *New York Times*, July 22, 1868.
66. Merrill, pp. 80–81. American residents in the Islands, always ready to believe in French and British intrigues, assumed that the treaty was fostered in Honolulu by the anti-American group headed by Charles de Varigny (Varigny, pp. 278–79).
67. Hamlin to Allen, July 16, 1869, Allen Papers.
68. *Pacific Commercial Advertiser*, April 25, Sept. 5, Oct. 10, 1868, June 19, 1869; Judd to Bond, April 2, 1867, Carter to Bond, May 16, 1867, Bond Correspondence; cf. *For. Rels.* (1894), App. II, 140–41, 149–51.
69. McCook to Seward, No. 24, Sept. 30, 1867, with Notes of Conversation Saturday, Sept. 14, 1867, encl., printed in *Sen. Ex. Docs.*, 52nd Cong., 2nd

sess., No. 77, but incorrectly dated Sept. 14, 1869. The *Lackawanna* incident was brought to the attention of the Cabinet by Seward on March 24, 1868, when he read a long dispatch addressed to McCook by Varigny. Secretary of the Navy Gideon Welles thought the positions taken by the latter were well founded and he believed there was a "spirit of mischief among those Islands, aggravated . . . by Reynolds" (*Diary of Gideon Welles* [3 vols., Boston and New York, 1911], III, 322). The most serious resentment against the *Lackawanna* was due to the conviction that it was retained in Hawaiian waters to take advantage of Kamehameha V's anticipated death. Cf. Wodehouse to FO, conf., Dec. 26, 1867, FO 58/136.

70. This protest was in part due to a memorial read before the New Orleans Chamber of Commerce on February 7, 1870, and forwarded to the representatives of Louisiana in Washington, which was a long plea for the welfare of the freedman in the southern Atlantic states who would suffer a reduction in wages and be left "unsheltered to the compulsory competition of his own race in bondage in Cuba and Brazil." A copy of this memorial is in the Justin S. Morrill Tariff Papers 1867–1872, AA (M874) Vol. 1, MSS, Baker Library of the Harvard Business School.

71. John Patterson, "The United States and Hawaiian Reciprocity, 1867–1870," *Pacific Historical Review*, VII (1938), 25–26.

72. Peirce to Fish, Nos. 15, 64, Sept. 11, 1879, July 30, 1870, USDS, Dispatches, Hawaii, XII, XIII.

73. *Fish Diary*, Oct. 18 and Dec. 20, 1870, II.

4

RECIPROCITY WITH PEARL RIVER

LAGOON

First Proposals

RECIPROCITY, though rejected by the United States Senate and shunned by Grant's Cabinet, did not long remain a dead issue. An unofficial proposition was submitted to Secretary Fish and to President Grant in July and September, 1870, by Colonel Z. S. Spalding, an annexationist formerly opposed to reciprocity but now associated with the Hawaiian King, the Minister of the Interior, Dr. Ferdinand W. Hutchinson, and Captain James Makee (one of whose daughters the Colonel later married) in a sugar venture on Maui.[1] Visiting Washington in the summer of 1870, Spalding sent a letter to Fish—at the latter's request—and, later, one to President Grant in which he stated that, while he had no official authorization, he felt justified in expressing the opinion that if the United States would enter into a reciprocity treaty, admitting free of duty Hawaiian sugar up to number 16 Dutch standard, the Hawaiian Government would grant or lease to the Government of the United States "for the term of ninety-nine years, at a nominal rental, sufficient land and water privileges upon the Island of Oahu near the port of Honolulu to enable the said U.S. Government to establish a Naval Depot . . . which shall at all times be free to and under the control of said United States Government." He further indicated that the Hawaiian Government "will agree that like privileges shall be granted to no other Country, and also that the United States may protect and defend their own property whenever the Hawaiian Government shall fail to do so."[2] In his letter to the Secretary of State, Spalding referred to the recently established line of British steamers between Honolulu and New Zealand and Australian ports, which opened a new market for Hawaiian products and might even absorb the entire trade of the

Islands, should the Australian colonies "be made 'free ports' by a treaty of reciprocity with Hawaii." Such a contingency might threaten the entire political and economic position of Americans in the archipelago. There is no record of any reply having been made to these unofficial letters.

The year 1872 brought a serious economic depression to Hawaii. Not only was the sugar crop short, but the average price was lower than that in past years. Custom House statistics for the year indicated a falling off of nearly five million pounds in the quantity of sugar exported. The accession of a new king, William Lunalilo, who was friendly to American interests, was the cue to commence agitation for a commercial reciprocity treaty which, as generally believed, would bring prosperity. In view, however, of previous failures of the United States Senate to ratify such treaties, there was general recognition that reciprocity alone was unacceptable to Washington and could be secured only through the offer of a *quid pro quo*.

One of the first to suggest the idea that the Pearl River lagoon might be leased to the United States for use as a naval station was Henry M. Whitney, who, on January 27, 1873, presented to the King a paper entitled "Reciprocity and How to Secure It," pointing out that the lease of the lagoon for a period of fifty years, more or less, "would materially aid our agricultural and other industries" and "tend to draw new capital here, with an increase of commerce and population, with their accompanying wealth and resources." At no expense to Hawaii, the lease "would secure the opening and improvement of one of the finest harbors in the Pacific Ocean, now lying idle and useless," and also "secure the expenditure of a large sum annually by its occupants, in necessary public improvements, and in the refitting of naval vessels and other vessels, which now go elsewhere." Whitney further maintained: "It will defeat and indefinitely postpone all projects for the annexation of these Islands to any foreign power, at the same time that it will secure to us all the benefits claimed by the advocates of annexation, and will guarantee our national independence under our native rulers as long as the treaty may continue. For this reason, it ought to receive the cordial cooperation of all the European Powers." It would also "provide for the permanent rule of the *native Aliis*, under the existing popular form of government."[3] Reportedly the King favored the proposal, but since it was believed the United States Government would not be interested in a lease and would consider nothing less than a cession of the territory in question, the idea was dropped.

Demands for reciprocity, however, were forthcoming elsewhere. The first days of the following month H. A. P. Carter and other businessmen and planters prepared and addressed a petition to the King urging prompt official action to meet the exigencies of the economic situation and the difficulties under which the planters were laboring. The petitioners emphasized the "importance of immediately providing for large accessions to our laboring classes and of making another effort to secure a Treaty of Reciprocity with the United States of America." They suggested that the negotiation of such a treaty would be more likely to succeed "if it could be aided by your Majesty's personal presence in Washington."[4] This memorial, which made no reference to Pearl River, though unpublicized was quietly circulated throughout the business community.

The first open and published proposal that the Pearl River lagoon be offered as *quid pro quo* for a reciprocity treaty appeared on February 8, 1873, in the *Pacific Commercial Advertiser*, whose editor had favored the reciprocity treaty of 1867. The editorial referred to the unsatisfactory business outlook and expressed the opinion that the time was propitious for the negotiation of a reciprocity treaty with the United States. Hawaii, if necessary, could offer "a position for a harbor and coaling station. . . . We refer, of course, to the Pearl River." Several "persons high in authority" had questioned Minister Peirce about the probable reaction of his Government to an offer of such a cession, and he had expressed the opinion that the United States would probably object to acquiring sovereignty over only a part of the island. Admiral A. M. Pennock of the U.S.S. *California*, that had brought Schofield and Alexander on a vacation to Honolulu, believed that such an offer, if made, would be accepted. General Schofield evidently shared the same opinion.[5]

The Honolulu Chamber of Commerce, several of whose members were actively considering reciprocity behind the scenes, debated the subject at its meeting of February 12, when Samuel N. Castle resolved that "a Committee of this Chamber be appointed to confer with the Government and ascertain if any measure can be devised to induce the Government of the United States to enter into a Treaty of Reciprocity with the Hawaiian Islands." Carter seized the opportunity to read to the Chamber the petition he and others had quietly circulated earlier in the month and asked the members to endorse this. During his remarks he spoke favorably of the cession of Pearl Harbor in exchange for the desired treaty. An attempt to substitute this petition for Castle's resolution failed, for there was opposition to the King's

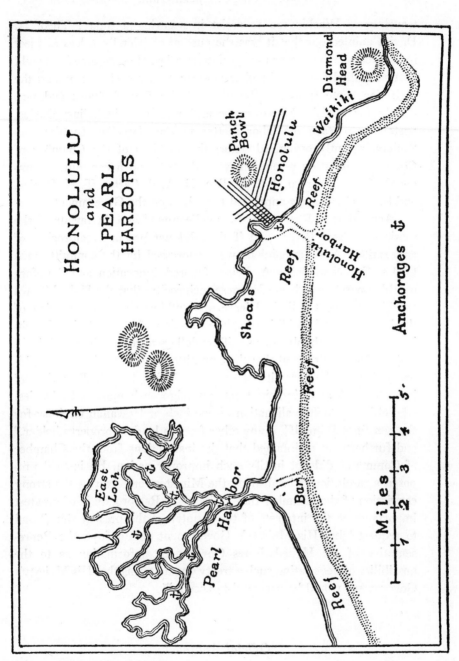

MAP OF PEARL HARBOR

traveling to Washington to assist in securing a treaty. Theo. H. Davies pointed out that it was the custom of friendly rulers to meet for conference, but never to negotiate treaties. He considered it would be undignified for the Chamber to suggest any such step unless the invitation came from the President of the United States and was simply for a visit. Moreover, several members, including Davies, preferred to leave the labor matter to the Hawaiian Immigration Society, recently organized under the auspices of the Chamber of Commerce. Castle's resolution was adopted, and a committee, composed of W. L. Green, J. S. Walker, H. A. P. Carter, T. H. Davies, and S. N. Castle, was appointed to wait upon the Government.

According to Davies, his four colleagues "were in favour of the cession of Pearl River—and if that did not procure reciprocity, of annexation." Various opinions were expressed by the committeemen to the effect that Henry A. Peirce favored annexation and therefore would oppose any scheme for mere reciprocity; that the United States would not accept a limited lease or anything short of a cession of the lagoon; that in addition to the remission of sugar duties, Washington would probably offer a million dollars to secure the naval depot and station.[6] A proposal that the committee should "wait on the Cabinet and urge the necessity of at once offering to cede Pearl River" in exchange for a reciprocity treaty was vigorously opposed by Davies, who objected to "the alienation of one inch of Hawaiian territory for the benefit of [himself] or any other foreign land or property holder," and furthermore maintained that the instructions from the Chamber of Commerce did not justify such improper action. He instead proposed a resolution to "wait upon the Ministers and express the strong conviction of the Chamber that a Treaty of Reciprocity is of greatest importance to the interests of the country at the present time," and to request "that His Majesty's Government obtain from the Representative of the United States Government information as to the possibility of negotiating such a treaty on any terms that His Majesty's Government would be prepared to accept."[7]

Official Approach

THE committee adopted this resolution and presented it to the Cabinet Ministers who promised to give it their serious attention. On February 26, Charles R. Bishop, Minister for Foreign Affairs, sent a

note to Peirce stating the desire of the Hawaiian Government to negotiate a reciprocity treaty with the United States and inquiring whether
there was "a fair prospect for success in a new project." He made
no reference to Pearl Harbor, but verbally stated that he was not
authorized to offer any new inducements other than what was proposed in 1866. The United States Minister replied that he was convinced of the value of a reciprocity treaty, but since he had no information in the present attitude of his Government, he would have to
await instructions.[8]

Peirce had already informed the State Department of the activity
in Honolulu and the proposed panacea; "the cession of the sovereignty
and proprietorship of the spacious, landlocked, easily defended harbor
or estuary known as Ewa or Pearl River, in this island, 10 miles
distant from Honolulu, and also to include the territory surrounding
it, say 10 miles square in all." Although an ardent annexationist, he
was of the opinion that neither the King nor the Hawaiian people
would at this time willingly agree to annexation. "The glitter of the
crown, love of power, and emoluments of office have too many attrac-
tions to prevent it." Consequently, he urged Fish to consider reciprocity. Now in forwarding to the Secretary of State Bishop's inquiry,
the Minister confided his belief that if the United States would open
negotiations afresh, the Hawaiian Government would be prepared to
propose an amendment to the Treaty of 1867, providing for the admission into the United States, free of duty, of all Hawaiian sugars up
to number 15 Dutch standard instead of admitting only those sugars
up to number 12, and would consent as a remuneration therefore, to
"cede to the United States, the proprietory title & sovereignty, to ten
miles square of its territory, with the harbor of Pearl River; situated
10 or 12 miles N W of Honolulu; a place highly valuable & adapted
for a Naval Depot for the United States." He mentioned the rumored
opposition of Theo. H. Davies, acting British Commissioner, and
Captain Ralph P. Cator, of H.B.M.S. *Scout*, to any cession of Hawaiian territory, but dismissed this handicap with the statement that
there was a sufficient number of Americans in Hawaiian Government
offices "to treat such unwarranted interference with the scorn it
deserves."[9]

Peirce was impressed with the necessity for United States action
to benefit his own as well as his countrymen's interests in the Islands.
Whether such action should be directed toward annexation, a reciprocity treaty based on the terms named with a defensive and offensive alliance, or a protectorate was for Washington to consider and

decide; otherwise, the United States must be content to see the greater portion of the trade with these Islands slip gradually into the channels of the British colonies in this part of the world. The Islands themselves sooner or later would become the possession of a European nation with whom some day the United States might be engaged in hostilities. To have to forcibly acquire the archipelago, at a great cost in blood and treasure, would be a calamity "that should be prevented in season."

The Minister pointed out that the duty on Hawaiian sugar in the United States was two and a half to three and a half cents per pound, in British Columbia and New Zealand two cents, and in Australia three-fourths to one cent. Unless preventive measures were taken, these low duties, with the establishment of a contemplated line of British steamers, were likely to give the British interests in the trade and navigation of the Pacific superiority over those of the United States. He was of the opinion that the cession to the United States of Pearl River Harbor would "undoubtedly lead, sooner or later to the cession of the entire Archipelago" and he suggested that provision might perhaps be made in the treaty "that the latter event shall occur on decease of the reigning sovereign; Thereby making the United States his successor to the sovereignty of the country."[10]

In mid-January, Major General John M. Schofield and Brigadier General B. S. Alexander, ostensibly vacationing, but in reality acting under confidential instructions of Secretary of War William W. Belknap, visited the Sandwich Islands to "ascertain the defensive capabilities of their different ports, examine into their commercial facilities," and collect information that would be helpful "in event of a war with a powerful maritime nation."[11] The two generals remained in the Islands for two months quietly obtaining the information they were seeking and keenly observing passing events.

Throughout the spring and summer, public and private debate raged over reciprocity, the cession of Pearl River, and annexation. Both the *Pacific Commercial Advertiser* and the *Hawaiian Gazette* carried numerous articles on these controversial subjects, the greater number opposing annexation; both newspapers, however, favored reciprocity and approved the cession of the lagoon. The February 22 issue of the *Pacific Commercial Advertiser* chose annexation rather than independence, which meant "possible and even probably retrogression." A resolution and a petition signed by numerous sugar planters and businessmen favoring the cession of Pearl River lagoon were published in its March 1 columns. Public meetings and forums, in which well-reasoned arguments were advanced, were held on the subject.[12]

In an address at the Hawaiian Hotel on March 11, Stephen H. Phillips, who had recently served as Attorney General, maintained that a reciprocity treaty was hopeless. As Attorney General, he had taken offense at President Johnson's remarks of December 9, 1868 to the effect that reciprocity would lead to a voluntary application for admission to the Union, now out of grace with the new King. Phillips believed that something more tempting must be offered, but entertained the gravest doubts that the Pearl River cession would recommend itself to Americans. Reciprocity, popular ten years before, was now odious. The advantage of such treaties was all on the other side; the Canadian treaty on the American continent and the Anglo-French treaty in Europe were found to work unequally. The principle of reciprocity was so exceptional and irregular that it disturbed normal commercial relations. According to Phillips, it was evident that the United States saw no advantage in such a treaty, and he was not aware of any new arguments by which it could be recommended. Hawaiian national life, nevertheless, required free access to the American markets, "and must be sustained if need be, by the sacrifice of national pride." In short, since absolute independence was no longer practical, annexation was inevitable. Phillips' former colleague, Charles C. Harris, apologized for these outspoken utterances by saying that he and his friend were born under free institutions where free discussion was the life of the nation; then he moved for a resolution of thanks for the speech and proposed that "a permanent organization be formed to sustain the interest which the address was meant to arouse."[13]

This interest was maintained throughout the summer and early autumn with a mounting opposition from native Hawaiians to any alienation of their soil, and was fanned by the violent editorializing of Walter Murray Gibson in the *Nuhou Hawaii*. The publication of this newspaper was undertaken not as a business, but in order to defeat the Pearl Harbor project and to establish an enduring sentiment on behalf of maintaining Hawaiian independence. Four days after Phillips' utterances, in a public address in the same hotel, H. A. P. Carter answered the lawyer by advocating reciprocity, insisting that it was essential and that it could be attained by the cession of Pearl Harbor. Annexation, though possible in the future, was neither necessary nor practical at this time.

Actually, the United States Government was not seriously inter-

ested in a reciprocity treaty even with the offer of a naval base. In
a long instruction, Hamilton Fish indicated that it was unsafe to
predict "how far the equivalent of a cession of Pearl Bay would
operate a change of opinion on the subject." "A proposition to that
effect, when regularly made, will receive due consideration." He,
however, held out little encouragement for the measure and for the
King's visit to the United States, which might have as its purpose
the attainment of that objective. The Secretary wrote Peirce that both
houses of Congress were more or less adverse to such a treaty, not
only because deference was granted to those states who had or hoped
to have sugar as one of their staples, or because under the most-
favored-nation clause the United States would be obliged to admit
Hawaiian sugar on the same terms, but also because regulation of
duties by treaty would deprive the House of Representatives of its
constitutional control over questions of revenue revision. The Secretary of State discussed at length the subject of annexation, and
referred to the strong support for it from "many persons in the Islands
representing large interests, and great wealth," and from people of
"influence and of wise foresight" in the United States. He also mentioned its influential opponents.

On receipt of this dispatch, Peirce, in a letter of June 3 addressed
to the Hawaiian Minister of Foreign Affairs, quoted only the first
part of his instructions relating to Pearl Bay, indicating the willingness of the United States to entertain a proposition. In the intervening
period, pressure and petitions from the planting and commercial
interests had led King Lunalilo, his adviser, ministers, and Chief
Justice Elisha H. Allen to consider various aspects of the question.
At Cabinet Council meetings on June 9, July 2, and July 5, the pros
and cons of reciprocity with the cession of territory, and the problems
involved in this particular case, were thoroughly discussed. Edwin O.
Hall, Minister of the Interior, and Albert Francis Judd, Attorney
General, the latter born and reared in the Islands, had a natural repug-
nance to the cession of any territory, but they, along with Allen, were
convinced that there would be no treaty without the cession of Pearl
Harbor. Since the only hope of pulling Hawaii out of the depression
and ensuring future progress rested with the prosperity of the sugar
industry, they were in favor of Bishop's proceeding with the negotiation. Robert Stirling, Minister of Finance, was the only cabinet
member who would not advise the cession. The situation would have
been different with an outlying island. But, he argued, the territory
desired "would contain one hundred and twenty square miles at the

least, making a long boundary line, upon which difficulties would arise, and although the United States were friendly to Hawaii now, they might not always remain so." The Englishman insisted that economic conditions in the Islands had been "painted in colors too dark to represent the truth"; that the depression in business was the result of a short crop and low prices the preceding year, a combination of unfavorable circumstances not likely to reoccur; that the tendency in the United States and elsewhere was towards lower duties, "and in a few years the duties on sugar might be so low that reciprocity, for which we would have parted with territory, past recovery, would be of no advantage"; moreover, he regarded the measure as class legislation to which he was opposed. Hall could not agree that the proposal was such, for all branches of trade and business depended upon the success of the sugar interest. "They are all bound together; the advantages of their success are distributed throughout the entire community, and their failure would be a serious detriment to all."

The Minister of Foreign Affairs refrained from expressing his personal opinion, but observed that by reciprocity, "under a proper treaty, our security as an independent nation would not be diminished, but rather promoted, and that there would really be less danger of encroachment with than without the treaty." He indicated on a map of Pearl River and surroundings what he understood from conversations with General Schofield and Admiral Pennock would be required by the United States, and discussed the nature of the cession. He told King Lunalilo that it rested with him to say what should be done; His Majesty replied that the Council favored the resolution to open negotiations.[14]

At the July 2 meeting of the Council, Justice Allen suggested that Bishop make a proposal to Peirce in general terms which would probably eventuate in an understanding. Stirling observed that the "general term 'Pearl River' was too indefinite, and more might be understood and claimed than was intended to be given." He favored postponement of an offer of cession to give time for petitions to be sent in, so that the popular opinion might be known; he believed that numerously signed petitions would be presented to the King. Allen opposed delay, thinking that nothing could be settled by petitions. Businessmen throughout the Islands were waiting with great solicitude for the action of the Government; if a treaty were negotiated it would not be final until approved by the Legislature. Hall felt that it was time for the public to know whether the Government had a policy or not; if it had one, "it ought to be adhered to and carried out with vigor."

The ministers were embarrassed by the undecided state of affairs; "if His Majesty was unable to make up his mind to cede any territory, there was no use in trying further for reciprocity . . . it must be supported by the king or dropped altogether."

King Lunalilo then said that he "had been warned and advised by old residents and some natives against cession of territory"; he did not like to cede; he knew that a few, "the planters and some others, would be benefited by reciprocity, but did not know how it would affect the mechanics and natives"; he was in favor of trying it, of having his ministers commence negotiation, and he would finally decide whether or not to sign the treaty.[15]

At a Cabinet Council meeting three days later, Bishop read a draft of a letter addressed to Peirce. King Lunalilo said that although he had determined to follow the advice which had been given by a majority of his Cabinet at the last meeting, "he did not wish to act hastily in this matter." His Minister of Foreign Affairs replied that reciprocity and the cession of Pearl River had been under consideration a long time, and "That unless it is really intended to try earnestly for reciprocity and to cede the lagoon and a reasonable extent of territory for a Naval Station, for national purposes, under proper restrictions and conditions, it is worse than folly to commence any negotiations; and he wished His Majesty to be satisfied in his own mind, so as to act decidedly with his Ministers for the accomplishment of the object in view." Hall, Judd, and Allen each favored signing the letter and proceeding with the negotiations. The King also approved the letter, authorized Bishop to sign it, and to negotiate a treaty upon the terms proposed. Stirling, however, was opposed to ceding any territory on any terms, and said that he "would favor reciprocity 'pure and simple,' " and be willing to expend considerable money in securing it; if the United States had "a proper sense of justice or were disposed to act generously, there was a fair basis for such a treaty between the two governments, without any cession, the imports from the United States and the exports to them being of about the same value." The Chief Justice again observed that "his experience and the results of all former efforts convinced him that reciprocity without cession was unobtainable."[16]

Bishop informed Peirce on July 7 that he had been authorized to negotiate at Honolulu a reciprocity treaty on the basis of the one signed May 21, 1867, subject to some changes and modifications, the most important of which would be to raise from number 12 to number 16 Dutch standard of color, the grades of sugars that would be admitted into the United States free of duty, and to include a "cession of land for a Naval Station under such reservations, restrictions and conditions as the interests of the contracting parties may seem to require."[17] In forwarding Secretary Fish a copy of Bishop's letter, Peirce strongly recommended prompt acceptance of the proposition. He had already warned the State Department that in case Hawaii failed to secure a reciprocity treaty with the United States, strong efforts would be made to negotiate one with the Australian colonies and British Columbia where Hawaiian products found a ready market at rates of duty much less than those imposed by the United States.

On July 3, writing of the prospects of a reciprocity treaty with the cession of Pearl Bay, "which would be approved by a large majority of the people outside Honolulu," the Minister observed that the nation did not seem prepared to adopt the measures necessary for annexation to the United States, but the death of the King or a general bankruptcy of the people would no doubt precipitate the event. In this dispatch he enclosed a cutting from the *Pacific Commercial Advertiser* of June 21, reporting that the people and Government of Canada would not only receive with favor any propositions coming from Hawaii looking to the establishment of reciprocal trade, but were actually considering initiating such negotiations. The *Advertiser* quoted the *Chicago Daily Tribune* of May 9, 1873, which stated that a resolution had been moved in the House of Commons in Ottawa favoring the establishment of reciprocal trade between Canada and the Sandwich Islands. The opinion in Honolulu appeared to be that the planters' needs could quite possibly be met by the British colonies of Australia and New Zealand or from the Dominion of Canada with less effort, negotiation and attendant expense than would be required to see a reciprocity treaty through the United States Senate. Yet, such an arrangement would be made only as a last resort. As the *Hawaiian Gazette* observed on August 31: "If we fail at Washington, then it may be advisable to make a similar effort with England, and one or more of her colonies, which, though not offering the same advantages, may be induced to negotiate with us for political reasons."

Meanwhile, on May 8, Generals Schofield and Alexander, in their report to Secretary of War Belknap, recommended securing the Pearl River estuary and estimated that approximately $250,000 would be required to remove the coral bar stretching across the entrance and thus open a channel deep enough for ocean-going vessels to enter "the fine sheltered sheet of deep water." They observed that neither the Government nor the native people of the Islands were at that time prepared to consider the question of annexation, even if the United States desired to propose it, "but the cession of Pearl River Harbor as an equivalent for free trade" was "freely discussed and favorably considered by the government and people." The officers warned that "if the United States is ever to have a harbor of refuge and naval station in the Hawaiian Islands in the event of war, the harbor must be prepared in advance by the removal of the Pearl River Bar. When war has begun it will be too late to make the harbor available, and there is no other suitable harbor on these islands."[18]

In forwarding to the State Department survey maps of Pearl Bay and a memorandum concerning stipulations which should be provided for in a treaty for the cession of Pearl Lochs, Peirce observed that "in view of the critical position of affairs in this country, I cannot too strongly urge the United States Government to obtain as soon as possible by means of Treaty, and on the general terms proposed by the government; of a legal status & foothold, in the territory of this country." According to the Minister, much influence was being exerted there privately and openly—chiefly by English residents—to prevent the consummation of an agreement. Although American capital and know-how had built up much of Hawaii's industry, particularly sugar, and the United States enjoyed almost a monopoly of the Islands' trade, English business interests there were still strong, and if trade were to swing to parts of the Empire, Hawaii might drift into the British sphere. Peirce's long dispatches repeated pleas to seize the opportunity to tie the Hawaiian Islands to the United States so strongly that they could not be drawn away into any competing or hostile political or commercial system.

In Washington, at a Cabinet meeting of October 3, 1873, Peirce's dispatch Number 221 of September 4 was read, and the maps of Pearl Bay accompanying it exhibited. Considerable conversation ensued and questions were asked relative to the status of trade and the internal politics of the Islands. President Grant decided to bring the subject to the notice of Congress and authorized a reply to Peirce to that effect, adding that "the proposition in the main is somewhat favorably regarded."[19]

Secretary Fish's communication contained the following observation: "It is possible that the acquisition suggested might in some respects be advantageous to the United States. No encouragement, however, can, under existing circumstances, be given that the proposition will be accepted upon the terms proposed. There is full experience that a reciprocity treaty with the Sandwich Islands is not palatable to the Senate, and the expediency of acquiring further territory abroad is doubted by reflecting members of Congress, whose opinions have much influence."[20]

Opposition

MEANWHILE, there was building up among Hawaiians a seething discontent and a bitter, insidious antagonism to the cession of Pearl Harbor, primarily because relinquishment of ownership of the bay was linked with the eventual loss of sovereignty over the Islands. Early in the debate, on February 22, 1837, the *Pacific Commercial Advertiser*, in an editorial entitled "Annexation—Independence," raised the issue and examined which course was better "for the *whole people* of the land, Hawaiians and all others," asserting:

> Annexation means the lifting of the great tax from our country's products, so that we shall be paid for and encouraged in our industry. It means the stimulus of industry to the Hawaiian, which will save him from extinction, if anything can. It means his independence *by his own chosen legislature and laws in all local matters*, as real as at present. It means prosperity to the schools, from the wise expenditure of funds granted by the U.S. Government. It means a reasonable pension or subsidy to those chiefs who have magnanimously given up certain political rights for the prosperity and good of *all* their people. . . . It means national prosperity instead of adversity. It means vigorous life of the people, instead of gradual decay and death. Which is best, and which must every lover of the Hawaiian race and of his own choose? It seemed as though there could be but one answer from Hawaiians, Americans, Britons, Germans, or any other else.
>
> Independence means a continued struggle for separate national life and prosperity, because our great staple products are so heavily taxed in our only reliable market that they will hardly pay for the raising in the best of times; but in less favorable times the struggle is so severe as to threaten ruin to our whole

commercial, industrial, and political system, our production, our labor, our mechanics, our carrying trade, our merchandising, our importing, our revenue. *Independence* then means possible and even probable retrogression, ruin to our laboriously and well built national structure, which all good men, both native and foreign, would mourn to see.

The editorial advocated "immediate annexation" as "undoubtedly the best thing for this people. . . . Gradual union would be the next best course to be pursued; that is a reciprocity treaty, based upon an immediate cession of a naval station and ultimate political annexation when the throne shall become vacant."

Native Hawaiians looked at the question differently. In the same issue of the *Pacific Commercial Advertiser* one observed that "from all indications a party in favor of annexation is now in process of formation in the islands." A proposition which strikes at the life of the nation, "the blow aimed at national existence—at national independence, comes not from the natives of the soil, but from men of foreign birth." Hawaiians believed that the question of annexation was "entirely of foreign growth, like the parasite that clings to and surrounds the tropical forest tree till it crushes out its life and usurps its place." The writer asked: "Would it not be wiser and more prudent of our foreign residents to wait until a single native of the islands raises his voice in favor of annexing his country to a foreign power, before they commence forming a party, or even giving publicity to the proposition?" He concluded:

Not a native has raised a complaining voice against his Government. Not one has asked for annexation. Not one has asked for a treaty of reciprocity. Not one has complained of a want of prosperity. They are contented with the King and Government, they love their country and desire its independence, and are prosperous and happy. They are better fed, clothed and housed and better educated than any other nation of people on our planet, and all they want, is, to be let alone. If the political tinkering of our foreign element, was only directed to a wise economy, not only in the administration of the Government, but in every department of life, and would exert themselves to aid in the development of the industrial resources of the country, they would benefit Hawaii, if not themselves. The annexation of these Islands to any power would be national death.

Those who wished to favor the prejudices of the people talked largely of a sacrifice of dignity in ceding any territory. Walter Murray Gibson, supported by Joseph O. Carter, elder brother of Henry, C. P. Ward, and Godfrey Rhodes worked diligently to prevent cession. The nationalist leader argued that the conditions of the treaty were "unpatriotic and unstatesmanlike," insisting that the United States should not be offered a bonus to induce negotiation of a reciprocity treaty, especially when she considered the Kingdom a "political foster child."[21] Also aligned against the cession were Queen Emma, the Princesses Bernice Pauahi and Liliuokalani, the latter's husband, John O. Dominis, Governor Paul Nahaolelua, and every chief, including David Kalakaua, who, because of his strong opposition to the project, gained considerable popularity with native Hawaiians.

The announcement in the *Pacific Commercial Advertiser* of June 14, 1873 of the Government's intention to cede Pearl River lagoon was the signal for the organization of public opposition to the scheme. The feud was intensified by the incomplete and inaccurate reporting in the Honolulu press, in early June, of Samuel N. Castle's letter which appeared in the New York *Evangelist* of April 17; the press had lifted from the long letter the latter part and asserted that he recommended "On the death of the King and a vacancy on the Throne, the United States have the power to take possession of and annex the Islands."[22] This "unblushing," some even claimed "treasonable," advocacy of annexation caused a furor among native Hawaiians, four hundred of whom met in an incendiary protest meeting in Kaumakapili Church on June 30, listened to an inciting address by Godfrey Rhodes, a British-born member of the Privy Council, and passed two resolutions disapproving of the cession of Pearl Harbor to the United States. A third resolution introduced by David Malo to banish Castle and his family from the Kingdom caused animated discussion and excitement which led the meeting to break up in confusion without acting upon the proposition.[23]

The *Hawaiian Gazette* reported: "a general feeling of profound patriotism seemed to prevail at the idea of ceding to a foreign power any part of the island"; many declared that outside "money and skill to develop the resources of the country were welcome, but any cessions of territory must be unalterably opposed."[24] The belief was widely held that the King at heart objected to the deal. This impression, added to the very active and effective efforts of Ward, Rhodes, Gibson, and others, created a strong prejudice in the minds of the Hawaiians not only against the ministers, but against foreigners and especially Americans.

Theo. H. Davies reported to the British Foreign Office at the end of August that "every week strengthens the opposition of the Hawaiians to the idea of an alienation of soil; and a most bitter feeling is being aroused in the native mind against the party, chiefly Americans, who have urged the cession."[25] In the same month Queen Emma, in writing to a chief, referred to the much discussed reciprocity treaty and the giving away of land and observed: "There is a feeling of bitterness against these rude people who dwell on our land and have high handed ideas of giving away somebody else's property as if it was theirs."[26]

In September the situation became serious when a number of the King's troops mutinied, a disobedience of authority attributed to their hatred of foreign officers. This unfortunate incident resulted in increased race hatred and a considerable loss of respect for the authority of King Lunalilo.[27] Peirce reported that much of the insubordination and disrespect of the people for the Government and their hatred of foreigners could be attributed to the secret machinations of David Kalakaua. In late October, Bishop pessimistically observed that "the people are very much influenced *against* what appears to me to be their best interests. Whether or not they can be made to see what is best, and to take advantage of any opportunities that may be afforded, is very doubtful. The ignorant and inexperienced are easily frightened and prejudiced."[28]

Gibson stepped up his campaign of opposition to the relinquishment of Pearl Bay, warning native Hawaiians in their own tongue against the cession in a semi-political prospectus published in the *Nuhou*, November 4, which appeared in translation in the *Pacific Commercial Advertiser*, November 15, under the title of "The Nuhou's Prospectus," and ran as follows:

> I am a messenger forbidding you
> To give away Puuloa,
> Be not deceived by the merchants,
> They are only enticing you,
> Making fair their faces, they are evil within;
> Truly desiring annexation,
> Greatly desiring their own good;
> They have no thought of good for you,
> A presuming set only are they,

A proud and a haughty set,
Ever soliciting at the same time flattering,
Desiring that *you should all die*,
That the Kingdom may become theirs.

The day before the appearance of this prospectus and a month
before Fish's instruction of October 15, 1873 reached Honolulu, the
subject of relinquishing the lagoon was discussed with the King in
Cabinet, at which time in very plain words the Sovereign was told
"that if he really was favorable to cession he should make it understood *decidedly*, but *quietly* if he chose, and sustain his Ministers"
or withdraw before any definite reply came from the United States.
Since he was of the opinion that "such a measure would not benefit
or promote the happiness of his people," Lunalilo said he "could not
favor and sustain it."[29] The Cabinet therefore decided to withdraw
that part of the proposal relating to the cession of the Pearl River
lagoon, and Peirce was so notified. At the same time he was informed
that the Hawaiian Government still favored a treaty of reciprocity
similar to that of May 21, 1867.[30]

Bishop reported to a Hawaiian consul abroad that it had become
so evident that the Hawaiian Legislature would not approve the
cession, and "that good faith and honesty seemed to require that we
should say so and stop unfounded expectations, useless negotiations,
and unprofitable discussion." The King and a majority of the people
would "strongly favor reciprocity without cession of territory; but
without reciprocity our situation is by no means desperate, either
financially or politically, with reciprocity our trade with the United
States would be greatly increased, for it is the habit of our people
to buy to the extent of their means."[31] Peirce, in informing Secretary
Fish of the withdrawal, explained and lamented:

> It has been evident for a short time past, that emissaries and
> political demagogues of foreign and native birth, were exciting
> the passions and prejudices of the people, against cession of terri-
> tory; stirring up strife and enmity between foreigners and natives;
> discrediting the King and government, and creating clamour
> for a change of Ministry. These agitators have succeeded in so
> alarming the government as to induce it, as a matter of pru-
> dence to withdraw the proposition to United States for cession
> of territory. . . .
> Several of the opponents to the cession of Pearl River Lagoon

to the United States, are warm 'annexationists' in reality—acting in the belief that the success of the former measure, would indefinitely postpone the annexation of the Islands to the United States. There are others, possessing but little principle, who aim to create disturbance and political complications; with the hope that a change in affairs, may bring to them office and emolument.

The Hawaiian Government in withdrawing the proposition alluded to, were no doubt influenced therein by a fear of a revolution among its people; reports received from the other Islands indicating excitement and turbulence of feeling among the masses.[32]

Continued Interest

THE withdrawal of the Pearl River offer did not terminate the movement for reciprocity which King Lunalilo claimed to favor. By his direction, the Minister of Foreign Affairs wrote to Justice Allen, then on leave in the United States, instructing him to go to Washington and find out whether a treaty similar to that of 1867 would receive the support of the administration and the approval of the Senate. Allen's mission did not achieve the desired results.[33]

The sugar planters of the Islands, apparently faced with continued high American tariffs, began to search for new export markets and found some hope in Australia, New Zealand, and British Columbia. The growth of population in the Australian colonies had gradually developed an improved market for Hawaiian sugar, and, after some experimenting, it was found that better prices could be obtained in the free trade port of Sydney than in San Francisco, and return cargoes would be brought to Honolulu much more cheaply. Thus the free trade system of the Australian colonies offered some promise of a solution to the planters' problem. The Hawaiian custom house statistics for the year 1873 reveal that 7,013,947 pounds of sugar were exported to Australia and New Zealand, and 1,270,102 pounds to British Columbia, which totaled was more than half the amount—14,828,313 pounds—entering the ports of the United States.[34] Allen reports that a strong effort was made to induce a negotiation with Great Britain for a treaty of reciprocity in order to supply her colonies in the Pacific, but resident Americans urged the

Government to make one more effort with the United States, convinced that "whichever country had the commercial supremacy would probably have the political."[35]

After David Kalakaua ascended the throne in February 1874, following the brief (less than thirteen months) reign of Lunalilo, the sugar factors and businessmen of Honolulu presented an urgent petition to the new monarch predicting economic disaster to the country unless relief to the plantation interests was speedily obtained. The Legislative Assembly in its 1874 session passed an act to initiate negotiations.[36] To conduct these the Cabinet Council appointed Chief Justice Elisha H. Allen Envoy Extraordinary and Minister Plenipotentiary to the United States, and associated with him as Special Commissioner was H. A. P. Carter, then head of the firm of C. Brewer and Company, the largest American exporting house and sugar plantation agency in Hawaii. At the King's request instructions were given the Plenipotentiary "to avoid all reference to any cession of Hawaiian Territory," as it could not be entertained. His Majesty proposed to follow the Chief Justice to Washington, but not as a special negotiator. Allen and Carter sailed for San Francisco on October 19, 1874.

On the same day the British mail steamer *Cyphrenes* reportedly brought to Honolulu an agent and a communication from Premier Julius Vogel of New Zealand to the effect that if the Hawaiian Kingdom desired to obtain a loan from one to three million dollars, for a term of years at an interest rate of five per cent per annum, the Premier would negotiate the same. The security was to be a lien on the property and revenues of the Kingdom. Allegedly assurances were also given by Vogel that efforts would be made to admit Hawaiian sugar free of duty into New Zealand and Australia.

Over a month before, on September 9, the *Hawaiian Gazette*, under the caption "A Grand Scheme, New Zealand and Polynesia," published Vogel's memoranda of October, 1873 and February, 1874 along with an editorial on the Premier's plan for a "Grand Dominion" of islands near and south of the equator.[37] The United States Minister informed Hamilton Fish of both the proposed loan and the scheme to establish a great Polynesian commercial company, enclosed in his dispatch the pertinent cuttings from the *Hawaiian Gazette*, and warned that if the Senate did not ratify the commercial reciprocity treaty already negotiated with Hawaii, the latter would, of necessity, look for its future prosperity to Canada and the British colonies in the Pacific, with the prospect of the Hawaiian chain becoming eventually an appendage of the British Empire. The State Department was informed that Hawaii's entire sugar crop of 1876–77 would flow to British possessions. This intelligence was submitted to the Senate Committee on Foreign Relations, along with warnings of other Americans interested in the fate of their Hawaiian investments and the destiny of the Islands, and caused some senators to realize that reciprocity was assuming a "graver importance, and, as political supremacy in the islands must inevitably follow commerce," a favorable atmosphere was created for an agreement.

Hawaii's Swing toward the British Empire: Myth or Reality?

ONE may pose the question, was there imminent danger in 1874 or thereafter of a Hawaiian swing toward Australasia? The official evidence available indicates there was absolutely none. First, the reports of the arrival in Honolulu of a New Zealand agent on the *Cyphrenes* and of assurances that efforts would be made by the Australasian colonies to admit Hawaiian sugar free of duty appear to be fabrications. A thorough examination of the passenger list of the *Cyphrenes* and of contemporary press items of arriving and departing visitors produced no evidence of any such agent visiting the Islands, and no reference to him is made in the British Consul General's dispatches of this period. Secondly, the question of Hawaii's receiving a loan from New Zealand was never mentioned or discussed in Cabinet Council meetings. There is nothing in the records of the Public Archives of Hawaii to indicate a visit of a New Zealand agent on such an important mission or even the receipt of an official communication on the subject. Moreover, the Julius Vogel Papers, preserved in the Parliamentary Library, Wellington, and the Prime Ministers Papers in the National Archives of New Zealand reveal no such inducement.[38]

A glance at the Hawaiian Custom House statistics and those of the British colonies discloses a definite decline in Hawaiian sugar imported into Australia and New Zealand after the peak year 1873. These colonies' imports of that commodity dropped from 7,013,947 pounds in that year to 4,945,647 pounds in 1874, to 846,166 pounds in 1875, to 55,880 pounds in 1876, to only 703 pounds in 1877, the year that the reciprocity treaty with the United States went into operation, and thereafter sugar ceased to be a significant item in Hawaiian exports statistics regarding those areas. The imports of paddy and rice, however, show a slightly different trend. From 8,000 pounds imported by Australia in 1873 (New Zealand bought none), the amount rose to the startling figure of 247,040 pounds in 1874, but dropped to only 73,804 pounds in 1875, 38,056 pounds in 1876, and to 6,820 pounds in 1877. New Zealand's imports of Hawaiian sugar fell from 369 tons in 1873 to 330 tons in 1874 and 198 tons in 1875, and she imported no rice in 1873 and 1874 and only 8 tons in 1875. Similarly, the value of her Hawaiian imports declined from £13,269 in 1873 to £5,244, £2,688, £1,719, and £382 in the succeeding years, reaching the amazingly low figure of only £47 in 1878.[39] Although the exports of Hawaiian sugar to British Columbia held steady in the years 1873 and 1874, these fell from a high of 1,285,183 pounds in 1874 to 372,517 pounds in 1875, increased to 1,003,330 pounds in 1876, but declined precipitously to only 12,561 pounds in 1877, and thereafter were negligible.[40] After the completion of the Canadian Pacific Railway, Canada commissioned Adjutant General Walker Powell to proceed to Hawaii to investigate the advantages that might accrue from a closer commercial relationship between the two countries. Powell made a careful analysis of the whole question, which he embodied in a report to the Council. The Government in Ottawa discussed the various phases of trade prospects, which were further considered by Theo. H. Davies, British vice consul in Honolulu and head of a prosperous mercantile house there, while he was on a trans-Canadian trip in 1887;[41] however, there is no evidence of any propositions having been made by any British colony in 1874.

In that year New Zealand's population was approximately half a million, and in 1891 it was only 634,058. Similarly, all of Australia, including Tasmania, claimed only 1,849,393 white inhabitants in 1874, and 3,240,985 in 1891.[42] On the other hand, the population of the American republic had advanced to 62,947,714 by 1890. Moreover, both Pacific areas were receiving and refining ample supplies of sugar from Fiji. Sir Frederick Whitaker, speaking on June 15, 1886, in the Legislative Council of New Zealand on the New Hebrides question, asserted that "Australasia had land for growing more sugar than would be needed for the next five hundred years. Fiji was sufficient to produce sugar for the whole of those colonies without any difficulty" and, in addition, there was all of Northern Australia.[43]

Furthermore, paddy could be obtained more cheaply from the East
Indies and Southeast Asia than from Hawaii. Never in history did
the British colonies, or any other nation, offer as attractive a market
for Hawaiian tropical products as did the large and growing population of the comparatively close United States. Ample documentary
evidence exists that some American, Hawaiian, and British officials
were cognizant of this indisputable fact. When the treaty had been
in operation less than two years, James Comly reminded Finance
Minister John M. Kapena that the great distance of other powers
from the products of the Hawaiian Islands served "as an effectual
bar to the enjoyment of reciprocity."[44] Similarly, Henry W. Severance,
Hawaiian consul in San Francisco, in commenting on the prospects
of a Hawaiian-German treaty wrote, "but our Treaty with the United
States is of more importance than all the others."[45] Eight years later,
when H. A. P. Carter mentioned the possibility of Hawaii's negotiating a reciprocity treaty elsewhere, Secretary Thomas F. Bayard
reminded the Minister that it was not within the power of other
states to offer what the United States afforded. In the spring of
1886, when there was talk in Washington of abolishing the treaty,
the Hawaiian Cabinet toyed with the idea—including a promise to
pay five thousand dollars and expenses—of sending Colonel V. V.
Ashford to Canada to take up the treaty if the Americans rejected it,
expecting that "Canada would hold a club over the United States,
as it were, and the latter would not give up the treaty not because
they greatly desire it themselves, but because they would not want
Canada to have it."[46] Finally, in July, 1897, when the British Colonial
Office was considering Richard Seddon's communication of June 23
that objected to the annexation of Hawaii to the United States, the
secret minutes on the draft dispatch of July 30, among other revealing statements, included this: "The trade between N. Zealand &
Australia & Hawaii is very small, nor is there much between Canada
& Hawaii."[47] Nevertheless, in the last quarter of the nineteenth
century the spectre of an economic swing by the Hawaiian Kingdom
toward the British Empire, with its resultant political consequences,
was frequently and effectively raised in Honolulu to excite fears and
to produce action in Washington.

NOTES

1. Testimony of Z. S. Spalding in *Sen. Reps.*, 53rd Cong., 2nd sess., No. 227, p. 238; Spalding's undated statement filed April 1, 1871 in USDS, Consular Letters, Honolulu, XII.
2. Spalding to Fish, July 18, 1870, *ibid.*; Spalding to Grant, Sept. 27, 1870, *ibid.*
3. This paper, not immediately made public, was published in the *Hawaiian Gazette*, Feb. 26, 1873.
4. *Pacific Commercial Advertiser*, Feb. 14, 1873; cf. Davies to Granville, conf., Feb. 11, 1873, FO 58/136.
5. Peirce to Fish, No. 190, Feb. 10, 1873, USDS, Dispatches, Hawaii, XV, printed in *Sen. Ex. Docs.*, 52nd Cong., 2nd sess., No. 77, pp. 148–49; cf. Schofield and Alexander to Belknap, May 8, 1873, *ibid.*, pp. 150–54; Pennock to the Secretary of the Navy, Feb. 15, 1873, encl. with chief clerk of the Navy Department to the Secretary of State, March 20, 1873, USDS, Misc. Letters, March, 1873, Pt. 2; Schofield to Gen. W. T. Sherman, Feb. 15, 1873, encl. with Schofield to the Secretary of State, Feb. 1, 1893, *ibid.*, Feb., 1893.
6. *Pacific Commercial Advertiser*, Feb. 15, 1873; Davies to Granville, conf., Feb. 11, 1873, FO 58/136.
7. Davies to Granville, conf., Feb. 15, 1873, FO 58/136.
8. Bishop to Peirce, Feb. 26, 1873, Peirce to Bishop, Feb. 27, 1873, both printed in the *Pacific Commercial Advertiser*, March 8, 1873; encl. in Peirce to Fish, No. 192, Feb. 28, 1873, USDS, Dispatches, Hawaii, XV. Since all of Peirce's dispatches for 1873 are contained in this volume, it will hereafter be omitted.
9. Peirce to Fish, Nos. 190, 191, Feb. 10, 17, 1873; *For. Rels.* (1894), App. II, 153. The most important of Peirce's dispatches of this period are printed in *For. Rels.* (1873), App. I, 480–515; *Sen. Ex. Docs.*, 52nd Cong., 2nd sess., No. 77, pp. 147–50; *Report of the Historical Commission of the Territory of Hawaii . . . December 31, 1928*, pp. 19–27.
10. Peirce to Fish, No. 192, Feb. 28, 1873.
11. *Sen. Ex. Docs.*, 52nd Cong., 2nd sess., No. 176, p. 150; *ibid.*, No. 77, p. 150; *For. Rels.* (1894), App. II, 154.
12. *Pacific Commercial Advertiser*, March 1, 15, 22, June 14, July 5, 1873; *Hawaiian Gazette*, Feb. 26, July 2, 5, 9, 1873; cf. *Nuhou Hawaii*, Feb. 28, 1873. The *Advertiser*, March 8, 1873, raised the question why necessarily a cession, and not a lease for ten years?
13. *Pacific Commercial Advertiser*, March 15, 1873; encl. No. 1 in Peirce to Fish, No. 198, March 17, 1873; cf. *Hawaiian Gazette*, March 19, 1873, for critical comments; encl. in Peirce to Fish, No. 201, April 10, 1873.
14. Cabinet Council Minute Book, 1866–1874, June 9, 1873.
15. *Ibid.*, July 2, 1873.
16. *Ibid.*, July 5, 1873. These persistent efforts to urge the King toward a policy of reciprocity with the cession of territory were reported by Davies to Granville in Nos. 8 and 9, conf., July 24, Aug. 26, 1873, in FO 58/136; cf. *Commercial Herald* (San Francisco), Aug. 21, 1873.
17. Bishop to Peirce, July 7, 1873, AH, FO & Ex. file; also encl. in Peirce to Fish, No. 213, July 7, 1873.

18. Schofield and Alexander to Belknap, May 8, 1873, *Sen. Ex. Docs.*, 52nd
    Cong., 2nd sess., No. 77, pp. 150–54; *For. Rels.* (1894), App. II, 154–58;
    American Historical Review, XXX (1925), 561–65.
19. Hamilton Fish Diary, Oct. 3, 1873, IV, pp. 175–176.
20. Fish to Peirce, No. 102, Oct. 15, 1873, USDS, Instructions, Hawaii, II.
21. Walter M. Gibson, *Address to the Hawaiian People*, January 31, 1876,
    pamphlet (Honolulu, 1876), p. 2. A copy is encl. in Peirce to Fish, No. 352,
    Feb. 3, 1876, USDS, Dispatches, Hawaii, XVII.
22. The letter, entitled "Sandwich or Hawaiian Islands," was reprinted in the
    Pacific Commercial Advertiser, July 7, 1873, copy encl. in Peirce to Fish,
    No. 214, July 16, 1873, and in Davies to Granville, No. 8, conf., July 24,
    1873, FO 58/136. Peirce had made the identical proposal to Fish in Feb-
    ruary (Peirce to Fish, No. 192, Feb. 28, 1873). See above, p. 88.
23. *Hawaiian Gazette*, July 2, 1873; *Pacific Commercial Advertiser*, July 5,
    1875; cf. encl. No. 2 in Peirce to Fish, No. 212, July 3, 1873.
24. *Hawaiian Gazette*, July 30, 1873. On December 8, 1873, the *Gazette* empha-
    sized that reciprocity was promoted by the planters to improve their fortunes
    and was neither desired nor needed by the mass of the population of Hawaii.
25. Davies to Granville, No. 9, Aug. 26, 1873, FO 58/136.
26. Queen Emma to Kelimoewai, Aug. 20, 1873, private letters of Queen Emma
    in AH.
27. William Alexander, *A Brief History of the Hawaiian People* (Honolulu,
    1899), p. 300; cf. Richard A. Greer, "Mutiny in the Royal Barracks," *Pacific
    Historical Review*, XXXI (1962), 349–58.
28. Bishop to Allen, Oct. 25, 1873, AH, FO Letter Book No. 52.
29. Cabinet Council Minute Book, Nov. 14, 1873.
30. Bishop to Peirce, Nov. 14, 1873, AH, FO Letter Book No. 52. Bishop's letter
    and Peirce's reply of November 17, 1873, were published in the *Hawaiian
    Gazette*, November 17, 1873. Davies reported that the publication of these
    documents "filled the cessionists with disappointment and almost rage." He
    was jubilant over all these events "for he had been from the first a firm
    upholder of the integrity of Hawaiian soil" (Davies to Granville, No. 13,
    conf., Nov. 27, 1873, FO 58/136). Cf. my "British Opposition to the Cession
    of Pearl Harbor," *Pacific Historical Review*, XXIX (1960), 381–94; "Great
    Britain and the Sovereignty of Hawaii," *ibid.*, XXXI (1962), 327–48
    (Louis Knott Koontz Memorial Award Essay, 1963); "Twisting the Lion's
    Tail over Hawaii," *ibid.*, XXXVI (1967), 27–46.
31. Bishop to Odell, Dec. 4, 1873, AH, FO Letter Book No. 52.
32. Peirce to Fish, No. 228, Nov. 18, 1873; cf. No. 229, Nov. 24, 1873, printed
    in *Report of the Historical Commission of the Territory of Hawaii . . .
    1928*, pp. 31–32; cf. *Commercial Herald* (San Francisco), Aug. 12, 1873.
33. Bishop to Allen, Dec. 2, 1873, AH, FO Letter Book No. 52; Allen to Bishop,
    Jan. 6, Feb. 5, 20, 1874, AH, FO & Ex. As early as January 31, 1873, a
    suggestion had been made that Allen be sent to Washington to negotiate
    a reciprocity treaty. He had delayed taking his leave in June, 1873 until
    the treaty matter could be settled (Allen to Mrs. Allen, Jan. 31, June 6,
    1873, Allen Papers).
34. *Custom House Statistics, Hawaiian Islands for Year 1873*, prepared by
    Collector General (Honolulu, 1874), p. 6. *Cong. Record*, 44th Cong., 1st
    sess., Pt. 2, p. 1430, states that in 1873 the Hawaiian Islands exported
    11,595 tons of sugar, of which 4,191 tons were sent to the British colonies.
    Cf. *Hawaiian Gazette*, Feb. 4, 1874.

35. *Remarks of Mr. Elisha H. Allen, Hawaiian Minister, and Geo. S. Boutwell, Counsel, on the Bill for the Termination of the Hawaiian Treaty . . .* (Washington, 1882), p. 8, in Allen Papers.

36. *Laws of His Majesty Kalakaua, King of the Hawaiian Islands, Passed by the Legislative Assembly, at Its Session, 1874, Honolulu, 1874,* Chap. XL, pp. 37–38. Hereafter cited as *Session Laws.*

37. *Hawaiian Gazette,* Sept. 9, 1874.

38. The writer was assisted in this search by the Chief Archivists in charge of the respective Archives.

39. *Custom House Statistics, Hawaiian Islands for Year 1873* (Honolulu, 1874), p. 6; *Statistics of the Colony of New Zealand, 1873, 1874, 1875, 1876, 1877* (Wellington, 1874, 1875, 1876, 1877, 1878), pp. NANZ. See my "Australasian Interest in the Commerce and the Sovereignty of Hawaii," Australia and New Zealand, *Historical Studies,* XI (1964), 500–01.

40. *Custom House Statistics, Hawaiian Islands for Year 1873,* pp. 2, 6, *1874,* p. 6, *1875,* p. 6, *1876,* p. 6, *1877,* p. 6, *1882,* p. 8, *1884,* p. 7.

41. *The Daily Colonist* (Victoria, British Columbia), Nov. 3, 1887; Davies to Salisbury, conf., Nov. 17, 1887, FO 58/241. A year earlier, in the spring of 1886, W. M. Gibson's cabinet considered sending V. V. Ashford to Canada to negotiate a trade treaty (Honolulu *Bulletin,* Aug. 20, 1887). See my "Canada's Interest in the Trade and Sovereignty of Hawaii," *Canadian Historical Review,* XLIV (1963), 20–40, especially pages 23–26.

42. Commonwealth Bureau of Census and Statistics, *Official Year Book of the Commonwealth of Australia,* I, 1901–1907 (Melbourne, 1908), 57.

43. *New Zealand Parliamentary Debates,* LIV (1886), 478.

44. Comly to Kapena, No. 140, July 1, 1878, encl. No. 4 in Comly to Evarts, No. 43, July 8, 1878, USDS, Dispatches, Hawaii, XVIII.

45. Severance to Allen, Oct. 10, 1879, Allen Papers.

46. *Bulletin* (Honolulu), Aug. 20, 1887; Merrill to Bayard, No. 139, Aug. 29, 1887, USDS, Dispatches, Hawaii, XXIII; encl. in Wodehouse to FO, No. 2, pol., Jan. 14, 1891, FO 58/258.

47. Minute on draft dispatch of CO to Seddon, July 30, 1897, CO 537/136; cf. my "Myth of Hawaii's Swing toward Australasia and Canada," *Pacific Historical Review,* XXXIII (1964), 273–93, especially p. 293.

5

RECIPROCITY AND ITS RESULTS

Reciprocity Achieved

ON NOVEMBER 17, 1874, a month after the departure of Allen
and Carter, King Kalakaua, accompanied by Henry A. Peirce,
Governor Dominis, and several other Hawaiian dignitaries, followed
on the U.S.S. *Benicia* as guests of the United States Government.
At first the Cabinet did not favor his making the journey to Washington. At a Cabinet Council meeting called to consider the subject,
out of twenty-five or more present, only Judge Allen, C. C. Harris,
and Henry M. Whitney favored it, while others brought up various
objections. Allen was determined to carry his point, and finally
obtained the removal of every objection, and the ways and means
pledged. The resolution recommending His Majesty to make the
proposed visit was passed unanimously, and from that day the Cabinet, which had all along favored reciprocity, earnestly endorsed the
proposed royal embassy.[1]

So far as the British Consul General was able to ascertain, the
majority of the King's subjects disapproved of his leaving his Islands
so soon after the riots attending his election, for they believed it better
for him to remain home and endeavor to strengthen the foundations
of his Kingdom. King Kalakaua, however, was convinced that a
reciprocity treaty would revive prosperity and declared that "it was
for the good of his people, and not for his own good, that he was
leaving his native land."[2]

The Sovereign spent December 12 to 23 in the nation's capital,
where at 12:30 p.m., on the eighteenth, he was received officially in
the House of Representatives by the Vice President of the United
States and the Speaker of the House in a reception well-attended by
the members of both chambers and their ladies, who crowded the
galleries and occupied places on the floor behind the members. The

King, who was so affected with a cold and hoarseness that he was unable to respond to the Speaker's address of welcome, requested Justice Allen to read a prepared statement, which contained the following: "For our success in government and our progress in a higher civilization we are very much indebted to the government and people of this great country. Your laws and your civilization have been in a great degree our model. I reciprocate most cordially the hope for the continuance and growth of friendly relations between the two countries." A reception given that same evening at the White House by the President was attended by members of the Supreme Court, the Cabinet, Congress, the diplomatic corps, and officers of the army and navy. Without hesitation or debate, Congress appropriated twenty-five thousand dollars to defray the expenses of the visit of His Majesty and suite,[3] which included the cost of a "splendid Pullman car," all food and beverages, and three thousand dollars for a ten-room suite at the Arlington Hotel.

New York wanted to entertain a king, so King Kalakaua spent five thousand dollars of the city's money in ten days, while his popularity soared, and Americans warmed to reciprocity with his Kingdom.[4] He was the first sovereign of any country to visit the United States; his triumphal goodwill tour, well publicized by the press, was helpful in promoting a friendly feeling toward Hawaii among the American people and Government officials and undoubtedly smoothed the way for the treaty negotiations. He, however, took no part in these. The *Hawaiian Gazette*, the San Francisco *Alta California*, and the *Pacific Commercial Advertiser* credited the visit with materially aiding in the passage of the treaty, and the latter complimented the royal visitor on his exemplary behavior, reporting: "He came, although a King, democratically, and as far as possible, without any of the ponderous formalities which monarchs are so fond of wrapping themselves up in. He proved himself an agreeable, intelligent, well-behaved gentleman."[5]

While in the nation's capital, Peirce confided to the Senate Committee on Foreign Relations his views of the threats to the independence of the Hawaiian Kingdom and the urgency of negotiating a reciprocity treaty. On the morning of January 12, 1875, he presented to Senators Simon Cameron, Hannibal Hamlin, Thomas McCreery, and Carl Schurz his arguments on the subject and revealed the alleged secret efforts of New Zealand to loan money to Hawaii in exchange for her sugar, the same information which in October he had disclosed to the Secretary of State. There were, the Minister claimed, strong indications that the archipelago might not much longer retain its present status, for a scheme had been "set on foot, and powerfully supported by the chief officials of New Zealand, by which the Hawaiian Islands may be confederated with the groups of the South Pacific under British rule." In his paper he included long excerpts from Julius Vogel's "scheme" for a Grand Dominion and stated that a loan to the Hawaiian Government had already been offered by New Zealand of from one to three million dollars. What security for its payment at maturity was asked of Hawaii, Peirce did not know. But the matter was not "of much consequence, inasmuch as the loan, if taken, can never be repaid." The offer was made by New Zealand, no doubt, "to obtain a lien upon the islands, sap their sovereignty, and avert their political and commercial tendencies toward a closer union with the United States, and finally to make a British colony of them." The proffered loan was a secret and was held "under advisement" by the Hawaiian Government, "awaiting the result of her proposed treaty with the United States for reciprocity." The Hawaiian assembly had authorized a loan of one million dollars to be made, but it had not yet been put upon the market by the Government. Therefore, Peirce suggested the incorporation into the reciprocity treaty of a provision binding the Hawaiians against effecting hereafter any loan needed by their Government for national purposes, without at first having offered said loan to the Government of the United States, which power should have the opportunity of contracting for or guaranteeing the payment of the same. This proviso would, "in effect, confer on the United States government a kind of guardianship over the Hawaiian Islands, and justify intervening in their political relations whenever found proper and necessary."

Under the existing circumstances Peirce considered the cession of a port in the Hawaiian Islands of doubtful expediency. "Patient waiting will give us the whole group of islands. A single port would be a snare and an injury to our real interests." At that moment King Kalakaua was opposed to the relinquishment of Pearl River lagoon for two reasons: the cession of a harbor and its improvement, eight miles west of Honolulu, would destroy the value of property in the capital of the Kingdom; and the act of cession to the United States would complicate Hawaiian relations with Great Britain, who, it was feared, would immediately seek the acquisition of the port of Hilo, in Hawaii, as a counterpoise to that acquired by the United States at Pearl River.

Peirce was convinced that "the acquisition of the Hawaiian Islands by the United States sooner or later must become a national necessity, to guard the approaches against hostile attempts on the Pacific States, and to protect and succor the navigation and commerce of the United States on that ocean, as well as to prevent disasters to our country, similar to those experienced in past times, from operations of vessels of war, privateers, and blockade runners issuing from Bermuda, Jamaica, Nassau, and other British possessions lying off our coasts." He warned the senators that the "Hawaiian Islands, if in possession of any European or Asiatic Power, would be a standing menace to all the vital interests of the United States on our Pacific shores."[6]

Allen's and Carter's assignment was not easy, for Secretary Fish, unenthusiastic regarding reciprocity, would not press it until he had reasonable expectations of favorable action by Congress. At times he was annoyed with the unpunctuality of the Envoys and bored by Allen's verbosity and Carter's statistics. They intimated their willingness to add to the list of articles to be admitted free into the Islands and also, if desired, to strike out rice from the articles to be admitted free into the United States. The Secretary indicated to the eager, optimistic agents the difficulties which he anticipated not only from general objections to any reciprocity treaty, but also those arising from the pendency of such a treaty with Canada, which would be opposed on grounds other than those which would apply only to a convention with Hawaii.[7] Nevertheless, on January 30, 1875, a treaty of commercial reciprocity was concluded.

Realizing that they had to be lobbyists as well as diplomats, the Envoys brought all possible influence to bear upon senators who would lend them an ear. Allen attended before the Committee on Foreign Relations and grew "tired of this kind of life"—of "dancing attendance on Congress."[8] Hawaii's representatives found a warm friend in Senator Hannibal Hamlin and were heartened by the fact that the President was "decidedly for us." But they had to contend with the opposition of Justin S. Morrill, who remained a strenuous opponent of reciprocity, as well as with that of the producers of cane sugar who protested that the treaty would greatly stimulate the production of sugar in Hawaii; that the enterprise would be developed by American capital which would otherwise be attracted to expanding the home cane and beet sugar industry; and that the agreement would eventually lead to the annexation of the Islands by the United States. Another strong objection to the treaty was that it would inure to the benefit of a few individuals, particularly to those who might control the sugar interests. A sizable portion of the active opposition to the treaty in the East originated with the great grocery house of Thurber & Company in New York, which had a considerable trade in sugar with San Francisco and attempted to raise alarm among the sugar planters of Louisiana and the rice planters of South Carolina. Their opposition, however, was neither vociferous nor formidable enough to defeat the measure, for in 1876 they were unable to provide a sufficient quantity of sugar and rice to supply the growing population of the Pacific coast.

The representatives of that area steadfastly supported the treaty. To the arguments of its opponents that the Hawaiian Islands were too far away to be of any national value and that a great expenditure would be required to establish there a costly naval station, difficult to defend in time of war, Senator Aaron A. Sargent of California replied that the Islands were midway in the direct line of trade between the United States and Asia, and the possession of this point by a foreign government would subject American commerce, which promised to be great in the future, to the mercy of an adversary in war time. He referred to the havoc wrought by the *Shenandoah* on the whaling fleet during the Civil War, and reminded his colleagues how much more devastating the Confederate cruisers would have been had they been able to operate from Honolulu rather than from Sydney. It would not be necessary to expend a large sum in establishing a naval station, and if the Islands were captured in time of war, they would be returned when the conflict ended. The California senator argued that the native population of the Islands was decreasing so rapidly that unless the treaty were ratified, the Hawaiian Government would be compelled to offer the control of the Kingdom to Great Britain.[9] He brought up the possibility of a trade agreement between Hawaii and New South Wales. The latter wanted its commercial advantages as well as "the influence which England would have, by means of such an arrangement, in getting possession of the islands"; the United States would have no right to complain, for the Hawaiian Government had three times "offered us this power over their islands." But if the treaty were ratified, no foreign state could gain a foothold during the time of its operation, and at the end of that period the fruit would be ripe to fall into the hands of the United States, while the productions of the Islands would also be those of American citizens.[10]

Both Sargent and John P. Jones of Nevada called attention to the character of the sixteen items included in the treaty to be admitted free to Hawaii. Woolen goods, watches, and other manufactured articles were almost exclusively valued as the products of labor; although Americans paid about ninety per cent in gold for what they imported from other countries, they paid an equal amount in the products of their labor for sugar and other articles imported from the Sandwich Islands.

Senator Jones, after arguing that the political considerations involved were of themselves sufficient to decide the question in favor of ratification, further contended that the commercial importance of the treaty had been generally overlooked. For example, the Islands imported from the United States annually more than $100,000 of wooden ware, which represented an expenditure of over $90,000 for wages in this country, and $40,000 worth of clothing, of which only one-third of the value could be credited to raw materials.

There appeared simultaneously in several Boston papers on February 25, 1875, a letter from David A. Wells, who in 1867 had been requested to investigate the bearing a reciprocity treaty would have upon the revenue of the United States. Wells was of the opinion that a treaty would not be advantageous. To admit sugar free of duty would be equivalent to voting an "annual subsidy out of the treasury of the United States to some twenty-five pleasant American gentlemen." He claimed that "for every dollar taken from the treasury an equivalent dollar would have to be contributed by the people of the United States, through some form of additional taxation"; reciprocally, the same would be true for Hawaii, "and there was no class on whom the additional tax would bear more heavily than on the planters themselves."[11]

Although the Envoys from Honolulu hoped to succeed in their mission, the result was uncertain, for, on March 11, the Justice found himself in a severe contest for the treaty. Only seven days later the first stage of the struggle was over; the man who for eighteen years had worked for a treaty, sent a joyous message to his son "to give 3 cheers and jump into the air." Commissioner Carter returned home with the treaty on April 8, and was welcomed with a popular demonstration. At the Government Building, King Kalakaua received him with a speech of appreciation, and the crowd added three cheers for the treaty.[12]

This time the Senate had required only a month and a half to act, and on March 18, after inserting an additional article, it advised ratification of the treaty by a vote of fifty-one to twelve, which was eight more than the required two-thirds. The appended Article IV, without which the treaty probably would have been rejected, stipulated that: "It is agreed, on the part of His Hawaiian Majesty, that as long as this treaty shall remain in force, he will not lease or otherwise dispose of or create any lien upon any port, harbor, or other territory in his dominions, or grant any special privilege or rights of use therein, to any other power, state, or government."

The treaty itself provided that unrefined sugar, rice, arrowroot, castor oil, bananas, fruits, nuts, vegetables (dried and undried, preserved and unpreserved), undressed hides and skins, *pulu*,[13] seeds, plants, shrubs or trees, and practically all other Hawaiian products would be admitted free of duty to the United States. On the other hand, American goods to be imported into Hawaii duty free would include virtually every product conceivable, with major emphasis on wool, iron, steel, and textiles. The treaty was to continue in force for a term of seven years; thereafter, it could be terminated by either party after twelve months' notice.[14]

In the language of the treaty, the sugar to be admitted free was "muscovado, brown, and all other unrefined sugar," which meant sugars of the lower grades, boiled in the open train, as was the almost universal custom of American sugar producers in Louisiana and Texas at the time the treaty was negotiated. Muscovado was an unfortunate term; it had no place in the treaty and later tended to mislead, as no muscovado sugar had been made in the Hawaiian Islands for more than twenty years prior to the treaty. Centrifugals were manufactured and introduced there as early as 1850 or 1851, and had been in use exclusively for purging sugars since that date. Vacuum-pans were also generally used as early as 1865, and in 1875 there was but one or possibly two mills which retained the open train.

The *San Francisco Morning Call* of March 19, 1875, believed that the motivation for ratification of the reciprocity treaty was probably the conviction that if this offer for closer commercial relations were refused, the Islands would fall into the hands of England or France. "It would be very annoying," explained the *Call*, "if for want of a little assistance on our part at a time of need the Islands should pass into the hands of a maritime nation with which at some future day we might be at war."

General Schofield wrote to Representative John K. Luttrell of

California, pointing out the strategic value of the Hawaiian Islands, "the only natural outpost to the defenses of the Pacific coast. In the possession of a foreign naval power in time of war, as a depot from which to fit out hostile expeditions against this coast and our commerce on the Pacific Ocean, they would afford the means of incalculable injury to the United States." The Islands never would be able to maintain their own neutrality and their necessities forced them to seek alliance with some nation which could relieve their embarrassment. The British Empire stood ready to enter into such an alliance, "and thus complete its chain of naval stations from Australia to British Columbia." The United States could not refuse the group the little aid they needed, and at the same time deny their right to seek it elsewhere. The time had come to secure forever the desired control over them or let it pass into other hands. Schofield concluded: "The financial interest of the United States involved in this treaty is very small, and if it were much greater it would still be insignificant when compared to the importance of such a military and naval station to the national security and welfare."[15]

Representative James Garfield of Ohio sounded a similar warning in the House on April 6, 1876, arguing that if the United States failed to ratify this treaty, some other alliance would be sought by King Kalakaua, and after rejecting his overtures, any objections to such a course could not consistently be raised. Great Britain and France stood ready to make satisfactory arrangements with the Hawaiian Government in case the United States should reject the convention. The Congressman favored the treaty as a satisfactory substitute for all probable schemes of annexation that might come up if this failed; it was the best solution of the question. He proceeded to read a letter from J. F. B. Marshall in support of the treaty, indicating the vital importance of the half-way house between the Old and New Worlds in securing a paramount influence over the rapidly increasing Pacific commerce. Garfield also called attention to an article in the New York *Evening Post* of April 5 which questioned whether or not the products of American industries were to be admitted to Hawaii as freely as they are admitted to Florida, whether we would be allowed to do the carrying trade between Hawaiian marts and our own, and whether we were to have "a commodious and secure naval station in their sheltered waters" and thus escape the result which otherwise threatened to give the Islands into the hands of Great Britain. "A station which lying north of the equator, puts into her hands the key of the Pacific, completes the mighty chain of her dependencies from the remotest south to Vancouver's Island on the northwest coast of our continent, and links together the isles and coasts subject to her sway."[16]

King Kalakaua ratified the treaty on April 18; President Grant did so on May 31, 1875. Congress, however, delayed over a year in passing the necessary legislation for implementing the treaty. During this period it was received with varying degrees of enthusiasm in Hawaii and in the United States, depending upon the political or economic interests concerned. The principal objection voiced by Americans in the Islands was that reciprocity would postpone annexation, whereas in the United States the sugar and rice planters claimed that reciprocity would lead eventually to annexation. Another group of opponents felt that the terms of the treaty had been dictated by California refiners, and by one in particular because his grade sugars were not allowed free entry. In general the Pacific coast favored closer economic and political ties with the Hawaiian Islands. The San Francisco Chamber of Commerce urged California's representatives to exert their influence in securing passage in the House of the implementing legislation.[17] H. W. Williams of Williams, Blanchard and Company, a leading mercantile house on the Pacific coast, was a faithful supporter of the treaty and, with other West coast merchants interested in Hawaiian trade, called the attention of Senator A. A. Sargent, chairman of the Finance Committee, and Senator Newton Booth, both of California, to the approaching presidential election and warned that the Pacific states almost unanimously favored the treaty, both in its business and political aspects, and the Republican Party would doubtless be defeated in all these states if this important measure was rejected by the Republican Senate in failing to concur with the Democratic House. The San Francisco merchants further counseled that should the treaty fail, the Hawaiian Government would make a treaty of reciprocity with Australia and New Zealand, establishing British supremacy there, and nearly destroying the West coast trade with the Islands.

The enabling legislation was finally carried in the House by a vote of 115 to 101 on May 8, 1876, and passed the Senate on August 14, with a vote of twenty-nine for, twelve against (six senators were paired and twenty-four were absent). The treaty was put into operation by a special protocol on September 9, 1876,[18] an occasion for great rejoicing in Honolulu, and the date became a significant one in Hawaiian history.

Political considerations certainly prompted the ratification of the Treaty of 1875. Not even its supporters claimed that the pecuniary advantages would be equally shared by both nations, but frankly conceded that they would inure preponderately to the little Kingdom. However, it cannot be denied that trade was also a significant factor in the agitation for reciprocity. As stated above, the margin of American dominance in Hawaiian trade in 1873 was not comfortable. In that year the exports of sugar to the British colonies more than equaled half the amount of that product shipped to the United States. Since the availability of a market in parts of the British Empire would naturally influence the sources of imports, American businessmen and politicians sought to reverse this condition.

The Reciprocity Treaty of 1875 was a perfect example of a commercial and economic negotiation dictated by political motives. It was designed primarily to extend American influence over the Islands and, only secondarily, to secure economic benefits. The annexationist-minded Grant administration was aware of the prevailing anti-annexation feeling in the Congress. Hence, there was achieved through the execution of a commercial instrument the substance of a policy which would have been defeated if brought to an open fight on the floor of the Senate. This agreement prevented any European power from gaining a political foothold in Hawaii, and—from the commercial point of view—rendered the archipelago a significant appendage of the United States.

Results of Reciprocity

BUSINESS in Hawaii was by no means brisk in 1875: plantations were languishing; tracts of good land were uncultivated. There was little capital to invest, and the wages of the laboring men on the wharfs were low; there was, in fact, a depression. The following year, when the Kingdom finally got reciprocity with the United States, the effect was immediate and proved to be cumulative. According to the *Hawaiian Gazette* of May 24, 1882, "everything sprang into life." In six years the revenue was more than doubled; the public debt which in 1876 amounted to $459,187.59 was reduced until in 1882 it stood at $269,200. Every part of the Island showed the greatest activity. "The swamps where the plover and wild duck used to find a home, are now yellow with rice. The mountain slopes, the valleys are green with cane, the landings and harbors are busy with small craft; instead of one steamer we have half a dozen; there is not a business in town which has not been able to increase; it matters not that men are not directly interested in our leading product, indirectly they have all shared in the prosperity."

The Reciprocity Treaty of 1875 made the Hawaiian Islands the sugar-raising field of the Pacific slope and gave West coast manufacturers therein the same freedom as in California and Oregon. So far as the staple growths and imports of the Islands went, the treaty made "them practically members of the American Zollverein in an outlying district of the state of California."[19] The convention provided Hawaii with its first great impetus in trade, and developed that activity of production which attracted the eager attention of European powers anxious to share in the prosperity and advantages which the United States had created in mid-ocean.

The effects of reciprocity exceeded the most sanguine expectations and the most extravagant predictions. A spectacular result was the immediate increase in the output of sugar and rice. In four years the production of sugar more than doubled and that of rice increased nearly as much. Reciprocity transformed a million-dollar industry into a multi-million-dollar enterprise. Before the treaty United States imports of Hawaiian sugar had never risen to twenty million pounds; after its passage they reached that figure in the very first year. The total imports into the United States of sugar from the Hawaiian Islands rose from 17,063,133 pounds for the fiscal year ending June 30, 1875, to 115,325,077 pounds for the fiscal year ending June 30, 1883.[20] From 1877, the first full year succeeding the conclusion of the treaty, to 1880, the imports from Hawaii to the United States nearly doubled, increasing from $2,550,335 in value to $4,606,444, and in the same period the exports from the United States to Hawaii rose from $1,272,949 to $2,026,170.[21] The total exports from the Kingdom rose from $2,241,000 in 1876 to $8,958,000 in 1885, of which sugar accounted for no less than $8,356,000. The preponderance of this trade was with the United States. In 1885 the total value of Hawaii's exports to and imports from this country amounted in round numbers to $11,874,000 slightly over ninety-two per cent of the value of the whole foreign commerce. Great Britain came next, though with only three and three-fourths per cent, thus leaving only a trifle over four per cent to be divided among the rest of the world.[22] By 1890 Hawaii's foreign trade had mounted to $20,105,030. In that year $5,259,154 of her imports out of a total of $6,962,201 came from the United States. Of her exports, totalling $13,142,829, the United States took ninety-nine per cent, or $13,073,477. The Hawaiian Kingdom's imports during 1890 were at the rate of seventy-five dollars per capita, and exports of domestic produce at the rate of $144 per capita, whereas those from Canada and the United States during 1889 were respectively forty dollars and twenty-two dollars per capita.[23] A consistently favorable balance of trade in Hawaii facilitated the accumulation of capital.

The treaty heralded an unprecedented boom in the Islands and initiated the second era of development in the Hawaiian sugar industry. Now that capital was assured a profitable market, and the duty of fifty or sixty dollars per ton of sugar was transferred from the United States Treasury into the pockets of the planters, money flowed in an increasing volume into agricultural enterprises. This capital, much of which was American, created not only the best customer the United States ever had, considering Hawaii's population, "but produced one of the most remarkable exhibitions of creative industrial energy in history."[24] Heavy application of capital and labor in sugar operations became a regular practice with the result that nowhere in the world did organization become more complete or science more effectively applied to cane raising. Vast tracts of land were bought or leased at exorbitant prices. Three new plantations went into operation in 1875, five in 1876, eight in 1877, nine in 1878, eight in 1879, four in 1880, and one in 1882, bringing into cultivation over twenty thousand acres of additional land, with a new capital investment of about ten million dollars. A sugar plantation required for the most economical work a large outlay of capital, $500,000 being very moderate for a single plantation and $25,000 being about as small as prudent.[25] Heavy machinery for tilling the increased acreage was important; and unbelievable exploits in engineering were accomplished. Mountains were tunneled and rivers of life-giving water were carried across seemingly impassable gulches, through dense tangles of tropical vegetation, and even were forced to flow uphill on their mission to make barren lands yield their quota of cane and rice.

The first major venture in water diversion was made by Samuel T. Alexander and Henry P. Baldwin, both sons of missionaries and pioneers in large-scale sugar production. With a loan from a few other men they formulated and executed a plan to bring water from the dripping windward slopes of Mount Haleakala ("House of the Sun") to the arid northern side of east Maui where they developed plantations at Paia and Haiku. The Hamakua Ditch, seventeen miles long, with a daily capacity of forty million gallons, cost eighty thousand dollars—an immense sum in 1878.[26] This irrigation scheme was followed by many others including the drilling of artesian wells to tap the great underground reservoirs of fresh water on the volcanic islands of the Hawaiian chain. The first successful one was bored in 1879 by John Ashley on the property of James Campbell at Honoulilui, Ewa district. On the advice of Samuel G. Wilder, organizer and principal owner of the Wilder Steamship Line, and for a time Minister of the Interior under King Kalakaua, the McCandless brothers—James Sutton, John, and Lincoln, engineers whose experience had been gained in the mines of Colorado and the oil fields of California—came to Hawaii. In a period of fifty-five years—1880-1936 —singly, and together as partners, they drilled more than seven hundred "good" artesian wells, that is, wells flowing around one million gallons of water in twenty-four hours.[27] A huge project of water diversion was completed in December, 1915, when a tunnel three miles long pierced the backbone of Oahu—the Koolau mountains —to carry twenty-five million gallons of water daily from the windward to the leeward side of the island. Finally, the Wailoa Ditch, the largest aqueduct constructed in the Islands before 1923, costing $1,500,000, delivers one hundred and forty million gallons of water daily at an elevation of over eleven hundred feet.[28]

Under the impulse of the treaty, Hawaii increased her population from 58,000 in 1876 to about 75,000 in 1882, and anticipated a figure of 100,000 if the treaty remained in effect.[29] Proponents of the treaty, however, neglected to say that much of this population increase was due to the importation of Oriental and other contract laborers. Of the entire 35,908 laborers of all kinds employed on the fifty-nine large sugar estates in 1899, 31,623 were Japanese and Chinese, 2,700 were Portuguese and other foreigners, and only 1,326 were Hawaiians.[30]

Tariff preference proved a tremendous stimulus to Hawaiian industry, especially to sugar culture and the carrying trade between the Islands and the Pacific coast. The sugar industry more than doubled its export tonnage every decade as indicated in the following table:[31]

Sugar production, which included that locally consumed as well as exported, increased more than eight-fold between 1877 and 1887

SUGAR EXPORTS FROM HAWAII 1872–1896

1872–1876 (two year average)	26 million pounds
1877–1881	54 " "
1882–1886	152 " "
1887–1891	251 " "
1892–1896	325 " "

and doubled in the next eight years. During the last quarter of the nineteenth century exports of Hawaiian sugar increased from 25.1 million to 545.4 million pounds, and in dollar value from $1,200,000 to $21,900,000. Sugar became the largest contributor to the gross product of Hawaii, rising from fifty-seven per cent of the total exports in 1875 to over ninety-six per cent in 1899.[32] This extraordinary result was accomplished by expanding old plantations and establishing new ones, by building bigger mills and equipping them with more efficient machinery, by applying commercial fertilizer—including guano—to the cane fields, and by developing huge irrigation projects.

Sugar planters and refiners elsewhere and some United States congressmen were disposed to doubt the accuracy of the published large yields of Hawaiian plantations. Obviously, irrigation of rich virgin lands, upon the warmer leeward sides of the Islands, in a climate almost perfect for maximum growth, greatly increased the average output of the archipelago; but the carrying of the largest portion of the crop in plant cane, according to William C. Stubbs, was unquestionably the main cause of the large yield. "Ratooning" or "stubbing" was not largely used in the Hawaiian Islands. Only first year ratoons or stubbles were cultivated. Whenever these would not, in the judgment of the manager, produce thirty tons of cane per acre, they were plowed up and the land replanted, a practice which contrasted with the procedure in several other sugar-growing lands. Here was one of the secrets of the large success attending sugar culture in Hawaii, where two-thirds, if not three-fourths, of the area each year was in plant cane.

The large sums of money needed for the expansion of and improvements in the sugar industry were brought into the Islands principally from the United States. The greater portion was in the form of loans to plantation companies and agencies. The agency system developed out of the need for specialization and division of labor. The struggling planters had enough to do just to grow cane.

For financing, warehousing, marketing, and purchasing of supplies and equipment, they turned to the Honolulu merchants, and both groups prospered from the arrangement. This system, well-established before 1875, became increasingly important after that date as large amounts of capital were invested in sugar culture. The most powerful agent in the 1880's was the firm of Wm. G. Irwin and Company, in which Claus Spreckels was a partner. Other important agents were H. Hackfeld and Company, C. Brewer and Company, with whom Wm. G. Irwin and Company eventually amalgamated, Theo. H. Davies and Company, Castle and Cooke, Ltd., G. W. Macfarlane and Company, and F. A. Schaefer and Company.

Ratification of the Reciprocity Treaty fostered the emergence of the largest, most conspicuous, and notorious of the Hawaiian sugar planters, processors, shippers, and agents—Claus Spreckels. Born in Lamstedt, Hanover, in 1828, of poor parents, he migrated to the United States in 1846. Arriving in Charleston, South Carolina, with two or three dollars in his pocket, he worked in a grocery store for his board, and by rapid promotions, increases in wages, and thrift, he was able to buy out his second employer within a few years and operate a grocery of his own. Nine years thereafter he went to New York and later to California, where he achieved still greater success in the grocery business among the miners on the Pacific coast. In 1856 he bought his brother's store and soon had increased his capital to fifty thousand dollars. This he invested in a brewery which, along with his grocery, he sold a few years later for over one hundred thousand dollars. His next venture was in the field in which he was to become famous. With his brother and brother-in-law, Claus Mangels, in 1863 he started the Bay Sugar Refinery, which proved a lucrative business and grew rapidly. Still not satisfied with his success and anxious to expand further than were the hesitant directors, Spreckels decided to learn every angle and trick in the sugar business and to make a new start. He sold his business at an enormous profit, returned to his native Germany, donned workingmen's clothes, and secured a job in a refinery at Magdeburg. In the course of a couple of months he learned every step of processing refined sugar, as it was done in Europe, which then had the best refineries in the world.[33] He was back in San Francisco in 1867 and the following year organized the California Sugar Refinery Company, securing raw sugar from the Philippines and Hawaii. Spreckels invented a process by which the time for making hard sugar was reduced from three weeks to less than twenty-four hours.[34] Incidentally, he introduced cube and crushed sugars to Americans.

Meanwhile, his son John D. was working in Hawaii, first as a clerk for H. Hackfeld and Company, the leading German firm in Honolulu, and later on one of their plantations, where he acquired knowledge of the processing of sugar and saw the profit to be made in the purchase and sale of raw sugar. His friend, William G. Irwin, an Englishman, was selected to buy the product for the California Sugar Refinery Company. Originally an opponent of reciprocity because of his plans for creating a large beet sugar industry in California and his fear of competition from Hawaii's high grade sugars, the elder Spreckels, after the treaty had been ratified in the Senate by a large majority, came to believe that he could benefit by its terms. He determined "to work body and soul" for the immediate passage of the enabling legislation, furnished the manager of Hackfeld and Company with letters of introduction to several California congressmen whose influence could be relied upon and whose support of the treaty would carry great weight,[35] and decided to visit the Islands. He booked passage to Honolulu in August, 1876 on the *City of San Francisco*, the same ship which carried the news that the Senate had just passed, on August 14, the necessary bill for implementing the Reciprocity Treaty. Within a period of three weeks, half the estimated fourteen thousand ton sugar crop for 1877 had been brought up before the full price rise caused by the good tidings could take effect. After conversing with his son and making a visit to the barren central plains of Maui, the astute Spreckels saw a promising future in combining the profits of Hawaiian planting with those of refining, and decided to expand his operations by developing and managing his own plantation. Land and water, however, were the prerequisites of this objective.

On a second visit to the Islands in 1878, the California entrepreneur was able to buy from Henry Cornwell an undivided half interest in 16,000 acres on the Waikapu Commons and to lease 24,000 acres of adjoining crown lands for thirty years at $1,000 per annum, upon which he proceeded to develop a sugar plantation, called Spreckelsville, and to incorporate the new ten-million-dollar Hawaiian Commercial Company. With the exception of the former governor of California, Frederick F. Low, the five directors of this company had been bitter opponents of the treaty. The Hawaiian consul in San Francisco commented to Allen: "How things change when capital comes in to interest and strengthen commercial relations."[36] Yet thirty years' security appeared far from adequate for Spreckels' future plans. Expensive investments and improvements necessary to conduct a multi-million dollar enterprise might be lost if the lease were terminated; a fee-simple title would be far more satisfactory.

Learning that the Legislature of 1862, in settling the claims of the *aliis* against the crown lands, had omitted to provide for those of Princess Ruth Keelikolani, half sister of King Kamehameha IV (the King had died intestate), Spreckels purchased from her, for ten thousand dollars, all the interest that this last "claimant" of the Kamehamehas might have had in land estimated to be worth three-quarters of a million dollars. Although he knew that this claim was of doubtful validity, having been ignored in a Supreme Court decision of May 27, 1864, and in an act of January 3, 1865, establishing and, at the same time, declaring the crown lands inalienable, this nominal payment bought the influence of a member of the royal family and placed the Government on the defensive.[37] Spreckels intended the claim "as color of title" for his next step, which was to make threats of bringing a suit against the Government for the full amount of Princess Ruth's claim, now his.[38] To the King he proposed that the Legislature convey to him in fee-simple the crown lands of Wailuku, amounting to approximately twenty-four thousand barren acres—adjacent to the sixteen thousand he had already leased—much of which, however, if irrigated would produce cane; in return he would quitclaim his remaining interest to the Government. Instead of contesting the claim in the Supreme Court, Spreckels' proposal was approved by the Legislature of 1882, which was dominated by Kalakaua and Gibson and described as "one of the weakest and most corrupt that ever sat in Honolulu."[39] The "Maui land deal," which brought Spreckels' total holdings up to forty thousand acres at a ridiculously low price, aroused bitter opposition in the community. It produced the argument that Princess Ruth had no title to the crown land and, therefore, Spreckels had nothing to convey to the Government in exchange for the land of Wailuku. Nevertheless, a loan of $35,000 to Premier Gibson, a "gift" of $10,000 to King Kalakaua, and lawyers' fees previously paid to the new Attorney General, Edward Preston, served to obligate the Government to the Californian. Moreover, Simon K. Kaai, Minister of the Interior and a Gibson and Spreckels man, as manager of Princess Ruth's estate, was won over to the scheme.

In the meantime Spreckels had set about assuring himself of an adequate water supply, of which sugar culture demands an abundance—approximately one hundred and twenty inches a year,[40] depending upon the relative humidity of the area, the frequency and volume of water, and other factors. To grow enough cane to produce one pound of sugar requires well over eight hundred pounds of water, but the quantity used on various plantations has been as high as three to five thousand pounds. The true value of irrigation is measured not by the amount of water that is applied to the land, but the amount of moisture that is retained by the soil within reach of the roots, which in turn is dependent upon the character of the field, character of the cane, conservation of soil moisture, and so forth.[41] Spreckels endeavored to secure from the King and Cabinet a thirty-year lease on all the surplus water in certain streams of Maui, but Attorney General A. S. Hartwell and the Premier, Minister of the Interior John Mott Smith, refused to grant these rights on the terms offered. A large personal loan to Kalakaua induced him to request unceremoniously in the early morning hours of July 2, 1878, the resignation of the Ministers and to appoint more amenable ones who granted the requested rights for thirty years at the nominal fee of five hundred dollars annually.[42]

Spreckels then brought Hermann Schussler, a leading irrigation engineer in California, to Maui. Schussler, after an examination of the configuration of the terrain, constructed a second ditch *makai* (seaward) of the Hamakua. This "grand piece of engineering," running from the northern slopes of Mount Haleakala in east Maui to the central part of the island, involved some thirty miles of ditch, tunnels, pipes, flumes, and trestles. It crossed thirty gulches, some over two thousand feet wide and four hundred feet deep, and required the construction of twenty-eight tunnels and fourteen bridges. The mammoth project cost $500,000, but on completion it delivered up to 3,600 cubic feet of water a minute, or approximately sixty million gallons daily, enough to produce fifty thousand tons of sugar annually. On the land thus made arable, the entrepreneur founded the Hawaiian Commercial and Sugar Company, which took over the assets of his privately owned Hawaiian Commercial Company. As a majority stockholder, he retained control of the Company which under his management developed into the largest sugar plantation in Hawaii.

This plantation also became the most modern in the world with the optimum utilization of manpower, water, agricultural machinery, and technological processes in the harvesting and milling of cane. Spreckels had a complete topographical survey made of the plantation which resulted in an extensive and ingenious irrigation network in which two main ditches were connected with a series of supply ditches that in turn fed their contents into a larger number of water courses constructed on each acre of tillable land. This enabled the furrows to be filled with water in about twenty minutes, with the result that in ten hours one man could irrigate twenty-five to thirty acres, as compared with the previous record of two acres a day.[43] For the cultivation of his well-watered cane, Spreckels replaced the traditional bullock and mule team with the first five-furrow steam plows to be used in Hawaii. In an effort to reduce the amount of idle mill time, he constructed the Islands' first intra-plantation railroad system, which transported the harvested cane rapidly from the field to his centrally located mill. This was achieved by the unique employment of both permanent and portable tracks, the latter used to extend the railway to whatever area of the plantation was being harvested.

The mill at Spreckelsville was one of the largest and most modern, having a capacity of one hundred tons daily and thirty thousand tons annually. Here each carload of cane was weighed before milling and the trash (bagasse) was weighed afterward to ascertain the percentage of juice extracted. Here was used the first five-roller mill in the Islands, replacing the old three-roller mill. The additional rollers resulted not only in increased juice extraction, but also in greater quantities of cane that could be milled at a given time. Fuel and labor costs were decreased, since the crushed cane was left dry enough to be burnt immediately. Automatic feeders fed this refuse to the furnaces, thus eliminating moving it to and from trash houses. Running the juice through heaters and a subsequent liming[44] process prevented loss of sugar through inversion. Other innovations included continuous clarifying of juice through clarifiers and sweeping pans and the use of electric lights.[45] The entire plantation and milling system at Spreckelsville was so efficiently managed that the tycoon reportedly was eventually able to realize annual profits of fifty per cent or more on his investment.

To facilitate the marketing of his product as well as to gain control of a large portion of the output of other planters, Claus Spreckels, in 1880, became the sole partner of William G. Irwin in Irwin and Company, a sugar agency which had been founded in 1874. The combination of the Englishman's Island contacts with the American's financial resources resulted in a partnership which soon became preeminent among the agencies, holding a grip on other plantations with loans that at one time amounted to about $2,500,000. The Company acted as an agent of the Hawaiian Board of Immigration in bringing in Japanese contract laborers and transporting them to their destination; it dealt in real estate and also acted as a real estate agent; it conducted a banking business, and was the first agency to make fire insurance on growing crops available to Hawaiian planters. Spreckels claimed in June, 1893, that the firm had direct control of forty-five thousand tons of sugar and provided agency service for an additional twenty thousand tons, a total of sixty-five thousand tons, or about half of the 1892 crop. This was transported to the Pacific coast in vessels of the Oceanic Steamship Line, founded by John D. and his father in 1881, which in 1883 started a semi-monthly steamer service between San Francisco and Honolulu. A few years later the service was extended to Australia. Irwin and Company served as the Honolulu agent of this steamship line as well as of the Matson Navigation Company in its formative years, the Pacific Oil Transportation Company, the Japan-Seattle line, Nippon Yusen Kaisha, and the Union Steamship Company.[46] Although this factor failed to establish a complete monopoly over the ocean shipping serving the Islands, it maintained, by providing the most frequent and regular transportation facilities between Hawaii and the West coast, a decided advantage for the plantations under its agency. Moreover, a majority of the planters at first used Oceanic ships. After failure to secure a franchise from the Hawaiian Legislature of 1884 for a National Banking Corporation with power to issue notes receivable as legal tender for taxes and customs and to serve as a Government depository and fiscal agent, Spreckels owned and operated a private bank in Honolulu without these powers.

In spite of opposition, Spreckels acquired an ascendancy in the Hawaiian Islands where "sugar was a dominant fact of economic life"; and in sugar he was king. Through his Spreckelsville plantation, his partnership with William G. Irwin, the Oceanic Steamship Company, and the California Sugar Refinery, "Spreckels controlled Hawaiian sugar more completely than any man before or since his time." Moreover, he established the pattern of vertical integration which the industry still follows.[47] None of the planters or agents individually could challenge his power—the nearest competitor of the Irwin-Spreckels combine handled an annual output of only twenty thousand tons of sugar—and regardless of how much his rivals resented his tactics, they were not, in the 1880's, inclined to take collective action against him. The capital stock of the Hawaiian Commercial and Sugar Company was valued in 1892 at ten million dollars, or approximately one-third of the total investment in the Islands' sugar industry.[48] This company was controlled by the Spreckels family until 1898, when a syndicate composed of Samuel T. Alexander, Henry P. Baldwin, and James B. Castle and associates bought the majority of the capital stock.

Thus it is evident that "the outlander, the interloper, the invader from the mainland," through his own ingenuity, secured the maximum advantage of the Reciprocity Treaty and spurred economic progress in the sugar industry. There was no competitor in the Islands to match him. Professor Jacob Adler, an authority on Claus Spreckels, doubts that without him the Island sugar industry would have developed as rapidly as it did. "No other person brought in such a large amount of foreign capital, or had comparable technical knowledge of sugar." Spreckels also possessed the dynamic drive and bountiful energy necessary to transform apparently fantastic dreams into functional reality.

As sugar production soared, so did construction, merchandising, banking, transportation, and other business activities associated with a sugar and rice culture. In addition to the transformation in agriculture and sugar milling, the Hawaiian Kingdom underwent a revolution in transportation and communication, with American firms or investors playing a leading role. Fifteen years before the treaty, in 1862, William E. Matson of California founded the Matson Navigation Company which supplied service for the Chinese immigrants composing the main labor force on the Hawaiian sugar plantations. William Henry Webb, a businessman of New York City, established the American Pacific Mail Steamship Company in 1871. The carrying trade was particularly responsive to the increased demands created by reciprocity. These two firms prospered, grew strong, and eventually controlled sugar freighting. The second company placed an intermediate steamer in the trade in 1878 to ply alternately with the regular Australian line, giving the Hawaiian Islands a fortnightly, instead of the previous monthly, service. Later Webb and his associates organized the American Pacific Cable Company and began scouting for cable and coaling stations for their transoceanic enterprises. The Oceanic Steamship Company inaugurated regular monthly service in 1882, and, in 1883, semi-monthly service, between Honolulu and San Francisco with a fleet of vessels purchased from a Philadelphia shipyard. Later, in an attempt to break away from Spreckels' control over shipping, other planters and sugar factors turned to the Matson Navigation Company which, in the twentieth century, supplanted the Oceanic Steamship Company. Samuel G. Wilder, owner of the Wilder Steamship Company, played a leading role in the development and expansion of inter-island navigation. Through private initiative in 1877 there was erected on Maui the first telegraph line. The next year the service was extended to the remainder of the Islands. The initial outlay was provided by Charles R. Bishop and the Hawaiian Government.

Benjamin Franklin Dillingham, who shipped to Hawaii as a sailor on the bark *Whistler* and was left behind with a broken leg, remained there permanently to work as a clerk in Henry Dimond's hardware store. With Alfred Castle, he purchased Dimond's business and formed the firm of Dillingham and Company in 1869. After twenty years of success and large profits he retired from the firm to devote his attention to plantation promotion and to linking Honolulu with the back country of Oahu by means of a railroad. The latter project was at first much criticized and dubbed "Dillingham's folly." Back of the enterprise, however, was the vision of turning miles of wild, barren land into a vast sugar-producing area serviced by a railroad. Through his untiring efforts and enthusiasm he finally succeeded in interesting capital in the project of irrigating land around Red Hill with artesian well water raised to the necessary level with pumps. The Ewa plantation was organized, and on September 4, 1889, the first train to run out of Honolulu took an excursion party one half mile into the Palama rice field. With the extension of the railroad there was a need for more freight, and Dillingham proceeded with the organization of the Oahu and Honolulu plantations. The Waianae, Waialua, and Kahuku plantations were expanded, and the Oahu Railway was finally extended to Kahuku, thus providing railroad transportation to practically all of the extensive sugar growing areas of Oahu. Later Dillingham extended his operations to the islands of Hawaii, Kauai, and Maui, where he promoted several plantations and built what later was known as the Hawaii Consolidated Railway that served the large sugar-growing areas of the Big Island.[49] Dillingham's son, Walter, subsequently became president of the Oahu Steam Railway and Land Company. His other interests included sugar plantations, builders' supplies, real estate, and publications. Eventually the Dillingham family came to control sixteen Hawaiian corporations.

Thus, powerful economic ties cemented earlier cultural and political relations, and the diminutive island Kingdom became inextricably bound to the great mainland Republic. Hawaii's continued prosperity certainly depended upon her favored treatment in a large and expanding, contiguous market. With the exception of a few anti-American foreigners and some Hawaiians who feared that too close economic ties with the United States might lead to annexation, most people in the archipelago were anxious to have the Reciprocity Treaty renewed.

NOTES

1. *Hawaiian Gazette*, March 6, 1876. In preparation for the visit, Peirce urged the United States Government to bestow upon King Kalakaua the same attention planned for the trip of the late King Kamehameha V. (Peirce to Fish, Nos. 277, 279, Aug. 8, 20, 1874, USDS, Dispatches, Hawaii, XVI). Peirce's dispatches for 1874 are in this volume; cf. James Scott to Fish, Nov. 24, 1874, *ibid.; Pacific Commercial Advertiser*, Nov. 14, 21, 1874.
2. Wodehouse to FO, pol. and conf., No. 24, Nov. 26, 1874, FO 58/136. Peirce reported that the strong opposition to the King's departure was headed by the British and French commissioners who declared that "if the king goes as proposed he will be dethroned in his absence" (Peirce to Fish, Nos. 283, 291, Sept. 10, Oct. 21, 1874).
3. *Cong. Record*, 43rd Cong., 2nd sess., pp. 143, 556; *Evening Star* (Washington), Dec. 18, 19, 1874.
4. Blake Clark, *Hawaii: The 49th State* (New York, 1947), p. 83.
5. *Hawaiian Gazette*, March 8, 1876; *Pacific Commercial Advertiser*, April 10, 1875. Hawaiians were delighted with the reception their King received in the United States (Scott to Fish, No. 230, Jan. 18, 1875, USDS, Dispatches, Hawaii, XVII).
6. [Confidential] An Argument before the Committee on Foreign Relations of the Senate of the United States, with regard to a treaty of reciprocity between the United States and the Hawaiian Islands, pp. 1, 4, 7, encl. in Peirce to Fish, Jan. 12, 1875, USDS, Dispatches, Hawaii, XVI. This statement was ordered to be printed for confidential use of the Committee on Foreign Relations, but no other action was taken.
7. Hamilton Fish Diary, Nov. 25, Dec. 5, 1874, IV, 675, 698. Unexplainedly, Allan Nevins, *Hamilton Fish, The Inner History of the Grant Administration* (New York, 1937), an apparently exhaustive and definitive study of the distinguished Secretary of State, completely ignores Fish's Hawaiian policy.
8. Allen to Mrs. Allen, Feb. 14, March 1, 1875, Allen Papers.
9. See my "Decadence of the Hawaiian Nation and Proposals to Import a Negro Labor Force," *Journal of Negro History*, XLVII (1962), 248–63.
10. *Cong. Record*, 44th Cong., 1st sess., pp. 4266, 4267, 5485–86.
11. "Hawaiian Reciprocity Treat Not a 'Fraud' or a 'Swindle,' " *Evening Transcript* (Boston), Feb. 25, March 1, 1875.
12. *Hawaiian Gazette*, April 14, 1875; Peirce to Fish, Nos. 324 and 344, April 29, Nov. 9, 1875, USDS, Dispatches, Hawaii, XVII. Peirce's dispatches that follow are contained in this volume. Allen was called back to the capital in January and again in May, 1876 to labor for the passage of enabling legislation to carry the treaty into effect. Dr. Fernando Wood of New York, a member of the Committee on Ways and Means, to Allen, May 25, 1876 (telegram), Allen Papers.
13. *Pulu* is a silky or wooly fiber which grows at the base of the fronds of the tree fern and was used as a filling for mattresses and pillows. It was exported to San Francisco for about thirty years, 1851–84.
14. For a text of the treaty see *United States Statutes at Large*, 44th Cong., 1875–77, XIX, 200, 666; *For. Rels.* (1894), App. II, 166; cf. *New York Times*, March 19, 1875; *Daily Alta Californian* (San Francisco), March 19, 1875; *Pacific Commercial Advertiser*, April 10, 1875.

15. Schofield to Luttrell, Dec. 30, 1875, *American Register*, a journal of politics, literature, science, and news, I (Jan. 6, 1883), 8.
16. *Cong. Record*, 44th Cong., 1st sess., pp. 2273–74; *Evening Post* (New York), April 5, 1876; cf. *American Register*, I (Jan. 6, 1883), 12.
17. H. W. Williams to Allen, July 1, 1876, Allen Papers; cf. *ibid.*, Jan. 22, 1876, with encl.; *San Francisco Chronicle*, April 22, 1876; United States Tariff Commission, *Reciprocity and Commercial Treaties* (Washington, 1919), p. 109.
18. *United States Statutes at Large*, 44th Cong., 1875–77, XIX, 666–67; cf. *For. Rels.* (1877), p. 296.
19. Blaine to Comly, No. 113, Dec. 1, 1881, USDS, Instructions, Hawaii, II, printed in *For. Rels.* (1881), p. 636.
20. Report of the Commission Appointed by the Secretary of the Treasury to Investigate Alleged Frauds Under the Hawaiian Reciprocity Treaty, Washington, D.C., Aug. 29, 1883, in U.S. House of Rep. Committee on Ways and Means, *Statement of the Committee on Ways and Means on the Morrison Tariff Bill and on the Hewitt Administrative Bill, the Hawaiian Treaty, etc.* (Washington, 1886), p. 20; cf. Frank William Taussig, *Some Aspects of the Tariff Question* (Cambridge, Mass., 1929), p. 59.
21. Blaine to Comly, No. 113, Dec. 1, 1881, USDS, Instructions, Hawaii, II.
22. *The Times* (London), Sept. 23, 1886; U.S. Dept. of Commerce, *Statistical Abstract of the United States, 1907* (Washington, 1908), p. 555.
23. Lorrin A. Thurston, "The Sandwich Islands, I, The Advantages of Annexation," *North American Review*, CLVI (1893), 279.
24. United States Tariff Commission, p. 130.
25. *Sen. Reps.*, 53rd Cong., 2nd sess., No. 227, App. X, "The Hawaiian Treaty. A Review of its Commercial Results," p. 465.
26. Lorrin Thurston, *Memoirs of the Hawaiian Revolution* (Honolulu, 1936), p. 81; Ralph S. Kuykendall and A. Grove Day, *Hawaii: A History* . . . (Englewood Cliffs, N.J., 1961), p. 153; John W. Vandercook, *King Cane* (New York, 1939), p. 68. In 1872 an effort to get an appropriation from the Legislature for the construction of such a ditch had been unsuccessful. Irrigation had been tried in a small way before this period, the first plantation ditch having been dug as early as 1857 at Lihue, Kauai; but it was only after reciprocity that the big ditches were opened. S. N. Castle recommended that the "government take up the ditch at once and dig it of a size to irrigate several thousand acres more than the immediate wants of the applicants so as to stimulate agriculture in the district that only lacks water to make it fertile" (Suggestions for the Cabinet from S. N. Castle, 1876, Haiku Water Ditch, AH, FO & Ex., Misc. Local); William P. Alexander, *The Irrigation of Sugar Cane in Hawaii* (Honolulu, 1923), p. 1.
27. James Sutton McCandless, *A Brief History of the McCandless Brothers and Their Part in the Development of Artesian Well Water in the Hawaiian Islands 1800–1926* (Honolulu, 1936), Foreword, pp. 17, 20.
28. Alexander, *Irrigation*, p. 2.
29. H. M. Whitney, "The Hawaiian Reciprocity Treaty."
30. *Sen. Docs.*, 57th Cong., 2nd sess., No. 206, p. 2.
31. U.S. Dept. of Commerce, *Statistical Abstract of the United States, 1925* (Washington, 1926), p. 668.
32. *Ibid., 1907*, p. 555; cf. Jacob Adler, *Claus Spreckels: The Sugar King in Hawaii* (Honolulu, 1966), p. 12 (hereafter cited as Adler, *Claus Spreckels*).
33. Jacob Adler, "Claus Spreckels' Rise and Fall in Hawaii with Emphasis

on London Loan of 1886," HHS Sixty-Seventh *Report*, 1958 (Honolulu, 1959), pp. 7–8; Adler, *Claus Spreckels*, pp. 21–29.

34. D. Billam-Walker, "Claus Spreckels, the Sugar King," in "Adventures in the History of Hawaii," *Honolulu Star Bulletin*, Aug. 17, 1934, Sec. 3, p. 5; Thurston, *Memoirs*, p. 81. In 1882 Spreckels moved his refinery to the water front at the foot of Twenty-third Street, where ships from the Islands could unload the cane directly into the refinery.

35. J. C. Pfluger, manager of Hackfeld & Company, to Allen, Dec. 7, 1875, Allen Papers.

36. Severance to Allen, Oct. 5, 1878, *ibid.*

37. William D. Alexander, *The Later Years of the Hawaiian Monarch and the Revolution of 1893* (Honolulu, 1896), p. 8; Thurston, *Memoirs*, pp. 82–83. The most comprehensive treatment of the Hawaiian activities of Spreckels is Adler, *Claus Spreckels*. For his career as a mainland refiner, see W. W. Cordray, "Claus Spreckels of California" (unpublished Ph.D. dissertation, University of Southern California). Included in the latter is a chapter on Spreckels' activities in Hawaii.

38. Billam-Walker, "Claus Spreckels"; Shelly M. Mark and Jacob Adler, "Claus Spreckels in Hawaii: Impact of a Mainland Interloper on Development of Hawaiian Sugar Industry," *Explorations in Entrepreneurial History*, X, Oct., 1957 (Research Center in Entrepreneurial History, Cambridge, Mass.), 25; cf. Adler, *Claus Spreckels*, pp. 54–56 for details of the Maui land deal. Later genealogical detective work casts considerable doubt on whether Princess Ruth was of the Kamehameha line. Cf. John F. G. Stokes, "Kaoleioku: Paternity and Biographical Sketch," HHS Forty-third *Report*, 1934 (Honolulu, 1935), pp. 15–44.

39. W. D. Alexander, *Hawaiian Monarch*, p. 8.

40. Stubbs, "Report on the Agricultural Resources and Capabilities of Hawaii," p. 95. Later scientific experiments showed that the sugar crops of 1898 and 1899 required, respectively, 865 and 859 pounds of water (*ibid.*). Kuykendall and Day (p. 28), state that 4,000 pounds of water are required to produce one pound of sugar. This figure represents amounts used but not *required*. Obviously, there was a considerable waste of irrigation water.

41. W. P. Alexander, *Irrigation*, p. 73; cf. Alexander, *The Rational Distribution of Irrigation Water as Practiced on Ewa Plantation* (Honolulu, 1928), p. 27.

42. Comly to Evarts, No. 44, July 8, 1878, USDS, Dispatches, Hawaii, XVIII; Adler, *Claus Spreckels*, pp. 36–38, 44–45; cf. *ibid.*, pp. 39–41, 50–51; Mark and Adler, p. 25; Billam-Walker, "Claus Spreckels." Spreckels later secured a lease for a much smaller amount of water from private individuals for $100,000.

43. Adler, *Claus Spreckels*, pp. 48–49, 70–79; cf. *ibid.*, chap. VIII; "The Hawaiian Commercial & Sugar Company's Estate at Spreckelsville, Maui, H. I.," *The Planters' Monthly*, VIII (1889), 72; Mark and Adler, p. 26. In 1882 Spreckels built the Waihee ditch that tapped the streams on the mountain slopes of west Maui, thus becoming the first to bring water to the plains from both ends of the island.

44. In sugar processing free lime is calcium in the form of hydroxide or sucrate, which is removed by carbonation.

45. "Deeds of Claus Spreckels Recalled by Andrew Moore," *Honolulu Star Bulletin*, Dec. 6, 1924; Mark and Adler, p. 26.

46. *Sen. Reps.*, 53rd Cong., 2nd sess., No. 227, Vol. II, p. 1783; cf. *Pacific*

Commercial Advertiser, Dec. 2, 1882, *Pacific Coast Commercial Record*, May, 1892; Alexander, *Hawaiian Monarch*, p. 238.

47. Adler, "Claus Spreckels: Sugar King of Hawaii; Interaction of an Entrepreneur with an Island Economy" (Ph.D. Dissertation, Columbia University, 1959), pp. 404–06.

48. *Sen. Reps.*, 53rd Cong., 2nd sess., No. 227, Vol. II, p. 1782. For a general treatment of Spreckels' achievements, see W. W. Cordray, "Claus Spreckels of California" (unpublished doctoral dissertation, University of Southern California, 1955), included in which is a chapter on his activities in Hawaii.

49. Hawaiian Sugar Planters' Association, *Story*, pp. 20–21.

Part II

RECIPROCITY WITH PEARL

HARBOR, INDEPENDENCE, AND

ANNEXATION

6

TREATY IN JEOPARDY

Treaty Attacked

AS HAD BEEN the case with other trade conventions negotiated by the United States, the Hawaiian Reciprocity Treaty encountered opposition soon after it became law. When it had been in operation less than two years, allegations were made that the increase in exportation of sugar from the Islands from September 9, 1876, to June, 1878, was from ten to twenty-five million pounds, or fifteen million pounds in two years, and it was assumed that this growth in exportation could not have resulted solely from an increase in production. Secretary of the Treasury John Sherman, on June 28, 1878, communicated with James Scott, United States consul at Honolulu, requesting "information on the practical operation and results of the treaty as affecting the interests of the U.S." The consul's reply, in brief, stated that it had proved "a bonanza to these Islands, especially to the sugar and rice growers," that it had increased the price of "sugar and rice-lands 100 per cent," and that it was costing the United States more in duties than in the entire gain in exports to the Islands.[1] Much of Scott's information was incorporated in Sherman's annual report for 1878 with the Secretary's comment that "the advantages have thus far not been reciprocal, but, . . . have been largely in favor of Hawaii, and it is probable that the benefits in favor of Hawaii will increase largely."[2]

Before the appearance of this report the *San Francisco Chronicle* predicted that strong efforts would be made to secure a modification of the Reciprocity Treaty. The Committee on Ways and Means of the House of Representatives, in which the sugar interests of Louisiana had an effective representation, would be expected to favor this, and Secretary of the Treasury Sherman would strongly recommend such a step in his annual report. His opposition to the treaty dated back to the debate on its ratification in the Senate, when he claimed that the remission of duties would not lead to an increase in trade likely to be beneficial to the United States. Under his orders the Treasury Department prepared and released a statement revealing that the total duties remitted by the United States on Hawaiian sugar, molasses, rice, and paddy in the year ending September 9, 1877, amounted to $1,125,359.99, whereas the total value of goods imported into Hawaii from the United States free of duty under the treaty for the same period was $962,125.93, leaving a debit excess of $163,234.06.[3]

The San Francisco *Evening Post*, however, pointed out that this "apparent debit balance" was not dead loss to the United States. If Sherman "gave the subject intelligent consideration, he would soon be convinced that the loss of revenue was counterbalanced by the increased profits on exports."[4] The editor of the *Washington Post* took a similar position. He called attention to Sherman's own statement that the increased value of American goods imported by Hawaii was eight hundred and fifty thousand dollars over that of the previous year. Although this amount was not large, when considered to be an increase in trade procured among a people that numbered only fifty thousand, it made a very fair showing. No doubt this amount would be greatly augmented if the treaty were allowed to stand. The Secretary "should understand that we cannot have both the duties and the increased profits on trade. As between the two it will be found that increased trade is the more valuable in the long run. If we levy an exorbitant tax upon the produce of that country, she will not continue to send it to us in exchange for American goods, but will deal with England, where she can get better terms."[5] The consensus of the proponents of the treaty was that bare figures of imports and exports failed to convey a correct idea of the advantages which reciprocity had secured for the United States. At a time when the chief need of American producers was a large foreign market for their productions, it would be sheer folly to cut off even the moderate field recently opened in Hawaii, or to check the enterprises that the Reciprocity Treaty had evoked, by raising doubt as to the permanency of its operations.

Attacks on the treaty persisted. Representative Randall L. Gibson of Louisiana, convinced that the sugar and rice interests of his state were being ruined by the convention, attempted to secure its abrogation by an act of Congress, but his resolution to that effect died in committee. Meanwhile, an expert on customs, Henry Alvin Brown of Saxonville, Massachusetts, formerly a special agent of the Treasury Department and a special inspector of customs in the district of Boston and Charlestown, conducted a private investigation of customs evasions and frauds. During 1878 and 1879 he produced three pamphlets assailing the fraudulent sugar dynasty, the "one sided reciprocity treaty" with the Hawaiian Islands, and "a California refiner, who lords it over consumers of sugar on our Pacific Coast and taxes them most royally under government patronage."[6]

General accusations reached Washington as to frauds and contemplated frauds upon the revenue of the United States by the importation of sugar and rice from the Sandwich Islands that were brought there from other countries, repacked, and sent forward with certificates that they were the products of those Islands. Specifically it was alleged that a certain party who had a prominent interest in securing the treaty had purchased a large tract of unoccupied land on one of the distant islands that contained a fine harbor, a quiet place of refuge, where he could order cargoes of rice and sugar from various parts of the Pacific Ocean to be landed, repacked, and sent up by coasting vessels to Honolulu and other ports of export, to be shipped thence to the United States as the growth and product of the Sandwich Islands. Through these fraudulent manipulations, duty-paying sugar and rice, evading and defrauding the customs, could be landed in Atlantic ports from the Sandwich Islands at an expense of about a half a cent per pound, a saving in duties of about two and a half cents.[7]

Secretary Sherman requested "that a full report be obtained from Honolulu concerning the frauds alleged to be committed in the importation of sugars, and also of rice from the Hawaiian Islands" into the United States. Minister James Comly communicated with the Hawaiian Foreign Office and the American consulate on the matter. Foreign Minister John M. Kapena responded that "any allegation that there has been any sugar or rice exported from this country to any ports of the United States, being the product of any other country than this, is utterly without foundation." He explained that Spreckels' land on Maui was not on a remote island, but in the midst of a large population, and Kahului, which was the harbor adjacent to his estate, was not within his property but was public land, "from which on all sides the ground rises to the mighty dome of Haleakala, so that it is overlooked for many miles, and every action can be observed by every plantation in the district, and that it is quite impossible that any cargo could be landed from any vessel without being observed by those interested." The harbor was used by all the planters of that region for the export of their sugar and the reception of their supplies; since the treaty went into operation no vessel had arrived there from any foreign port other than ports of the United States.[8]

Vice-consul F. P. Hastings informed Comly that he knew of no frauds, either actual or contemplated, upon United States revenue by the repacking and exporting of sugar and rice not the product of the Islands, nor did he "think it possible that a cargo of any kind could be landed or transhipped from one vessel to another, at any port or place on these Islands, without the fact coming to the knowledge of this office." He pointed out that the difference in size, shape, and polish of Japanese rice imported into the Kingdom to be fed to Chinese servants and laborers on the plantations could easily be detected in any of the ports of entry of the United States. Moreover, the vice-consul disclosed that an examination of the tables of domestic exports failed to indicate any such increase as the reported fifteen million pounds in two years. Actually the amounts of sugar produced in the Hawaiian Islands and exported to the United States for the years ending December 31, 1875, 1876, 1877, and 1878 were 23,762,744, 25,001,397, 25,506,478, and 38,399,862 pounds, respectively.[9]

Nearly a year earlier Minister Comly had reported that there was no reason to suspect that any of the Oriental rice in the Islands was or would be exported as Hawaiian rice. It was all fed to the laborers on the plantations, who preferred it to the better and more costly Hawaiian rice. The latter was a different species, much larger, finer, better, and different in shape and appearance. The Minister, who was no expert, could pick out the Hawaiian grains from a quantity of mixed rice as fast as he could pick out grains of wheat from mixed grains of wheat, rye, and oats. Nevertheless, in representations to the Hawaiian Government he insisted that these large importations must necessarily be looked upon by United States officials as a constant menace of frauds, and that it made very little practical difference whether this very same rice, grain for grain, was sent to the States, or whether it merely released Hawaiian rice to go in its place, free of the duty the foreign rice would have paid into the United States Treasury. Comly maintained that the United States was not only practically defrauded out of the revenue on this foreign rice, but was being used to add that much more to the Hawaiian revenues, for the Hawaiian Government received one half cent on every pound of this foreign rice, and exported to Americans an equivalent amount free of duty.[10]

The result of his interviews on the subject in almost every case was an expression of regret that rice was ever placed in the treaty. The Minister was informed that the rice industry was totally in Chinese hands, that only their capital and labor were invested in it. The sugar planters all preferred to have Hawaiian rice pay duty in the United States and have their own purchases of Chinese, Japanese, or East Indian rice freed from the Hawaiian duties. This would have brought down the cost of their own supplies and would have made even Hawaiian rice cheaper in the home market, for the price of the local product depended upon San Francisco.

Hawaiian officials did everything within their power to prevent the importation of sugar and rice from the Orient for fraudulent reshipment to the United States, duty-free under the treaty. As evidence of good faith, the Legislative Assembly of 1880 imposed a tariff of two and a half cents per pound upon such importation of rice, an impost designed to be prohibitive, and thus relieve further apprehension on the matter in the United States. Conviction under the act was punishable by a fine not exceeding one thousand dollars or imprisonment at hard labor not exceeding two years. Officers, called "export guards," skilled in detecting and distinguishing different growths of rice, were appointed to examine all packages of that article.[11]

In spite of these precautions allegations of sugar frauds continued to be made. In January, 1881, Secretary of the Treasury Sherman received from Henry A. Brown his three pamphlets on the sugar question and samples of sugar with data that explained and illustrated the practice of outwardly discoloring semi-refined sugars to evade duty.[12] The editors of several respectable periodicals published in New York and San Francisco, where sugar refining was an important industry, and New Orleans, which was in the heart of the sugar cane area, came out openly against the treaty. The campaign was inaugurated by the *San Francisco Chronicle*, a strong protectionist organ owned and edited by Michael de Young. On October 11, 1881, this newspaper attacked the "infamous treaty and the Spreckels monopoly" fostered by it, and in several editorials and articles denounced the convention, luridly depicting the evils of the contract

labor system under such headlines as: "Hawaiian Island Slavery,"
"Hawaii's Hideous Slave System," "Slavery and Sin," "Hawaiian
Helots," "Hawaiian Law and Labor," "Wrong and Oppression,"
"Norse Serfs," "Forty Percent, Awful Mortality of the Hawaiian
Laborers," "To Sin and Shame, The Pathway Prepared for Hawaiian
Handmaids," "Planter and Peon," "House of Bondage," "Hawaiian
Sugar-Coated Slavery," "Hawaiian Slavery," and "Sugar Planters and
Their Slavery." The newspaper inveighed against the "odious com-
mercial despotism" of what the *American Grocer* called "Sir Claus
Spreckels, knight by the grace of King Kalakaua; king of the
sugar trade by virtue of the Hawaiian Reciprocity Treaty, and
monopolist by the grace of the Pacific Railroad." The refiner allegedly
paid "the railroad $40 a ton upon 2,500 tons of freight annually,
which it does not carry from New York to San Francisco."[13] Through
this subsidy of one hundred thousand dollars per annum to keep
eastern sugars out of the West coast market, Spreckels was enabled
to charge two cents a pound over the New York price. An article of
October 23 maintained that the "autocrat of the breakfast table" was
realizing for himself a clear profit of six thousand dollars daily. Not
only was he holding "a rod of terror over every merchant in this
city and State," so that the chambers of commerce and boards of
trade were afraid to act, but he had even extended his sugar empire
eastward to include Colorado, New Mexico, Texas, Kansas, and
western Missouri, and was underselling eastern refiners in all those
markets.

In three editorials de Young resurrected and referred to a memorial which Claus Spreckels, president of the California Sugar
Refinery, and the presidents or managers of the Pacific Sugar Refinery, the Golden Gate Sugar Refinery, and the Bay Sugar Refinery,
had submitted to Representative John K. Luttrell in 1875, in protest
against the treaty. He claimed that their predictions that it would
crush the beet sugar industry, flood American markets with sugar
and rice produced in the Hawaiian Islands, and compel American
consumers "to pay more for an article of absolute necessity" had been
fully realized. But much worse, "the infamy" had virtually converted
the Islands into a funnel through which sugar and rice produced in
the Orient were being poured duty-free into the United States. Not
only was this a fraud upon the Treasury, it was destructive of all
of California's "tentative efforts at the production of beet and sorghum
sugar." In brief, the *San Francisco Chronicle* asserted: "Reciprocity
is a huge fraud, and the quicker the treaty is abrogated the better it

will be for the Government and for all consumers of sugar on this coast."[14]

The editor of this San Francisco newspaper, wishing to anticipate former Governor F. F. Low's efforts in Congress to break the force of the attacks on the Reciprocity Treaty, formulated twelve questions to which that prominent member of the Hawaiian Commercial Company and president of one of the sugar refineries of San Francisco should give satisfactory answers before senators and representatives committed themselves. Among others were these queries: Does not sugar, which pays the Government an average duty of two and a half cents a pound, sell in the East for from two and a half to eight cents a pound less than the sugar monopoly on this coast charges for the duty-free product of the Hawaiian Islands? Has not the sugar monopoly entered into contracts with Central and South Pacific Railroads by which the latter agreed to raise the charges of west-bound freights on sugar, which had been twenty dollars a ton previous to the contract to forty dollars a ton? Is it not a fact that no merchant of this city would dare to import his sugar from the East? Has not the Hawaiian Treaty been nearly fatal to the beet sugar industry in this state? Has not every reputable paper in California condemned the Reciprocity Treaty? Has a decent paper in this state raised its voice in defense of the treaty?[15]

The *San Francisco Chronicle* never considered the "Eastern refiners a whit better or less selfish than the Pacific coast monopoly. They are a corps who aim to do the best for their stockholders, and have as little regard for the rights of the people as the railroad corps." These were not the kind of people who ought to influence Congress in the adjustment of the tariff on an article which was the foremost source of revenue from customs. The duty on sugar was primarily for the protection of the planter, "to encourage home production, and not in the interest of the refiners, who always manage to secure for themselves the lion's share of the profits on sugar, whether the duty is high or low. Spreckels will never be drawn into a fight with them." The bills introduced into Congress providing for the abrogation of Hawaiian reciprocity had all been inspired by the planter interest. The editor of the *Chronicle* considered it preposterous to claim that the planters of Louisiana were in league with the eastern refiners. Their interests were directly opposed, and if the Reciprocity Treaty were abrogated, it would be without the assistance of the refineries.[16]

Moreover, de Young did not go along with the claim that the

treaty was politically valuable, that its retention would Americanize the Islands and eventually lead to annexation, but took the ground that the latter could only be accomplished by force. He questioned whether the American people were prepared "in order to build up the private fortunes of a few persons here, to incorporate into the body politic a piebald mass of humanity such as no one except those who have seen it can appreciate? and as for the morals of the people . . . the less said the better." Furthermore, if the Hawaiian Islands were annexed, their defense would cost infinitely more than they could possibly be worth. To the argument that Great Britain was "hovering in the vicinity of the Islands, ready to gobble them up," the *Chronicle* was of the opinion that the United States could rely with confidence upon the pledge which the British Government had given in 1843.[17] The editor went further and quoted a leading article entitled "Hawaiian Nationality and Independence," which appeared in the *Pacific Commercial Advertiser* of February 25, 1882, to prove that "the native people to a man and a large majority of the foreigners in the Kingdom" were devoted to the preservation of Hawaiian nationality and independence and that they were not "tempted by the glory of being part of a great political organization of fifty millions," but scorned the idea of merging into any other nation.

Although the *Chronicle* was the only one of the eight daily newspapers of San Francisco to campaign against the Spreckels monopoly and the Hawaiian Treaty, several Pacific slope papers lent their support. The Portland *Oregonian*, reflecting the general opinion in the district north of San Francisco and west of Minneapolis, criticized the agreement for its failure to cheapen sugar on the West coast, whereas the people of Oregon generally complained that the treaty favored San Francisco at the expense of other Pacific seaboard communities. In addition, some periodicals east of the Rocky Mountains were aroused. In its issue of November 21, 1881, the *Chronicle* listed the names of seventy-seven journals which during the preceding three or four weeks had "expressed their detestation of the Hawaiian contract system." Many were in the Midwest and East, including the *St. Louis Republican*, the *Chicago Tribune*, the *Cleveland Leader*, the *Ohio State Journal*, the *Cincinnati Commercial*, the *Cincinnati Times Star*, the Louisville *Courier-Journal*, the *Philadelphia Chronicle*, the *Providence Star*, and the Boston *Commercial Bulletin*. All but two or three demanded the repeal of the Reciprocity Treaty.

In whatever light the New Orleans *Times-Democrat* studied the treaty, it was found injurious to the sugar cane interests of this country. It encouraged coolie or slave labor, defrauded the government of $2,800,000 of revenue a year, created a balance of trade against the interest of the United States, opened up no new trade, injured home interests (the Louisiana sugar planters and the New York refineries), and benefited only one man—"a certain Claus Spreckels, a Hollander, who went to Hawaii a pauper a few years ago and who is now, thanks to the Reciprocity Treaty, a millionaire." The treaty, passed at the request of the Pacific slope, under the delusion that it would decrease the price of sugar by letting in the Hawaiian sugars free, had brought about the contrary effect, with sugar ranging from eleven to thirteen cents a pound in San Francisco —higher than anywhere else in the country. Only where Hawaiian sugar came into competition with Cuban sugar refined in New York, as was the case in Colorado, had Spreckels been compelled to decrease the price. The editor observed that the further one gets from Hawaii the lower is the price of its sugar, and complained that "so profitable is this reciprocity that Hawaiian sugar is now carried as far east as Texas and Missouri with profit."[18]

The New Orleans *Daily Picayune* also denounced the Hawaiian convention, intimating that the Islands served as a funnel, as a base of operations, for defrauding United States customs of duties on goods other than sugar. Since the Hawaiian Kingdom charged a duty of only ten per cent ad valorem on silks, satins, velvets, etc. and the United States sixty per cent, a shrewd merchant could bring "into the United States from Hawaii a big invoice of silks, satin, velvets, etc., mixed in with a cargo of duty free sugar, and make a handsome margin of 50 per cent on his venture. Gloves, hosiery, glass beads, champagnes, high priced brandies and other things present nearly as large inducements." Moreover, since the eighteen thousand Oriental laborers on the plantations in the Islands were obliged to eat the cheaper rice of China imported under a nominal duty, seven or eight million pounds of Hawaiian rice were released to be funneled into the United States duty-free. The convention was not a treaty but an instrument to subsidize the manufacture of Hawaiian sugar at the expense of the United States. The editor of the New Orleans *Daily Picayune* claimed that the "loss by this beautiful reciprocity fraud" amounted to nearly four million dollars in one year, and he called upon senators and congressmen to move immediately and give notice of its abrogation in 1883.

The editor of the *New York Times* observed that the Reciprocity Treaty "was intended to be of mutual benefit to the islands and to the United States," but a greedy Prussian had turned it into a charter of monopoly. The treaty undoubtedly benefited the Islands, for Spreckels and the Islands were synonymous so far as reciprocity was concerned, but it worked a positive injury to the people of the United States. "Fastening one hand upon the sugar plantations of the Hawaiian Islands and the other upon the sugar refineries of San Francisco, he puts his girdle of his monopoly half-way round the globe, and exacts his own price for the sweetening of the entire Pacific slope. His greatness comes of his persistently following out a single idea." In contrast to Jay Gould, who dealt in railroads, telegraphs, and newspapers, "Claus Spreckels sticks to sugar, and his faithfulness is rewarded by a return of $5,000 a day."[19] In another issue of the same newspaper the argument was advanced that fraudulent importations had so encouraged sugar production in the Islands that the Pacific coast refiners could no longer take all the Hawaiian crop and that it was finding its way to market on the Atlantic seaboard.

Campaign to Abrogate

THE *American Grocer* cited figures of the Bureau of Statistics which disclosed that during the year ending June 30, 1881, imports of merchandise from the Hawaiian Islands amounted to $5,533,000, whereas the value of domestic exports to the Islands was $2,694,583. Of the imports, sugar, valued at $4,927,021, amounted to over eighty-nine per cent of the total. Thus the people of the United States actually paid to the Hawaiian Islands, "in the way of surrender duties, not less than $1,500,000 as an inducement for them to purchase our products to the extent of $2,694,583, equal to a premium of over 55 per cent on last year's exports. That is reciprocity with a vengeance."[20] The periodical called upon the Government to give notice at once of "an abrogation of the Sandwich Islands Treaty."

Meanwhile, Henry A. Brown, who had acquired considerable recognition as an authority on sugar, was invited to a monthly meeting of the sugar planters in New Orleans. There, in an address of November 10, 1881, he reported on the plans resorted to by foreign parties to evade the payments of import duties on sugar of high grades brought into this country, and called attention to the injury which the United States was sustaining from the free imports of sugar made in the Sandwich Islands. The product now manufactured there had ceased to be of a low grade, and none of that class was sent to this country as the planters of the Islands had called to their aid the best machinery used for the manufacture of sugar.[21] The American people should be awakened to the necessity of abrogating the treaty.

Early in the new year Brown reiterated these arguments in an open letter to President Chester A. Arthur, maintaining that the convention was injurious to the sugar consumers of the Pacific coast, to the sugar planters of Louisiana, to the sugar refineries of the East, and to the United States Government which, allegedly, had been deprived of $10,162,749 in sugar duties alone. The Hawaiian planters were regularly defrauding the Treasury by exporting under cover of the treaty semi-refined sugars which were not legally exempted from duty. Reciprocity, while enriching "the Spreckels dynasty," was permitting wholesale, systematic, customs evasion. In his opinion the treaty could not be abrogated too soon.

Brown elaborated all his previous contentions in a forty-page pamphlet entitled *Concise Resumé of Sugar Tariff Topics, in Defense of American Sugar Industries*, published in January, 1882. In it he appealed for the protection of "our sugar producing and refining industries" against semi-refined sugars. He disclosed that "a Claus Spreckels & Co. 'ring,'" having unlimited means, was seeking in Washington to prevent the abrogation of the Hawaiian Treaty monstrosity. Failing in this, their lobbyists were instructed to push annexation of the Hawaiian Islands. "Should this 'ring' succeed as a precedent, this nation would soon become a general hospital for the support of semi-defunct countries and petty kingdoms, and reciprocity with such would be forced upon the people of this country with the terrors of annexation, staring them in the face whenever a ring of interested capitalists see their way clear to enrich themselves by the method of robbing the people and destroying American industries, now practised and sought to be perpetuated by the Claus Spreckels dynasty." The pamphleteer insisted that it would be "far better and cheaper for this nation to donate a trifle to the Hawaiian Islands as a matter of charity, and levy duty on their sugars, than to continue in any form or manner the annual payment of the enormous sugar bounty tribute now levied upon American consumers, sugar industries and revenue, by said treaty, simply for the support of the kingdom of Hawaii, and the enrichment of the Spreckels dynasty."[22]

Simultaneously with this unofficial activity, the opponents of the treaty in Congress were busy in an effort to bring about its abrogation. During December, 1881, and January, 1882, Representatives Randall L. Gibson and C. B. Darrall of Louisiana and John Hardy of New York introduced into the House two joint resolutions and one bill providing for the termination of the treaty. On January 9, Senators Benjamin H. Hill of Georgia and Benjamin F. Jonas of Louisiana introduced similar resolutions into the Senate which were referred to the Committee on Foreign Relations. During the opening week of the Forty-seventh Congress, the Board of Trade and Transportation, the chambers of commerce in New York City and state, the boards of trade of Providence and Philadelphia, and several other community organizations petitioned for the abrogation of the treaty on the ground that it had been used by a syndicate of capitalists to develop enormously the production of sugar in the Sandwich Islands, sugar which was admitted free of duty into the United States, thus discriminating against other sugar-producing nations and injuring domestic sugar interests. The first named petition was signed by several hundred firms, including all the sugar importing and refining trade, together with a large representation of manufacturers and merchants doing business with sugar-producing countries.

Questions and problems which arose from the operation of the treaty were referred to the appropriate committees in Congress, and the consequences of reciprocity with Hawaii were much discussed in both chambers. At hearings on the subject held in February and March, 1882, before the House Committee on Foreign Affairs, John Hardy, speaking for the sugar-refining interests of the East, and four of Louisiana's representatives argued against the continuance of the "infamous Hawaiian reciprocity treaty" on the ground that gross frauds had been perpetuated by the introduction of Chinese, Indian, and Manila articles under the title of Hawaiian sugar, as well as by exporting semi-refined sugars free of duty in violation of the convention, and that these imports injured the interests of their constituents. Representative Darrall showed the Federal Treasury was robbed of at least $2,500,000 annually in the introduction of free Island sugar. Henry Brown, on behalf of the sugar planters, appeared before the Committee on February 17, substantiated these allegations of frauds with an impressive array of statistics, and reiterated his previous charges. He warned that annexation of Hawaii would not alleviate, only aggravate, the difficulties of the American industries and require the United States Government to maintain a large navy for the protection of the outlying islands.[23]

These persistent demands for the abrogation of the Reciprocity Treaty naturally impelled its beneficiaries and friends to marshal their forces in defense. The San Francisco *Merchant*, reportedly the instrument of Claus Spreckels, and the San Francisco *Post* attacked the *San Francisco Chronicle* as the hired organ of the New York refiners. These newspapers insisted that reciprocity benefited California, first by establishing in San Francisco the largest sugar refinery in America, if not in the world, and, secondly, by stimulating shipbuilding for the sugar trade with Hawaii. They denied that it was injurious to eastern refiners or Louisiana planters and contended that it was politically advantageous to the United States as a whole. The *Merchant* insisted that "the Hawaiian planter spends his profits mainly in the United States as the Louisiana planter does. They stand exactly upon an equal footing, and it was the intention in making the treaty to put them on an equal footing."[24] To relieve somewhat the criticism directed against him and the treaty, Spreckels made two concessions: he reduced the price of sugar on the Pacific coast and terminated his agreement with the railroads, which served to exclude eastern sugars from the western markets. Furthermore, in January, 1882, a distinguished group of lobbyists, including Frederick F. Low, journeyed to Washington to exert pressure upon congressmen in favor of reciprocity. Spreckels himself traveled to the nation's capital in February. Nevertheless, by early 1882 he was manifesting a strange indifference to the treaty and talking of building a refinery in New York.[25] He became less vigorous in defending the convention, claimed he had his own policy, withdrew his lobbyists, and declined to contribute to the maintenance of anyone in Washington to work for the treaty in the interest of San Francisco and the Pacific coast.

The Hawaiian Minister to the United States, Elisha H. Allen, and his counsel, George S. Boutwell, former senator from Massachusetts and former Secretary of the Treasury, appeared at the hearings before the House Committee on Foreign Affairs on February 19, 20, and March 6, 1882. Allen refuted the charges that the sugar plantation laborers were being debased and degraded to the status of slaves and explained that the terms of service—six, twelve, eighteen, or twenty-four months—were entirely at the option of the laborers, except in the case of those procured at much expense from foreign countries, in which case the period was from three to five years. Furthermore, nine or ten hours constituted a day's labor; twenty-six days made a month. And, he added, the laws which regulated this service were enacted by Hawaiians for their own protection and benefit and were partial to the laborer.[26] He denied the charge that part of the Islands' sugar export was the growth and manufacture of other countries and proved this by reading a letter from Minister Comly. While the growth and manufacture of Hawaiian sugar had rapidly increased in an honest and legitimate manner, American investments in and the commerce of the United States with the Islands had also grown in like proportion. Of the estimated twenty million dollars of capital invested in the Kingdom, two-thirds was owned or furnished by Americans and the rest by English, Germans, Hawaiians, and Chinese. About two-thirds of the machinery used in the fifty-eight sugar mills had been manufactured in the United States and Hawaii and one-third in England and Scotland. The United States now supplied the Islands with as much produce and manufacture as the amount of duties remitted under the treaty. Instead of paying coin to China and Manila for sugar supplied for her Pacific states and territories, she paid in the products of the soil and the workshops which her own laborers had prepared for export. Allen said that it might "safely be stated that every dollar credited to the island planters for sugar sold in San Francisco, is expended for produce and manufactures, or in freight, commissions, and profits, earned by American ships, merchants and insurance companies." It had been estimated "that $1,000,000 were earned by American vessels engaged in the carrying trade with Hawaii in 1881, and an equal amount by merchants and insurance companies." Although the national revenue was reduced by the operation of the treaty, American farmers, laborers, mechanics, merchants, ship-owners, ship-builders, and capitalists derived profit from the trade with Hawaii which they could never have enjoyed had the treaty not been made, and had the sugar supplies of California been obtained, as formerly, from China and Manila. This important point was too often overlooked. The Minister maintained that the opposition to the treaty came only from the refiners of the Atlantic seaboard and some other persons interested in the sugar trade. He reminded the committee that Marcy, Seward, Sumner, Grant, and other eminent Americans all dreaded the future possibility of the Hawaiian Islands falling under the protection or sovereignty of some power other than the United States. Boutwell, reinforcing the Minister's arguments, asserted that the treaty contributed "to the security of the Pacific Coast," and that in view of the great trade of the future with the countries of the Pacific, it was of more consequence to the United States "than the production of $20,000,000 worth of sugar on this continent." If it were abrogated, he added, Great Britain would promptly conclude a similar convention with the Islands, having in view their eventual annexation.[27]

The *San Francisco Chronicle*, in reporting the arguments and inferred threats of the "Envoy Extraordinary and Minister Plenipotentiary from the sugary little kingdom of Hawaii," declared: "We have no use for the Islands as an integral part of our country. If we had them in case of a war with France, England, or Germany we could not hold them, save at a much greater cost than they are worth." There would be time to talk about securing or protecting these Islands when we acquired a navy able to cope with the naval forces of the European powers. The defense of reciprocity by "Boutwell of Boston 'culture' " was also excoriated by the *Chronicle*, which condemned a policy of fostering "trade and commerce in the Hawaiian kingdom at an expense of $4,000,000 a year to the Treasury, and $1,100,000 a year to the people of the Pacific coast states." Although at that time the price fell heaviest on California, the *Chronicle* predicted that if the treaty ran seven years more it would "fall with still more telling force on the Louisiana planters and the Eastern refiners, representing an actual investment of more than $120,000,000." The Washington correspondent of that newspaper, in an article entitled "What We are Losing," referred to an annual loss of eight million dollars and concluded that "there is not a single valid commercial or diplomatic reason that will justify Congress in continuing this Hawaiian Treaty fungus—this 'profound foreign policy' which is doomed ere long in any event."[28]

The New Orleans *Times-Democrat* stepped up its campaign against the Reciprocity Treaty, which it considered "but the first of a series of blows directed against one of our most flourishing and profitable agricultural interests," as obviously "it was to be speedily followed by similar treaties with other sugar producing countries. Such legislation would certainly culminate in the utter and entire destruction of our flourishing sugar producing industry." There were vast regions in Texas and bottom lands of several of the rivers and streams of the state of Mississippi on which rice could grow almost as well as in the most optimum regions of Louisiana. Under favorable circumstances, the South could produce all the sugar required to supply the nation for many years to come, and at the same time this industry would give employment to many.[29]

A petition requesting the abrogation of the Hawaiian Reciprocity Treaty was circulated and extensively signed by Louisiana sugar and rice merchants during February, 1882, and was later presented to the planters for their signatures. The editor of the *Times-Democrat* urged action in this matter, for Hawaiian coolie-raised sugar was finding its way further and further east and entering into competition with that produced in Louisiana and Cuba; the latter was refined in New York and had a large duty levied against it. Moreover, Hawaiian rice, about which little had been said, was being exported to the United States in such large quantities "as to give rise to the suspicion that a great deal of East Indian and Chinese rice passes through Honolulu in order to avoid payment of duties." Rice raised by coolie labor was "proving a serious and dangerous rival to the product of Louisiana and South Carolina." Twelve carloads of Hawaiian rice, about one thousand barrels, were delivered in an Ohio town at the same or a lower price than the domestic product, "a difference against the Louisiana and Carolina product of three-eighths to one-half cent per pound, and this, after paying freight nearly across the continent." During the year, one lot of a thousand packages of Hawaiian rice was purchased in New York at a price less than an equivalent grade of Carolina or Louisiana rice could be bought at the producing point. Before the treaty went into effect Louisiana had a large and increasing rice trade with the Far West from Denver to San Francisco. The editor estimated that "rice would have sold at least one-half cent higher last season if we could have had the Pacific coast and the trade west of the Missouri river—heavy rice consuming regions."[30]

True, Hawaiian sugar had penetrated the Midwest by early 1882. The visit of W. H. Dimond to St. Louis resulted in an offer for five hundred tons per month, a large sale effected at a satisfactory figure, and said to be the same as the contract rate with San Francisco for 1881. The *Saturday Press*, published in Honolulu, commented: "Thus while the extreme East and West markets are fighting over our produce we enter a middle field and find a ready market for all we are disposed to send them." The success of this project was largely due to the reduced rate on sugar by the railroads, and it was hoped in Hawaii that "they will see it to their interest to adopt a figure that will encourage this trade, instead of our sending cargoes East by way of Cape Horn."[31]

Defense of the Treaty

WHILE scores of journalists and Henry A. Brown penned their caustic attacks on the treaty, two apologists, R. P. Spalding and Thomas Welles Bartley, brought out pamphlets in defense of it. The former emphasized that "as we do not seek to increase our national domain by the annexation of territory outside of the Continent of America," we must secure the key to the Northern Pacific by conciliating the inhabitants of the archipelago, and this had been done most successfully in the Treaty of 1875. No power on earth could gain the ascendancy over the United States in those Islands so long as the Reciprocity Treaty was continued in force. But let it be abrogated and England would "not be true to her own history" if she did "not speedily endeavor to convert the Hawaiian Islands into British Provinces." The sugar interest was the arterial blood of the Hawaiian people. They could not subsist without it, and it could not be maintained without a free market. If a duty of two and a half cents on the pound were imposed, the most prosperous plantations would fall back into cattle ranches unless England favored the Kingdom with a treaty and enabled it to transfer the sugar traffic to Australia.[32]

American residents in the Islands and visiting United States Navy officials cautioned the President and Secretary of State against abrogating the Reciprocity Treaty, for its existence was of such vital importance to the Islands that anything endangering its perpetuity was calculated to weaken American influence among the people while affording a powerful stimulant to forming a similar arrangement with Great Britain, Germany, or France, who would at any cost be glad "to obtain such a footing as we undeniably hold."[33] Some maintained that the English were secretly hostile to the continuance of the treaty, hoping to divert the great bulk of trade between the United States and the Hawaiian Islands to Canada and the mother country the moment the Canadian Pacific Railway was completed. George E. Belknap wrote that the Reciprocity Treaty, if renewed, "will continue to Americanize the group—foster American interests in the Pacific, and establish a commercial protectorate over the islands that will substantially make them a possession of the Republic without the trouble of their annexation or the expense of their government."[34]

On the other hand, Captain C. E. Dutton warned that if the treaty were abrogated, the investments of over fifteen hundred creditors and stockholders in the United States would in large part be sold at immense sacrifice to English capitalists. It was "obvious that the entire commerce with the islands would pass into British hands. It is now exclusively American. . . . The state of society would be revolutionized in the islands. Today it is as distinctly American as any part of New England. In a very few years it would become as distinctly British as that of Jamaica and Trinidad. . . . With a large influx of East India coolies, with the principal ownership and control of the islands' industries vested in British planters, with the capital and commerce of the islands in the hands of British merchants, the question of political ascendancy is not worth discussing."[35]

While the House Ways and Means Committee weighed the arguments for and against the retention of the treaty, Henry A. Brown denounced "this treaty abomination" and called for its abrogation in order to reduce the price of sugar on the Pacific coast and to protect "Louisiana planters, beet and sorghum sugar producers, and Eastern refiners."[36] On May 3, 1882, he addressed to the chairman of the Committee on Foreign Affairs a letter reiterating the charges that the convention was being circumvented by unscrupulous Hawaiian interests. Not satisfied with these efforts, he proceeded, on October 24, 1882, to present his complaints directly to Secretary of the Treasury Charles F. Folger in a statement alleging that "at least 80 per cent of the sugars now entering free from the Hawaiian Islands are not designated in or exempted by the treaty of 1875." In January, 1883, Brown brought out another pamphlet entitled *Hawaiian Sugar Bounties and Treaty Abuses*, which was a collection of statements made to Congress, letters addressed to the Committee on Foreign Affairs, the Treasury Department, and further arguments against Hawaiian reciprocity. He estimated the annual prospective increase in Hawaiian sugar and the loss to the United States through the treaty and its subversion, and concluded "we shall lose in the next five years, through said treaty, enough money to build a navy that would command the world";[37] the additional injury and loss to consumers and sugar producing and refining industries would be incalculable.

A new Tariff Commission conducted hearings in Boston, Philadelphia, and St. Louis before which representatives of the sugar refiners of Boston and New York, the Merchants Exchange of St. Louis, and the rice planters of Louisiana presented their grievances. Under the careful coaching of Commissioner Duncan Kenner of Louisiana, the general complaint was made that the Reciprocity Treaty enabled "one man and his associates" to monopolize the sugar markets of the Pacific coast and to exclude eastern sugars from these, and even from the markets in Kansas City and St. Louis. The sugar interests requested the Commission "to recommend to Congress that the treaty be abrogated," a request which the members did not feel free to grant and did not recommend to President Arthur in their final report.[38]

Spreckels Denounced and Defended

NEVERTHELESS, the opinion persisted and continued to saturate the public press that Claus Spreckels and other refiners on the West coast were the only Americans who benefited from the treaty. This false idea created a bitter personal prejudice against him, which by implication, illogically and unjustly, extended to the commerce and industries of the Hawaiian Islands. Less than a year after the treaty went into operation, the Portland *Oregonian* inveighed against it, stating that "every intelligent person on the Pacific Coast knows that the treaty operates directly and solely in the interest of a sugar ring in San Francisco, which controls the plantations at the Islands. Every intelligent person knows, too, that the ring is making immense sums, that the government is losing a very large revenue, and that consumers are paying more for 'free' sugar than they did a while ago for sugar subject to duty." At Portland alone the loss to the revenue was one hundred and twenty thousand dollars a year; at San Francisco it was many times as great. All this, plus the increased price of sugar, which amounted to fully as much more, was transferred by the treaty to the pockets of the sugar ring. The trade of the wholesale merchants of the former city had been practically cut off by reciprocity and transferred to San Francisco.[39]

Senator James K. Kelly apprised Judge Allen of the unpopularity of the treaty in Oregon and stated that the merchants of Portland believed that if the Hawaiian planters would produce sugars of the best quality which could be imported free of duty and sent to his state, the results would be beneficial to its people and would make the treaty more palatable.[40]

The *Hawaiian Gazette* answered the accusations of the *Oregonian*, asserting that "every American, and every cent of American capital which is now, or may be hereafter, invested in sugar plantations in the country, does and will participate in the advantages of the treaty." No sensible person believed that the free introduction into the United States of Hawaii's small contribution to the world sugar market could affect the price of sugar in that country. The statement that a sugar ring at San Francisco controlled the Island plantations was devoid of a shadow of truth. The owners of the sugar refineries in that city held an interest in one sugar plantation in Hawaii, and their "control" was limited to that. The greater number of plantations were owned in Hawaii, were free of debt, and were subject to no control outside of that exercised by their owners. It was true that a large proportion of the sugar crop was sold to the San Francisco refiners, but whenever the merchants of Portland, or any other parties, offered better terms they would get the sugar.

Similarly, a later report of the Foreign Relations Committee of the Senate attempted to prove that although Spreckels monopolized the manufacture of refined sugars on the Pacific coast "and ruled that market to the extent of his powers with a rod of iron," two false impressions prevailed in regard to his activities. The first was in supposing that the Hawaiian Treaty had assisted in establishing, maintaining, or conferring any benefit whatever upon his monopoly. The second arose out of the mistaken belief about his relations to the industry and commerce of raw sugar. In these he was only one of many men, and, though individually his relations were large, relative to the whole they were small; he could no more control the whole than the Cunard Company could dominate American commerce with England. Claus Spreckels, as a majority stockholder, directed only one plantation in the Islands. Until 1884 he had a minority interest in each of four others. He, his son, and friends together could not control more than a fourth part of the Hawaiian crop, except by buying it on terms satisfactory to the planters. As a monopolist of refined sugar, he could not escape the odium which always attaches to a monopoly. As a planter and stockholder, as a director of an American steamship company, and as a banker, his whole career and course of conduct would "compare favorably with that of any great and successful merchant in America."[41]

The Senate report answered the contention of the eastern refiners and the Louisiana planters that through the free entry of Hawaiian sugars, an entry which enabled the western refiners to purchase raw sugar more cheaply than they otherwise could, the treaty was discriminatory and unjust. The report stated the position of the San Francisco importers and the owners of Hawaiian sugar properties in California, who asserted that they got "their raw sugar no cheaper by reason of the treaty," but were obliged to pay the same price for it as for equivalent dutiable sugar from Asia, and that the ability of the Pacific refiners to compete successfully with the Atlantic refiners was founded upon conditions wholly independent of the treaty. First, because of much cheaper freight rates (five to six dollars per ton from Manila to San Francisco in comparison with nine to twelve dollars per ton to New York), unlimited amounts of Far Eastern sugar could be brought to San Francisco cheaper than to New York; second, because through eastward freights over the Pacific railroads were scantier than through westward freights, the railroads naturally preferred carrying sugar at lower rates to hauling empty cars. In brief, the San Francisco price of raw sugar was lower than the New York price by three-eighths to five-eighths of a cent per pound. The western refiners contended that this competition was a natural one, that it was destined to grow and would grow if the Hawaiian Islands did not exist, and that it was not aided by the treaty and would not be hindered by its abrogation.

The refineries did not obtain the benefits of the remitted duties in any degree whatever, for Hawaiian sugars were shipped by the planters or factors in Honolulu to commission merchants and importers in San Francisco and sold by the latter to the refinery. The terms of purchase after the treaty went into effect were known as the "Manila basis." The refiners agreed in substance to take the whole of each planter's crop at a price which should be equal to that of an equivalent quantity and grade of Manila sugar delivered, duty paid, in San Francisco. The price of a certain grade of sugar at Manila known as "extra superior," polarizing 91° and in color number 10 Dutch standard, was telegraphed daily to San Francisco. To this price were added six dollars per ton for freight, two per cent insurance, the cost of sixty days exchange, and a specific allowance for the remitted duty. This constituted the Manila basis for the day of quotation. Therefore, the western-shore importer of Hawaiian sugar had no treaty advantage over the eastern-shore importer of the article from Cuba, Brazil, or the Far East. The duty the former would have paid to the Government, he paid, in effect, to the seller in Hawaii. Most of the advantages resulting from the treaty remained with the planters or factors on the Islands. Much of the remitted duties went to shipping, banks, mercantile houses, investors, and so forth, not to Spreckels.

This, however, was the one big point of dispute between the sugar men of the East and those of the West and of Honolulu. New Yorkers refused to believe that Spreckels paid the full, normal price and the entire duty to the Hawaiian planters or factors. This question was repeatedly examined and investigated, and the universal verdict was that the entrepreneur dealt fairly in this matter; this was the testimony of both his friends and enemies.[42] In fact, Spreckels contended that he overpaid the planters and gave them more than Manila and China sugar would have cost him, and there is some indication that this is correct. But the technical problems involved in refining different standards of sugar—the Manila standard polarized 91°, whereas the average polarization of the whole Hawaiian crop was about 94°—required a detailed and complicated explanation which only sugar experts would easily understand.[43] Consequently, it was much simpler and more effective for avid journalists, subsidized pamphleteers, and concerned congressmen to single out Claus Spreckels as the principal benefactor of the Treaty of Reciprocity and to condemn him as the *bête noire* of the sugar industry.

Moreover, the great bulk of Hawaiian sugar arrived in San Francisco from December to March, inclusive, and Spreckels paid on delivery. Thus, during a great part of the year, he was forced to carry an enormous surplus stock worth three to four million dollars, and the interest on that was no trifle. If he had purchased Asian sugars as he wanted them or had been able to take advantage of the favorable fluctuations of the market, he would have had an advantage which he did not possess under the arrangement with the Hawaiian planters. All factors considered, it is probable that the practical working of the "Manila basis" caused Spreckels to pay more for Hawaiian sugar than for that from Manila.

In examining the nature of Spreckels' monopoly—his ability to raise the price of sugar materially above the price fixed by free competition—one must consider the possible sources of competition in the sale of refined sugars in California. There could be none from foreign-refined sugars because the duty on them was prohibitory. There could be no effective competition from eastern sugars because their price was established on the Atlantic seaboard, where Louisiana and Cuban sugars were costlier and the railroad transportation was too expensive. There was no local competition because in the 1880's and 1890's there was not enough work for two big refineries. A single refinery half as large as Havemeyer and Elders could supply the whole country west of Denver with sugar. If there were two refiners, as was actually the case, they must either begin a war of extermination, or else pool and divide the market, which they did. The causes which contributed to a monopoly were a prohibitory tariff on refined sugar, the isolation of California and its neighbors from eastern states where sugar was refined, the comparatively sparse population on the Pacific slope, and the fact that one ordinary refinery was ample for all needs. Nothing could stop the monopoly but time, and the changes which only time would ultimately bring. The treaty had no assignable effect whatever upon the sales of sugar in the Mississippi Valley. These would have been the same without the treaty as with it. San Francisco was the natural supply-source of sugar for almost the whole country west of the Kansas-Missouri line and of a considerable territory still further east. The only real competition to San Francisco in that region was the Louisiana planter, who had no more right to complain of it than of the competition of New York, except that the New York refiners bought his sugar. According to the Senate report, this competition was independent of the treaty. Congress could not prevent it, and ought not if it could, for it was a normal and healthy one. So far as Spreckels' monopoly was concerned, the Hawaiian Treaty had nothing to do with its establishment; it was fixed before that treaty.

Sixty-two sugar importing and refining companies of New York, Boston, and Philadelphia, in November, 1882, jointly protested to the Treasury Department the importation, free of duty, into San Francisco and other ports "of sugars from the Sandwich Islands, which are entirely different in quality from that contemplated and clearly specified in the Hawaiian Islands Treaty." This free importation, "considered an outrageous and illegal abuse" of the treaty, had stimulated the production of sugar in the Sandwich Islands to such an extent that it became necessary to find other United States markets. Already, cargoes imported into New York had been pronounced liable to duty for not coming within the stipulations of the treaty. However it was announced in the press that this question had been referred to the Collector of Customs at San Francisco; the petitioners protested this course maintaining that it was well known that such importations had "been very large and constantly increasing in San Francisco, and to refer the question raised to the Collector of that port, would constitute him a judge of his own importations, greatly to the detriment of the entire sugar trade of the country, without any benefit to the consumer." Acting Secretary of the Treasury, John R. French, replied to the effect that the Collector of Customs in San Francisco was in no way authorized by law or instructions from the Department to decide whether the sugar referred to as imported at New York should be treated as covered by the provisions of the treaty. The Department would decide after the facts regarding the matter had been ascertained.[44]

The opponents of the treaty persisted in their charges of illegal importation and implied that Hawaii also served as a funnel for the entrance of products other than sugar. The arguments that the treaty was used to cover fraudulent operations and that there was no real commercial reciprocity in it, only a drain upon the United States Treasury, were impressive, and taken together made a strong economic case against its retention.

Official Views on Termination

THE Secretary of the Treasury submitted a statement to the Committee on Foreign Affairs on January 16, 1883, at their request, setting forth his views on the commercial effects of the abrogation of the treaty with the Hawaiian Islands. So far as "the pecuniary interests of the United States" as a government were concerned, there had been a loss of $3,405,502 in tariff revenue during the previous year. He had information from an accredited representative of the Hawaiian Kingdom to the effect that, to a buyer from the United States, the price of the sugar in the Islands was made by adding to its Island value a sum equal to the duty on it at a United States port where the sugar was subject to tariff taxes. If this were true, the western-shore importer had no advantage over the eastern-shore importer by the freedom of duty. The Secretary was "not prepared to say that it would beneficially affect the business interests of this country to abrogate the treaty."⁴⁵

A majority of the Committee on Foreign Affairs, after deliberating for almost a year, reported they were of the opinion that the intent of the treaty had been violated by the introduction of grades of sugar under the Dutch standard of color which were not within the description of the treaty. It appeared that out of a total of one hundred and six million pounds of sugar entering the Pacific coast from Hawaii in the preceding fiscal year, ninety-eight million came properly within the Dutch standards of numbers 10 and 16, inclusive, whereas in purity the range was about ninety-five per cent. This result was not the intent of the contracting parties at the time the agreement was negotiated.⁴⁶ It, however, contained other important stipulations in favor of the United States. "The effect of the treaty has already been to give this Government the benefit of a satisfactory political influence with the Government of the Hawaiian Islands, and to enable it in all cases to secure the just rights of its citizens who have already very large pecuniary interests in Hawaii." Since the retention of this position was desirable in reference to the future, "it would be folly to take any step which might lose us the most important key to the commercial and naval situation." The Committee accordingly recommended that "the treaty should not be wholly abrogated with the consequent loss of all its provisions for our rights and security, but rather that modifications should be introduced which shall obviate the evils which have given just grounds of complaint." A minority of the Committee, however, saw fit to deal with the economic losses of the United States and alleged frauds under the treaty.⁴⁷

While this activity was taking place in the House of Representatives, the Senate did not remain passive. On January 9, 1883, Senator Lot Myrick Morrill, Chairman of the Committee on Finance, introduced a joint resolution providing for the termination of the treaty. In an able justification of his resolution he explained that reciprocity was a serious financial liability to the United States. Semi-refined sugars not stipulated in the convention were imported free of duty under its protection and the Treasury was losing large duties on Hawaiian imports, whereas the American export trade to the Islands was not making commensurate gains. The political advantages in the arrangement did not impress him; he had not much faith in "the idea of our establishing a jingo empire in the Pacific Ocean," for "in case of war these Hawaiian Islands will go to the strongest naval power, and it will not affect us one groat whether we have a treaty stronghold or not. Whoever has the largest navy and the most guns will take possession of those islands or any other in that open ocean." The senator requested that his resolution be referred to the Committee on Finance, and with the support of his colleagues from the sugar- and sorghum-producing and sugar-refining states his request was granted by a vote of thirty-one to twenty; twenty-five senators were absent.[48]

The majority of the Committee reported, on February 27, that by the use of the vacuum pan and centrifugal machines in the process of refining, the grade value of the sugars imported from Hawaii had been greatly changed; and now, instead of the larger portion coming in not above number 10 Dutch standard as previously, nearly the whole of it came in above that standard. Manifestly, the treaty had afforded an artificial stimulus to the growth of Hawaiian sugars and to the introduction of a grade of free sugars much above the standard of such as were to be lawfully admitted free of duty according to the very explicit terms of the treaty, "and their admission is an open and indisputable fraud upon the treaty." In other words, if there were no treaty, the sugars now received would be subject at least to one cent per pound more duty than the sugars to be received free of duty by the treaty. Since "it was no longer for the interest of the United States" to continue the Reciprocity Treaty in force, the Committee recommended its termination. The minority—Justin R. Morrill, Daniel W. Voorhees, and Nelson W. Aldrich—while agreeing with the majority, stated additional reasons for abrogation based upon the constitutional provision that revenue bills should originate in the House of Representatives as well as upon the "most-favored-nation" clause in the larger number of our treaties with other nations. They concluded "that experience shows, in every instance where a reciprocity treaty had been tried, that immense American interests have been sacrificed."[49]

After the treaty became terminable on September 9, 1883, Senators Benjamin F. Jonas and Gibson of Louisiana both introduced into the Senate joint resolutions calling for its termination. These were defeated by the timely report from the Committee on Foreign Relations to which the resolution of the Finance Committee had been referred. This report, presented by Senator John Morgan of Alabama on January 24, 1884, recommended the indefinite postponement of the resolution and was chiefly concerned with the refutation of the arguments and conclusions of the Committee on Finance. It emphasized the growth of American population and influence in Hawaii as a result of the liberal concessions made by the Hawaiian Government in the treaties of 1849 and 1875, and submitted a letter of October 15, 1883 from Minister Rollin M. Daggett to show that of the $15,886,800 which represented the entire value of sugar lands in the Islands, $10,235,464 belonged to Americans. Moreover, much of the profits which appeared to accrue to Hawaii really went to American shippers and sugar merchants. Considering the complaints of American sugar and rice interests, the Committee observed that since the overland freights on Louisiana sugars excluded them from California and Oregon, the Pacific states were compelled to look to the Hawaiian Islands for their chief supply.

The report stressed the importance of the archipelago as a base both in commercial and naval strategy, maintaining that "The Hawaiian Islands afford the only stopping place . . . between our coasts and those of Japan, Korea, and China; and from Panama to the heart of those countries they are in almost the direct line of travel. They are east of the meridian which touches the western shore of Alaska, and may be said to be properly within the area of the physical and political geography of the United States. They are nearer to us than to any other great power."

The Committee further observed that "the kingdom of Hawaii is the only Government in the North Pacific Ocean that is not a colonial dependency of some great power in Europe or Asia, and it is therefore the only neutral power in the North Pacific Ocean." The members contended that "if we abandon the treaty, we must also abandon the attitude we assumed when it was ratified—that our national interests are so identical with those of Hawaii that we cannot permit any other nation to gain such control in that country as will endanger our western coast or seriously impede our commerce on the Pacific Ocean." Australia, anxious to secure Hawaiian trade, "is but little further from those Islands than we are." The completion of the Canadian Pacific Railroad from Lake Superior to Puget Sound would induce the Dominion of Canada to make most favorable terms with the Hawaiian Government for the trade of those Islands. Furthermore, a canal through the Isthmus of Darien would cause Hawaii to seek better markets in Europe than Americans could offer for the purchase of the goods she needed, "so that every new route of transportation leading to Europe will put in jeopardy our trade with the

Hawaiian Islands unless we continue and make permanent our existing treaty agreement." The report concluded that whatever objections had been raised to the workings or results of the treaty were "greatly overbalanced by the advantages we have acquired in a national sense; and by the benefits to our people of a profitable trade with the Hawaiian people; and by the duty we owe to the people of both countries to give certainty and permanence to the gratifying prosperity which this treaty has created."[50]

In disagreement with this conclusion, the minority submitted a report signed by Senators John Sherman and Joseph E. Brown which embodied the adverse report of the Committee on Finance and emphasized that the fiscal losses to the United States entailed by the treaty were far greater than any benefit derived from it. This report recommended the termination of the arrangement "with a view to entering into such commercial relations with the Sandwich Islands as will be more nearly reciprocal than the provisions of the present treaty."[51]

Neither the Senate nor the House of Representatives as a body acted upon the reports of their respective committees. Consequently, the opponents of Hawaiian reciprocity continued to press their charges of fraudulent manipulations and customs evasion. During the congressional vote on the tariff in February, 1883, Senator Pope Barrow of Georgia and Representative John Van Voorhis of New York, along with other members of both houses, alleged that large quantities of both sugar and rice which were not produced in Hawaii were, nevertheless, being illegally imported into the United States as the products of that Kingdom under cover of the Reciprocity Treaty.

Meanwhile, under instructions of Secretary of State Frederick T. Frelinghuysen, the charges of the eastern sugar importers and refiners that sugars not of the standards stipulated in the treaty were being imported into the United States fraudulently through Honolulu were exhaustively investigated by Minister Daggett. His reports of March 5 and May 18, 1883, conclusively refuted these allegations, and he proceeded to account for all the sugar exported.[52] The number of acres cropped in 1882 was twenty-six thousand which yielded a fraction over fifty-seven thousand tons of raw sugars, all of which, with the exception of less than two tons, was exported to the United States. The average yield per acre was a little short of two and two-tenths tons, and that average on twenty-six thousand acres accounted for every pound of sugar produced in 1882.

In mid-summer an investigatory commission appointed on May 10 by Secretary of the Treasury Charles F. Folger and composed of Oliver Lyman Spaulding, who had served as congressman from Michigan and was at the time Assistant Secretary of the Treasury in Chester A. Arthur's Cabinet, John E. Searles, Jr., secretary of the American Sugar Company, and A. K. Tingle of the Treasury Department, visited San Francisco, Portland, Oregon, and the Hawaiian Islands. After a thorough investigation these gentlemen concluded that the formation of the Islands in itself was such as to forbid the successful smuggling of sugar. Only in the port of Honolulu could vessels lie with safety. All the others were open roadsteads at which landings had to be made by boats, and some of them were attended with no little risk, even at the most favorable season. In the state of society which existed on the Islands, where every new arrival or unusual event attracted attention, the presence of a sugar-laden vessel and the landing of her cargo would of necessity involve such publicity as to preclude the possible success of the venture, to say nothing of the necessary after-handling and re-shipment to the United States. This could be accomplished only by collusion between the shippers and the United States and Hawaiian officials of which there was no evidence or grounds for suspicion.

The members of the commission observed a significant fact, that though vague charges of fraud were made, no specific case had ever been brought to the knowledge of either government. The allegation seemed to have no other foundation than the fact that there had been a large increase in the quantity of sugars sent to the United States after the treaty, but this increase could be accounted for as the legitimate result of the treaty itself. The commissioners also found unwarranted by fact the charges that the treaty had created a sugar monopoly and had increased the price of that product on the Pacific coast. The increased cost of two to two and a half cents per pound was not the result of the treaty, but grew out of a monopoly of the refining business in San Francisco coupled with the still greater monopoly of railroad transportation.

There was no doubt in the minds of the visitors that the rice culture of the Islands had been stimulated by the treaty even more than that of sugar. According to the statistics compiled from official records of the Custom House in Honolulu, the exports of rice to the United States in 1874 totaled 885,646 pounds; in 1875, 1,146,835 pounds; and in 1882, 12,135,074 pounds, the latter being the entire exports of rice from the Islands, except for 34,401 pounds which went to other countries. The investigators also learned that the benefit of the duty remitted on rice went almost entirely to the Chinese, who, either by purchase or lease of lands, had secured control of rice cultivation.[53]

Although the Senate was unwilling to terminate the treaty, it was equally unwilling to make an explicit commitment for its extension and at the same time was undecided whether to abrogate it and then negotiate a new one. A verbal inquiry was made to Secretary of State Frelinghuysen as to whether the schedule of articles admitted duty free from the United States into Hawaii might not be enlarged and whether a supplementary provision—either by an additional article or by separate convention—for the establishment of a coaling station by the United States in the Islands might not be expedient.

The Secretary expressed the opinion that the introduction of changes in the text of the existing treaty "as a condition of its extension, would be, in fact, to negotiate a new treaty," which might call forth opposition and imperil the interests concerned. He was disposed to "an arrangement for establishing a coaling station, or even a naval and repair station, under the flag of this Government, at some available harbor in the Hawaiian Islands"; but considered it to be "inexpedient to join such a provision to the commercial treaty." He suggested that all the ends in view could "be most effectively and speedily reached" by the President saying to the Hawaiian Minister "that behind the Senate's vote of approval is a distinct expectation that Hawaii will grant us a revised and enlarged free list and a station."[54]

The Committee on Foreign Relations reported on June 19, 1884, a resolution favoring an extension of the agreement for seven years and advising the President to secure, "by negotiation with the Government of Hawaii, the privilege of establishing permanently a proper naval station for the United States in the vicinity of Honolulu, and also a revision and further extension of the schedule of articles to be admitted free of duty from the United States in the Hawaiian Kingdom."[55] The provision for the extension of the schedule was subsequently dropped and the resolution was passed. The Senate, however, on successive motions of Justin S. Morrill, voted to postpone action upon this resolution.

President Chester A. Arthur, who favored extending the Reciprocity Treaty and had urged action in his annual messages of 1882 and 1883, transmitted to the Senate on June 9, 1884, a report of the

Secretary of State communicating a proposal of the King of Hawaii that the duration of the existing treaty be extended for a further period of seven years. The following December 6, Frelinghuysen, on the advice of the Committee on Foreign Relations, concluded with the Hawaiian Minister, Henry A. P. Carter, a supplementary convention extending the duration of the treaty for a term of seven years from the date of the exchange of ratifications and beyond this period indefinitely, subject to twelve months' notice of termination—an agreement which was duly transmitted to the Senate and printed in confidence. On December 11, Senator John Franklin Miller of California presented a memorial from citizens of that state setting forth the benefits that had resulted from the operation of the treaty and the reasons why reciprocal relations should be continued.[56]

These positive steps did not mean that there was general agreement in Congress on the policy to be pursued, for there existed in the United States an influential party opposed in principle to all reciprocity involving one-sided concessions to nations of inferior populations and wealth, "involving the surrender of enormously unequal sums of revenue, involving the surrender of immensely larger volumes of home trade than are offered in return, and involving constitutional questions of the gravest character."[57] The views of this group were repeatedly and vigorously expressed by Senator Justin S. Morrill, the pro-tariff leader of Congress, and Representative Morrison. According to the latter, the United States was not "justified in incurring a loss of two or more millions per annum for the privilege of landing at the Islands which every other nation may do for nothing." He was of the opinion that whenever any other nation would pay more than the United States paid, Hawaii would abrogate with the Americans and treat with any competitors or rivals. "If we have any political rights in the Pacific they should be ours without hiring or paying for them."[58]

Henry Carter resorted to the press in an effort to counter what he considered misrepresentation of the facts concerning the treaty. The commercial advantages of Americans he knew to be greater than were generally understood. It was estimated that the American ownership in Hawaiian sugar plantations amounted to $10,500,000; in Oceanic mercantile marine to $3,500,000; in inter-island mercantile marine to $3,500,000; American banking capital to $3,500,000; American mortgages on foreign-owned property to $1,000,000, making a total of $22,000,000 as the investment upon which Ameri-

cans made interest and profit aside from that obtained from $12,250,-
000 of annual import and export trade. Six-sevenths of this capital
was created by and through the treaty. The export trade of the United
States to Hawaii in 1883 was $4,000,000, while the importations
amounted to $8,250,000. But no coin of any amount was sent to the
Islands in liquidation of the surplus. In fact, the surplus remained
in this country as profits on capital invested in the Islands.[59]

The Senate, hesitating either to abrogate or to extend the treaty,
failed to act during the remainder of Arthur's administration. Apparently, the view of the diplomatists that the value of American privileges and interests in Hawaii was far greater than the value of the
revenue lost by one-sided reciprocity prevailed and was strong enough
to save the treaty; in the absence of definitely adverse action by the
Senate, it continued in force.

Meanwhile, the treaty's foes, who had been somewhat discredited
by the reports that the alleged frauds had not been committed,
redoubled their efforts and lodged other charges against it. Two of
the most potent were that the nation had gained little directly from
its provisions and that the increase in export trade with the Islands
was more than counterbalanced by a loss of revenue. Their oft-
reiterated contention that the agreement was economically injurious
to the United States was reinforced by the 1885 report of the Bureau
of Statistics which indicated that the United States had imported
from the Hawaiian Islands in the course of the year, the astounding
amount of 169,652,603 pounds of sugar, although American exports
to the Islands had actually declined in value. Thus encouraged, Congressmen Randall L. Gibson and J. Floyd King of Louisiana, Roger
Q. Mills of Texas, and William R. Morrison of Illinois introduced
into the House of Representatives during December, 1885, and the
following January, resolutions calling for the termination of the
treaty, which were referred to the Committee on Ways and Means.[60]

Friends and Foes

WHILE these resolutions were under consideration, a report was
presented to the Committee by John E. Searles, Jr., who, as secretary
of the American Sugar Company and a member of the influential
sugar refining group in the East, commanded respectable attention.
He maintained that the treaty should be abolished because of the

enormous loss in revenue, a revenue which was practically paid out of the pockets of taxpayers to fill the pockets of a small company of sugar planters and speculators. Production in the Islands had assumed proportions never dreamed of when the treaty was made and the crop was still steadily increasing. The duties remitted during the nine years from 1876 to 1885 amounted to $22,808,085, but the total value of domestic exports to Hawaii for the same period was only $22,872,371, "or, in other words, if we had made the islands a present of every dollar's worth of goods they have bought in this country and collected duty on their sugars, we should have made no loss." The amount of duty remitted in 1885 was $1,225,508 *more* than the *total value* of American exports, and according to the estimates of the crop, the amount would be increased in 1886 "so that we shall give them $2,000,000." Also, the treaty had not, "either directly or indirectly, benefited the consumers of sugar in this country, but had brought the products of the islands into direct competition with our sugar producers and manufacturers." The imports of Sandwich Island sugars in 1881 exceeded the total consumption of the Pacific states, and in that year Spreckels shipped six million pounds east. The amount was increased in 1882 to thirty-two million pounds and in 1885 to fifty-nine million pounds, or more than twenty-nine thousand tons. The treaty had not benefited, but had, on the contrary, "injured the Sandwich Islands, demoralizing and destroying the native population, and substituting Chinese and other Asiatics," while American influence in the affairs of the Islands, except as it was exercised for the selfish interests of an individual, had been weakened.

In a second appearance before the Committee in February, 1886, Searles again vigorously attacked the treaty in an effort to show that its abrogation would financially benefit the United States and would cause no diminution of her political influence in the Islands. He was of the opinion that the United States need have no fear of any of the other great powers replacing her in the treaty matter. England had free trade in sugar and could not protect her own sugar-raising colonies against the beet crop of Europe; France, also with sugar-growing colonies, was an exporter of sugar, and Germany was the greatest sugar producer in the world, depending on other countries for a market. The reciprocity agreement with Hawaii was only a commercial treaty and otherwise had no material advantages or guarantees for the United States; neither had it the element of permanence.[61]

John Dymond, representing the interests of Louisiana planters and of eastern sugar refineries, pointed out to the Committee that Hawaiian duty-free sugars had not only penetrated the markets of Kansas City, St. Louis, and Chicago, but were competing directly with Louisiana sugars in that state. This fact and the fear of the extension of the treaty had caused sugar prices to fall from one-half to three-fourths of a cent between January 1 and March 10, 1886. On August 15 the entire Louisiana delegation in Congress—two senators and six representatives—presented to the Committee a "solemn protest against any further continuance of the unjust operation of [the] treaty."[62]

Although neither the Committee on Ways and Means nor the House of Representatives had in itself the power to cancel the convention, the representatives could withhold their approval of enabling legislation necessary to keep the treaty in operation. Supporters of reciprocity naturally marshaled their forces to counter the campaign of the enemies of the treaty and to create a favorable climate of opinion in the Committee. Henry A. P. Carter, who had assisted in negotiating the Treaty of 1875 and, after the sudden death of Elisha H. Allen on New Year's Day, 1883, had become Hawaiian Minister in Washington, appeared before the Committee on March 1, 1886. Through an array of statistics on the carrying trade, banking, insurance, and so forth, he sought to refute Searles' testimony about the unbalanced operations of the treaty and the unfavorable balance between exports to and imports from Hawaii. In an interview with a correspondent of the *New York Daily Tribune* on the preceding day, Carter had provided similar figures and had explained that thirty-six million dollars of American capital was invested in ships, plantations, and so forth, as a result of the treaty. Four ship lines, all of American ownership, were running to the Islands. Although Hawaii sold to the United States sugar worth eight million dollars, and imported goods worth only four million dollars, the exchange was always against Hawaii. The difference, the Minister explained, was made up in payments on freights and interests on American investments in the Islands.[63] Carter insisted that the treaty was not responsible for creating and perpetuating Spreckels' monopoly, and despite the Treasury's loss of revenue, reciprocity had actually been a commercial boon to the Pacific coast. George S. Boutwell, still serving as counsel for the Hawaiian Government, stressed the political advantages of the agreement and again warned that its abrogation would handicap the United States in the competition for the Pacific trade and would result in England, France, and Germany seeking control of the Islands. To surrender the treaty "would be the most unwise public act which this government since its existence has committed."[64]

The energetic Hawaiian Minister did not limit the dissemination of his formidable statistics to the press and the House Committee on Ways and Means; he wasted no time in making a formal presentation of them to the new Secretary of State. With some refurbishing of and additions to his compilations, he submitted to Thomas F. Bayard a fourteen-page communication with an annexed statistical statement of four pages and a two-column, printed list of products shipped from the port of San Francisco in 1885. This communication proved conclusively that the effect of the treaty was to open to American enterprise and capital a virgin field of operation. The arrangement was "avowedly made for the purpose of perpetuating friendly relations and 'consolidating' commercial intercourse between the two countries." The results had justified the wisdom of the treaty. Hawaii was "the largest consumer per capita of American products of any community outside the limits of the United States." Hawaiian trade, in proportion to its size, employed the most American vessels, paid the largest profits to those engaged in it of any other foreign trade of the United States, and was of the nature of interstate commerce. The fact that practically all the exports of Hawaii came to the United States and that the carrying trade, banking, insurance, and all the collateral advantages were in American hands, rendered it not difficult, with the full statistics kept in both countries, to account for all the so-called "balances of trade."

His statement showed "a balance in favor of the United States of over thirty millions during the operation of the treaty, after paying liberal wages to the working class in Hawaii, and adding to her material and permanent prosperity." By investing "in trade essentially natural in its conditions . . . an amount of twenty-three millions in a great variety of articles comprising food products and tobacco, and manufactures of all kinds which would not otherwise have found a market, and eleven millions in coin and exchange on foreign countries," American citizens had drawn from Hawaii over fifty millions in articles of necessity and had "acquired vested interests, profitable and safe, in Hawaii, to the amount of over fifty millions more." The contribution of the United States had been mostly in surplus production, yet the opponents of the treaty had complained that two dollars of Hawaiian products had been received for one dollar of the United States. Carter did not convey that this balance was all profit. It had gone largely, with the exception of money invested in Hawaii and in the United States, into the payment of American merchants, factors, mariners, carriers, insurances, bankers, and other money lenders, in the ordinary course of trade. To the objection that the treaty benefited only one section of the country, the Minister pointed out that a good proportion of the imports into Hawaii from the United States were of articles manufactured in the eastern states. He thought it safe to say that Hawaiian trade did not damage any existing American industry. The sugar product of the Islands was less than seven per cent of the importations of the United States. Careful consideration would show the treaty to have been profitable to the United States to an amount far exceeding any loss of revenue, and future profits would be greater as the investments in Hawaii began to make returns.[65]

In an appended statement intended to reinforce the points in his argument, Carter presented various statistics, assembled in the following table:

NATIONALITY OF VESSELS EMPLOYED IN THE CARRYING TRADE OF HAWAII 1885–1886		RATIOS OF HAWAIIAN TRADE BY COUNTRIES 1885–1886	
	per cent		*per cent*
American Vessels	89.05	United States	92.04
British	5.68	Great Britain	3.76
German	2.11	Germany	1.25
Hawaiian	1.81	China and Hong Kong	1.04
Norwegian	1.25	Australia	0.67
All others	.10	All other countries	1.24

Within a month Bayard received quite a different representation of the benefits of the treaty from William N. Armstrong, son of the Rev. Richard Armstrong and Attorney General of the Hawaiian Kingdom from 1881 to 1882 as well as Minister of the Interior ad interim during the absence of H. A. P. Carter. Since it was not in the interest of those who favored and profited by the treaty to furnish correct data regarding the social and political conditions of the Hawaiian Kingdom, Armstrong called attention to the fact that the enormous

BALANCE SHEET OF HAWAIIAN TRADE

CONTRIBUTIONS OF THE UNITED STATES: VALUE OF EXPORTS TO HAWAII 1877–1885		CONTRIBUTIONS OF HAWAII: VALUE OF HAWAIIAN PRODUCTS IMPORTED INTO THE UNITED STATES	
1877	$1,272,949	1877	$2,550,335
1878	1,736,099	1878	2,678,830
1879	2,374,918	1879	3,257,938
1880	2,086,170	1880	4,606,444
1881	2,778,572	1881	5,533,000
1882	3,350,775	1882	7,646,294
1883	3,776,065	1883	8,238,461
1884	3,523,353	1884	7,925,965
1885	2,787,922	1885	8,857,497
TOTAL	$23,686,323	TOTAL	$51,294,764

Bills of Exchange to pay for exports of other nations to Hawaii 1877–1885.	9,181,522
Total of coin shipped to Hawaii including $1,000,000 as a loan to the Hawaiian Government.	2,145,438
TOTAL	$35,013,283

From Appended Statement in Carter to Bayard, March 22, 1886, Bayard Papers, LXXVI.
Cf. *Reports of Collector General of Customs 1885–1892*, Honolulu, 1892, p. 3.

"bounty" (about four million dollars per annum in remitted duties) flung upon the Islands "was indiscriminately divided up among Chinese, Portuguese, Japanese, Norwegians, Germans, Englishmen, and Americans." As labor was the principal item in the cost of producing sugar, the largest part of the bounty went into non-American hands. He felt it safe to say that the twenty thousand Chinese were taking four million dollars of the money expended in raising sugar cane, of which probably two million dollars was remitted to China. Portuguese, Germans, English, and Norwegians received a considerable portion of the residue, whereas the sum which went to Americans in the Islands, including laborers, mechanics, merchants, and bankers, hardly equalled one-half of the amount received for the sugar crop. Instead of the Reciprocity Treaty of 1875, "there should have been enacted simply a federal law, by which all Hawaiian sugars, rice, and other articles, *the actual products of American labor, machinery, and capital*, should have been admitted into this country, free of duty, under such regulations, as the Executive might establish." Such legislation would have prevented the sudden and enormous expansion of sugar production which had "demoralized the white inhabitants of the Islands, and filled the Kingdom with a population, which makes it, in its social aspects, one of the foulest spots on the face of the earth."

Under such enactment the American planters would have been forced to divide their large tracts of land in order to induce immigration from the mainland. The profit on sugar production would have afforded rich and rare inducements to American laborers and their families to take up homesteads on the Islands. The growth of the sugar industry would have been healthy, safe, and gradual, and thus would have prevented the bitter hostility of the eastern sugar refiners towards the increased sugar production of the Islands. Armstrong was of the opinion that by 1886, the time in which he was writing, the best portions of the Hawaiian Kingdom would have been in the hands of a thrifty farming class of Americans whose number, including women and children, would have reached at least twenty thousand. The entire trade of the Kingdom would have been controlled by Americans, and the large sums of money, paid to England for sugar machinery, would have gone to the United States. The English and Germans would have put their capital wholly into American hands. The political result would have been "that the five or six thousand American farmers, mechanics, merchants, finding out the utter worthlessness of native Hawaiian rule, which had really no interest in the country, and also finding it intolerable, because of its absurdity, would have without the sacrifice of a life, or the loss of a dollar, reconstructed the nation, and, to-day, there would have existed on the Islands, a flourishing small American Republic."

Armstrong had often expressed these views in Hawaii, where it was admitted that these consequences would follow, but the results of the Reciprocity Treaty were so profitable that no American resident of the Islands desired that any modification of it should be made for fear of jeopardizing his interests. "The Americans in Hawaii," he wrote, "sought the treaty for no political purpose, but simply to save themselves from bankruptcy. If a political end may be gained, without disturbing their profits, they are in sympathy with it, but they are not willing to make any sacrifice for that purpose."[66]

There is further evidence that the sugar planters in the Islands were determined to go to extreme lengths—even to bargaining with their dangerous political opponents—to preserve the benefits of reciprocity. The conservative cabinet of William L. Green, an English businessman of long residence in the Islands and senior member of the firm, Janion, Green & Company, without a vote of lack of confidence, resigned on May 19, 1882, and declined reappointment. The resignation of this Ministry cannot be attributed solely to its unwillingness to alienate the crown lands of Wailuku to Claus Spreckels. This was only one and the most apparent reason. Its members were resolutely opposed to the dangerous schemes of increased expenditures to be met by large foreign loans and for some time had not enjoyed the support of the predominantly native Legislature and the confidence of the King, who depended more for advice upon Walter M. Gibson, leader of the native faction, than he did upon his constitutionally-appointed cabinet. Moreover, a letter written by Green to H. A. P. Carter eleven days before the former's retirement, but which indicated his intention to do so,[67] and one to the *Pacific Commercial Advertiser* six days after his resignation, refer to dissatisfaction with the Ministry from still another and very powerful source. The Planters' Association, an influential organization in the Islands, apparently anxious over the renewal of the Reciprocity Treaty then under severe attack in the United States, questioned whether the conservative Englishman's Ministry would be willing to make the necessary concession—to cede or lease Pearl Harbor—and cast about for a more tractable but still moderate body. An agent of the association approached Gibson and urged him to take a position in a new cabinet under certain conditions if it were offered to him. The latter declined to be made a tool, but was shrewd enough to recognize that the "game was in his own hands." When offered the premiership after the resignation of W. L. Green, the indisputable leader of the native Hawaiians "selected his colleagues to suit the king and himself without consulting his would-be supporters," "who retired crest-fallen and cried out that the country was in danger." Then the "red hot Reciprocity party . . . would have been glad to see even the old Ministry patched up, but it was too late, for a new set of performers had come upon the stage."[68]

On the question of "the large sums of money, paid to England for sugar machinery" about which several critics of the treaty complained in the 1880's and 1890's, Minister Comly reported to Secretary of State Evarts, in mid-1879, that there were eight complete sugar plants (a "plant" is all the machinery necessary for a sugar plantation) on their way to Hawaii from an energetic British manufacturer represented in Honolulu by G. W. Macfarlane and Company. This agency had "taken orders amounting to about $500,000 from these Islands, every dollar of which ought to have passed into the pockets of American manufacturers."[69] The Minister revealed that there were seven full plants and two nearly-full plants, besides other machinery, ordered from Great Britain in 1880. The four or five purchasers paid from forty-two thousand dollars to eighty thousand dollars for the plants. The bulk of the trade in sugar machinery was absorbed by British manufacturers. All of the sugar plants received in 1879 and early 1880 were from a Scotch manufacturer. Hawaiians purchased from the mainland chiefly steam plows, sewing machines, and other patented articles which could not be bought other than in the United States. During that period very little sugar machinery of any kind was shipped from the United States. This, however, was not the fault of the Reciprocity Treaty, but of American manufacturers, who neglected to work up a trade in the sugar machinery area until the best of it was already gone. The manufacturers of the Pacific coast enjoyed a lucrative business in mining machinery, and eastern manufacturers appeared to have ignored the Hawaiian field altogether.

The campaign against the Frelinghuysen-Carter Treaty was by no means confined to Congress. In the East the Philadelphia Maritime Exchange and in the Midwest the wholesale grocers of Chicago, groups which considered their interests adversely affected by the sugar clauses of the Hawaiian Treaty, petitioned the Senate for the abrogation of the agreement.[70] The *Sugar Beet*, a quarterly journal published in Philadelphia, but responsive to the interests of the sugar beet growers of California and the sugar planters of the Gulf states, protested against "the contemptible Sandwich Islands treaty." Henry A. Brown, who had remained comparatively quiet after his allegations of fraud were disproved by Secretary Folger's special investigation commission, resumed his attack upon the treaty in an open letter addressed to the Senate and the House in May, 1886. He brought out in the same year another pamphlet entitled *Hawaiian Treaty Chicanery Clearly Presented*, in which all his previous charges against the "treaty monstrosity" were restated and reinforced with a convincing array of statistics.

Treaty Retained

AFTER hearing evidence on both sides and conducting a thorough investigation, the House Committee on Ways and Means, ignoring the political benefits of the convention and viewing it strictly as a financial liability, reported through Roger Q. Mills, on April 20, 1886, that for the nine years from 1877 to 1885, inclusive, United States trade with the Islands amounted to $74,100,000, of which $51,300,-000 represented the value of imports from them and $22,800,000 the value of exports to them. Thus the imports were sixty-nine per cent and the exports thirty-one per cent of the whole trade. The claim made in 1876, when the treaty was pending before Congress, that it would greatly stimulate exports of lumber, food products, and manufactured goods, had not been fully realized. The United States Treasury had given the Hawaiian planters a bounty which had greatly stimulated the growth of population and wealth on the Islands, but the remission of duties had amounted to more than twenty-three million dollars, whereas the total exports to the Islands had amounted to little over twenty-two million dollars. This large bounty had gone into the pockets of the owners of estates on the Islands, and people in the United States had been compelled to pay higher prices for their free sugar on the Pacific slope than their kinsmen had paid for their dutiable sugar on the Atlantic seaboard. This majority recommended a resolution to terminate the treaty, but the adoption of such a resolution would not prevent the administration "from negotiating for such modification of the existing treaty as will more nearly equalize the benefits to be derived by the two governments from their commercial relations."[71]

William C. P. Breckinridge and Thomas W. Browne were not prepared to say that the treaty was commercially a good bargain, and they would have been glad to have seen it modified, yet there were "geographical and international reasons" which were "conclusive with them that the treaty ought not to be abrogated." They were unwilling to surrender any advantage that might be "given by that treaty to this Government to the possible future control of those islands."[72] On July 22, 1886, after a delay of more than three months, during which the House itself refrained from entering into the controversy, the report of the Committee was finally shelved by the overwhelming majority of 157 to 79.[73]

NOTES

1. *Report of James Scott, United States Consul at Honolulu, Hawaiian Islands, Relating to the Effects of the Reciprocity Treaty between Hawaii and the United States . . . August 9, 1878,* encl. in Comly to Evarts, No. 68, April 12, 1879, USDS, Dispatches, Hawaii, XVIII; cf. *Pacific Commercial Advertiser,* April 5, 1879. A copy is also in the Allen Papers. Scott arrived in San Francisco, October 8, 1878. Since he had never favored the Reciprocity Treaty, many people feared he was on his way to Washington to have it abrogated. Henry W. Severance, consul for Hawaii in San Francisco, dispatched a hasty note to Allen to keep an eye on Scott to find out if he was working against Hawaii (Severance to Allen, Oct. 9, 1878, Allen Papers).

2. *House Ex. Docs.,* 45th Cong., 3rd sess., No. 2, *Report of Secretary of the Treasury,* 1878, p. xxviii; United States Tariff Commission, *Reciprocity and Commercial Treaties,* pp. 107–108. It was believed that Sherman was hostile to Hawaii's interests (Severance to Allen, Oct. 28, 1879, Allen Papers). Cf. F. W. Taussig, *Free Trade, the Tariff, and Reciprocity* (New York, 1920), pp. 122–23.

3. *San Francisco Chronicle,* Nov. 27, 1878; cf. Letter to the editor, "Hawaiian Reciprocity," *ibid.,* Nov. 21, 1878.

4. *Evening Post* (San Francisco), Nov. 27, 1878.

5. *Washington Post,* Dec. 17, 1878.

6. Henry A. Brown, *Sugar Frauds and the Tariff* and *Revised Analyses of the Sugar Question* (Saxonville, Mass., 1878 and 1879).

7. Comly to Kapena, May 15, 1879, encl. No. 1 in Comly to Evarts, No. 75, June 9, 1879, USDS, Dispatches, Hawaii, XVIII.

8. Kapena to Comly, May 21, 1879, encl. 3, *ibid.*

9. Hastings to Comly, May 30, 1879, encl. 8, *ibid.* These communications are printed in *For. Rels.* (1879), pp. 533, 535, 540–41; Cf. *ibid.,* pp. 525–46.

10. Comly to Evarts, No. 120, July 30, 1878, USDS, Dispatches, Hawaii, XIX. For a similar contention see the New Orleans *Daily Picayune,* Nov. 4, 1881.

11. *Session Laws, 1880,* Ch. XXXIX, pp. 52–53, approved Aug. 14, 1880; cf. Comly to Evarts, No. 124, Sept. 20, 1880, Dispatches, Hawaii, XIX, copy encl.

12. Brown to Sherman, Jan. 21, 1881, John Sherman Papers, CCXLI, MSS, Library of Congress. This was not Brown's first disclosure of alleged frauds against the United States Treasury. Three years earlier he had sent Sherman a paper setting forth "illicit traffic, fraudulent and irregular practices, and abuses of the educational privileges of the free acts of 1872 and 1874, in the importation of books, apparatus, instruments" (Brown to Sherman, Nov. 12, 1877). For several years Brown had investigated every topic of the sugar tariff and had presented the matter to Congress in many ways, as a matter vital to the interests of consumers and sugar refiners in this country.

13. Quoted by the *American Grocer* (New York), Nov. 10, 1881, XXVI, 1043. This organ of the New York refiners is sometimes referred as to the New York *Grocer.* Cf. "Dead Sea Apple," *San Francisco Chronicle,* Oct. 23, 1881.

14. *San Francisco Chronicle,* Oct. 25, 27, Nov. 1, 29, 1881; cf. "Backers of Monopoly," *ibid.,* Dec. 1, 1881; editorial, "How it May Work," *ibid.,* Oct. 28, 1881.

15. Editorial, "Congress and the Sugar Monopoly," *ibid.*, Jan. 12, 1882.
16. *Ibid.*, Feb. 14, 15, 1882; cf. "Sugar Coated Fraud," *ibid.*, Feb. 17, 1882.
17. *Ibid.*, Dec. 1, 4, 1881, March 21, 1882; cf. *ibid.*, Nov. 1, 1881. The pledge was an Anglo-French declaration of November 28, 1843, to consider the Sandwich Islands as an independent state.
18. *Times-Democrat* (New Orleans), Jan. 9, 1882.
19. *New York Times*, Jan. 6, 1883; cf. April 12, Nov. 7, 1882.
20. *American Grocer*, Nov. 10, 1881, XXVI, 1043; cf. *ibid.*, Nov. 28, 1878, XX, 1455.
21. *Times* (New Orleans), Nov. 11, 1881. This journal was known as the New Orleans *Times* up to December 3, 1881, and as the *Times-Democrat* thereafter until April 5, 1914, when the *Daily Picayune* was merged with it.
22. Henry A. Brown, *Concise Resume of Sugar Tariff Topics, in Defense of American Sugar Industries* (Washington, 1882), pp. 23–24.
23. *Honolulu Bulletin*, March 18, 1882; Donald M. Dozer, "The Opposition to Hawaiian Reciprocity, 1876–1888," *Pacific Historical Review*, XIV (1945), 165.
24. Quoted by the *American Grocer* (New York), Nov. 10, 1881, XXVI, 1043. Cf. *San Francisco Chronicle*, Feb. 22, 1882. *The Merchant*, favorable to the treaty, carried valuable statistics and editorials on reciprocity. Henry Severance and Allen arranged to have some of its articles printed in eastern papers "to off set the malicious falsehoods of the New York *Grocer*" (Severance to Allen, Oct. 13, 1879, Allen Papers). *The Merchant* later became the *Pacific Wine, Brewing and Spirit Review*.
25. Henry W. Severance to Allen, Jan. 17, 1882, Allen Papers; Allen to Green, March 4, 1882, AH, FO & Ex., folder labeled "Minister and Special Commissioner to Washington, Jan.–March, 1882."
26. Allegations of slavery in the Hawaiian Islands, published in American papers, were copied in Berlin and Lisbon periodicals and called forth a letter from Theo. H. Davies to *The Times* (London), Jan. 25, 1882, reprinted in the *Hawaiian Gazette*, March 1, 1882.
27. *Remarks of Mr. Elisha H. Allen, Hawaiian Minister, and Mr. Geo. S. Boutwell, Counsel, Before the Committee on Foreign Affairs, House of Representatives, February 19 and March 6, 1882* (Washington, 1882). This pamphlet is in the Allen Papers. Cf. *Times-Democrat* (New Orleans), Feb. 21 and March 9, 1882 (editorials). The latter described Allen and Boutwell as representatives of the "Spreckels sugar ring." Cf. *San Francisco Chronicle*, March 10, 18, 1882. One feature of the hearing of March 6 was the introduction of a petition thirty-five feet long, signed by businessmen and firms of New York representing $110,000,000 of capital, and praying for the termination of the treaty as dangerous to the commercial interest of the country (Honolulu *Bulletin*, March 23, 1882).
28. "A Quick Witness," *San Francisco Chronicle*, Feb. 22, March 8, 10, 1882.
29. *Times-Democrat* (New Orleans), Feb. 21, 1882.
30. *Ibid.*, Feb. 28, 1882.
31. *Saturday Press* (Honolulu), March 4, 1882. This paper was owned and practically edited by Thomas G. Thrum. Cf. *Hawaiian Gazette*, March 22, 1888. Mott Smith, while in St. Louis in December, 1882, had interviewed the president of Belcher and Co. Sugar Refinery, who had purchased some 6,000 tons of Hawaiian sugar the preceding year (Mott Smith to Gibson, Dec. 8, 1882, AH, FO & Ex., folder labeled "Minister to Washington and Special Commissioner, Sept.–Dec., 1882").
32. R. P. Spalding, *A Bird's Eye View of the Hawaiian Islands with Some*

Reflections upon the Reciprocity Treaty (Cleveland, 1882), pp. 10, 13, 14.
Thomas W. Bartley, editor of the *American Register*, reprinted excerpts
from the Dec. 30, 1882, and Jan. 6, 1883, issues of that periodical in the
form of a pamphlet, *The Hawaiian Reciprocity Treaty; Its Policy and Merits*
(Washington, 1882).

33. H. H. Wells to the President, May, 1882, USDS, Misc. Letters, May 1882,
    Pt. 1.
34. Belknap to Secretary of the Navy, Nov. 20, 1882, *ibid.*, Dec., 1882, Pt. 1.
35. Dutton to Secretary of State, Feb. 6, 1883, *ibid.*, Feb., 1883, Pt. 1.
36. Dozer, "The Opposition to Hawaiian Reciprocity, 1876–1888," p. 167.
37. Henry A. Brown, *Hawaiian Sugar Bounties and Treaty Abuses* (Washing-
    ton, 1883), pp. 4–8, 22, 24–26.
38. *Misc. Docs.*, House of Rep., 47th Cong., 2nd sess., No. 6, Part 1, *Report
    of the Tariff Commission, Appointed Under Act of Congress Approved May
    15, 1882*, pp. 667–68, 675–78, 691, 695–97. For Kenner's opinion that the
    treaty was of no benefit to consumers and fostered a monopoly in California,
    see p. 691. Hereafter cited as *Report of the Tariff Commission*.
39. Quoted in *Hawaiian Gazette*, July 18, 1877.
40. Kelly to Allen, July 6, 1877, Allen Papers.
41. *Sen. Reps.*, 53rd Cong., 2nd sess., No. 227, App. X, "The Hawaiian Treaty.
    A Review of its Commercial Results." p. 470. In regard to Spreckels' rule
    with a "rod of iron," Severance informed Allen that a prominent whole-
    sale grocery in San Francisco who purchased New York sugar was refused
    a rebate on Spreckels' sugar. When increased purchases of eastern sugar
    were made the party was told they could buy no more sugar from the
    refineries in the area. A close watch was maintained for offenders, outside
    drays going to the offending houses were followed, the drivers interrogated,
    and the goods noted (Severance to Allen, Dec. 31, 1878, Allen Papers).
42. *Sen. Reps.*, 53rd Cong., 2nd sess., No. 227, App. X, pp. 471–72, 475; cf.
    Comly to Evarts, No. 19, Dec. 28, 1877, USDS, Dispatches, Hawaii, XVII;
    Taussig, *Free Trade, the Tariff, and Reciprocity*, p. 123. Carter insisted
    that the price of raw sugar imported into San Francisco was regulated by
    the market at Manila on the one hand, and at Cuba and Puerto Rico on
    the other. The San Francisco purchaser would not pay more for Hawaiian
    sugars than for Manila sugar, nor would the Hawaiian producer sell for
    less than he could get in New York, less of course the difference in freight
    and charges—about ¾ of a cent a pound.
43. For the technical details of polarization, the difference between 94°, which
    contained more pure sugar than 91° sugar, and the lower cost of refining
    the former, which was fully covered by a one-twentieth cent allowance for
    every color above number 10 Dutch standard, see *Sen. Reps.*, 53rd Cong.,
    2nd sess., No. 227, App. X, p. 472. C. Adolf Low and Company, which
    was pooled with Spreckels up to 1885, also seemed to think that Spreckels
    overpaid the Hawaiian planters, for, while having the option of taking as
    much Hawaiian sugar as it wanted, that company declined buying any
    on the ground that Manila and Central American sugars were cheaper.
44. *New York Times*, Nov. 7, 1882; Brown, *Hawaiian Sugar Bounties and
    Treaty Abuses*, pp. 26–27.
45. *New York Times*, Jan. 17, 1883. In a reply to an inquiry from the Secre-
    tary of State whether any other sugars than those known in 1875 as Sand-
    wich Islands sugars had been imported from the Hawaiian Islands under
    the treaty, Sherman stated that "so far as the facts are known to this

Department, it is not believed that any sugars other than those belonging"
to that class "had been admitted free under the treaty"; nor did it appear
that the value of the sugars imported since the treaty differed materially
from those previously imported, "except in so far as the grade of the
sugars had been improved by machinery used in their manufacture" (Sec.
of Treasury to the Sec. of State, Jan. 22, 1893, USDS, Misc. Letters, Jan.,
1883, Pt. 2).

46. On this point see John E. Searles, Jr., *A Few Facts Concerning the Reciprocity Treaty* (pamphlet, Washington, D.C., 1886), pp. 6–7. No. 13
Dutch standard is the clearly established line between raw or unrefined
and refined sugar.

47. *House Reps.*, 47th Cong., 2nd sess., No. 1860, Pt. 1, p. 2; Pt. 2, pp. 2, 4–5.
This report of January 29, 1883, recommended the adoption of a joint
resolution to the effect that further action respecting notice to terminate
should be postponed until a message from the President should be received
by Congress to reply to the resolution proposed by the majority of the
committee. Cf. *ibid.*, pp. 9–10; *New York Times*, Jan. 17, 1883.

48. *Cong. Record*, 47th Cong., 2nd sess., pp. 921–22, 1003, 1005.

49. *Sen. Reps.*, 47th Cong., 2nd sess., No. 1013, pp. 5–8.

50. *Sen. Reps.*, 48th Cong., 1st sess., No. 76, pp. 2, 7–8; *Sen. Docs.*, 56th
Cong., 2nd sess., No. 231, Pt. 8, pp. 228–29, 240.

51. *Ibid.*, p. 240; *Sen. Reps.*, 48th Cong., 1st sess., No. 76, Pt. 2.

52. Daggett to Frelinghuysen, Nos. 56, 73, March 5, May 18, 1883, USDS,
Dispatches, Hawaii, XXI; *Pacific Commercial Advertiser*, May 19, 1883.

53. Report of the Commission Appointed by the Secretary of the Treasury to
Investigate Alleged Frauds Under the Hawaiian Reciprocity Treaty, in
*Statements to the Com. on Ways and Means on the Morrison Tariff Bill,
and on the Hewitt Administration Bill, the Hawaiian Treaty, etc.*, pp. 20–
21; Reminiscences of Oliver Lyman Spaulding, Notes for the Information of
his Children, p. 59, Spaulding Collection; *Cong. Record*, 48th Cong., 1st
sess., pp. 127, 166.

54. Frelinghuysen to John F. Miller, June 17, 1884, *Sen. Docs.*, 56th Cong.,
2nd sess., No. 231, Pt. 8, p. 253.

55. *Ibid.*, p. 242; *Sen. Ex. Journal*, XXIV, 289. The advice concerning a naval
station was by no means novel, for as early as 1863 Minister James McBride
had suggested a naval depot in the port of Honolulu and ten years later
Henry A. Peirce recommended securing Pearl Bay. See above, pp. 46,
87–88. The *Boston Daily Globe*, July 10, 1873, referred favorably to
the proposition. Three years thereafter, on Oct. 5, 1876, the New York
Evening Post raised the question whether we should "have a commodious
and secure naval station in their [Hawaiian Islands'] sheltered waters and
escape the results which would threaten us if giving in to the hands of
Great Britain." On July 13, 1881, the *New York Times* suggested that the
United States acquire a naval station in Hawaiian waters.

56. *Sen. Ex. Journal*, XXIV, pp. 280, 376, 383.

57. *Cong. Record*, 48th Cong., 2nd sess., p. 506; cf. *ibid.*, p. 513.

58. Morrison to Bayard, March 16, 1886, Bayard Papers, LXXXVI. Similar
opinions were expressed in the *San Francisco Chronicle*, May 5, 1886.

59. "National Capital Topics The Hawaiian Treaty What it Has Done for the
United States Views of Mr. Carter," *New York Daily Tribune*, Jan. 5, 1885.

60. *Cong. Record.*, 49th Cong., 1st sess., pp. 137, 486, 581, 895.

61. John E. Searles, Jr., "A Few Points on the Hawaiian Treaty," in *State-*

ments to Com. on Ways and Means on the . . . Hawaiian Treaty, pp. 17–18, 81–82. The *New York Times*, December 11, 1884, produced similar statistics for the six years 1876–1882, indicating that for that period the duties relinquished upon sugar and rice alone were estimated to have been $13,717,436. On the other hand, the entire value of our merchandise exported to the Islands in the same period was only $13,033,314.

62. *Statements to Com. on Ways and Means on the . . . Hawaiian Treaty*, p. 239; *ibid.*, pp. 82–83.

63. *New York Daily Tribune*, March 1, 1886; cf. "The Hawaiian Treaty," *ibid.*, Jan. 5, 1885.

64. *Statements to the Com. on Ways and Means on the . . . Hawaiian Treaty*, pp. 60–74.

65. Carter to Bayard, March 22, 1886, Bayard Papers, LXXXVI.

66. W. N. Armstrong to Bayard, April 21, 1886, *ibid.*, LXXXVII. This private letter was mailed from Hampton Normal School, Virginia, where Nevin's brother, General Samuel C. Armstrong, was principal. Cf. Blaine to Comly, No. 114, conf., Dec. 1, 1881, USDS, Instructions, Hawaii, II, for the possibility of homesteads in Hawaii for Americans.

67. Green to Carter, May 8, 1882, AH, FO & Ex., folder labeled "H. A. P. Carter."

68. *Pacific Commercial Advertiser*, May 27, 1882. For a description of these performers, see my *The United States and the Hawaiian Kingdom*, pp. 61–63, 320, 324–26, 329, 334.

69. Comly to Evarts, No. 76, June 9, 1879, USDS, Dispatches, Hawaii, XVIII, printed in *For. Rels.* (1879), pp. 542–53.

70. *House Reps.*, 49th Cong., 1st sess., No. 1759, pp. 1–2.

71. *Cong. Record*, 49th Cong., 1st sess., pp. 3657, 4447.

72. *House Reps.*, 49th Cong., 1st sess., No. 1759, p. 3; *Cong. Record*, 49th Cong., 1st sess., p. 3638.

73. *Ibid.*, p. 7339.

7

"CESSION" OF PEARL HARBOR

Pearl Harbor Amendment

SOMETIME during the last months of Arthur's administration, before the supplementary convention was submitted to the Senate in December, 1884, Senators Miller and Morgan, former Senator Gwin, and others remarked to Carter that they had heard something of Pearl Harbor, "and asked if any use was made of it, whether it was private property, etc.?" The Minister claimed that he "thought but little" of the incident "as the parties did not speak as if attaching much importance to it."[1]

President Grover Cleveland assumed his duties in March, 1885, with Thomas F. Bayard as the new Secretary of State, but the official United States policy toward Hawaii remained unchanged. Although the Chief Executive did not look with favor upon reciprocity in general and withdrew the Spanish and other treaties, the Frelinghuysen-Carter Convention was left with the Senate for action. The successive administrations of Ulysses S. Grant, Rutherford B. Hayes, James A. Garfield, and Chester A. Arthur recognized this Reciprocity Treaty as an important instrument of American policy in the Pacific, and the political factor—not the economic—still remained the more important one in the equation of Hawaiian-American relations.

When, during the new session of Congress, Carter heard that a resolution asking the President to take steps to secure Pearl Harbor was under preparation, he at once told several friends that the Hawaiian King and Government would not entertain or consent to the proposition, that the United States did not need the harbor, and that Congress would certainly refuse to entertain the project. Reportedly, Senator George Edmunds of Vermont, after a visit to San Francisco, was inspired with the idea of acquiring Pearl Bay and insisted upon raising the question. He thought there was a strong feeling in California in favor of the cession of that harbor to the United States, but, being almost alone in favor of it, his idea was not sustained in the Committee on Foreign Relations. But, after the completion of the Canadian Pacific Railroad to Vancouver in early 1886, which made Canada a formidable competitor for the Pacific trade practically monopolized by the United States, and the reported subsidy of a line of British transpacific steamships, coincident with German aggression in the South Pacific, the necessity of owning Pearl Harbor was ardently emphasized by Edmunds.[2] In executive session on April 14, 1886, Senator Morgan, whose Committee on Foreign Relations had two years earlier justified the treaty upon "higher considerations," presented another favorable report, but on this occasion proposed a significant insertion after Article 1 to the effect that the King of the Hawaiian Islands would grant "to the Government of the United States the exclusive right to enter the Harbor of Pearl River, in the island of Oahu, and to establish and maintain there a coaling and repair station for the use of vessels of the United States, and to that end the United States may improve the entrance to said harbor and do all other things needful to the purpose aforesaid."

The report called attention to the vexatious complications with European and Asian powers which might arise if the question of the control of the Hawaiian Islands should be reopened. The proposed concession would provide a safe refuge for the United States in case of a foreign war and at the same time would afford political security to the Islands. The commodious harbor required only a slight deepening at its entrance to admit the largest ships. It could be easily defended, and as there were forty miles of shore, including the indentations, all vessels would be out of reach of bombardment. In the unanimous opinion of the Committee, this concession would be of great political advantage to the United States.[3]

Since the Pearl Harbor proposal was made in secret session, Carter did not know its exact terms, but he made it a point to tell several of Hawaii's friends that he hoped no amendment regarding a cession of any harbor or territory would pass, for it would not be consented to by the King, and it would be better to let the new treaty be defeated than to approve it with such an amendment. He was informed, however, that one senator had been assured that the amended convention would be accepted. Carter called on Bayard, with whom "no word had ever passed" regarding the cession of Pearl

River, to say that he had heard that such a proposal was being discussed. The Secretary indicated that no intimation had reached him of such a proposition and that he was opposed to it, but he recommended waiting till the Senate communicated with him. To Gibson, the Minister reported his conviction that there was no need for anxiety about the matter, that if such a proposition were made it would be returned by Bayard to the Senate with the information that the President did not approve it.[4] When on May 6 the press reported the text of the new treaty with the amendment, Carter thought that the Secretary had yielded to Senator Edmunds' representations.

This was not the case, for Bayard had not been apprised of the action of the Committee and was unacquainted with the nature of the amended treaty until the afternoon of May 6, when he was waited on by an agent of a New York paper who showed him an extract from the *New York Daily Tribune* of that date which carried a copy of the text of the amended treaty and in an accompanying statement reported that "the Senate and the Administration both favor it, but the free traders in the House, under Mr. Morrison's lead, apparently care little or nothing for the political advantage of a safe harbor for American vessels at the Sandwich Islands in case of war."[5]

Actually the correspondent of the *Tribune*, edited by Whitelaw Reid and historically an organ of the Republican Party, was in closer touch with the members of the Committee on Foreign Relations than was the Secretary of State. This, however, was not due to lack of interest on his part, for as early as January 16, 1886, he had written Senator John Franklin Miller with reference to the Hawaiian situation and had expressed the desire to meet with the Committee, observing, "The growing importance of our Pacific Ocean commerce and the group of Islands which seems just now to be in great demand with some of our Commercial rivals, makes it more than ever of consequence that a steady and well considered line of policy should be entered upon."[6]

Regardless of the opinion of Bayard, who at first objected to the Pearl Harbor article, the proponents of the Hawaiian Treaty welcomed the amendment as a means of acquiring a political counterweight to the economic disadvantages of reciprocity. Senator Edmunds, who during the incapacity of Senator Morgan served as chairman of the Committee on Foreign Relations, predicted that Pearl River Harbor would be worth fifty million dollars to the United

States.[7] Newspaper reports concerning rumors of German interest in Hawaii and of an agent sent on a mission to Hawaii, coupled with the expansive activities of that country elsewhere in the Pacific, reinforced political arguments. The editor of the Washington *Evening Star* opined: "Germany is not especially friendly to us, and is on the lookout all the while for opportunities to 'cut into' American trade. The Germans, for instance, stand ready to seize our Hawaiian advantages the moment we relinquish them."[8] In spite of these warnings, the Senators still refused to be hurried into a decision of the renewal of the treaty.

Much more sensational news was required to activate the Senate. This came in the autumn of 1886 when it was learned that negotiations had been opened through the Colonial Office in London with the Dominion of Canada, having in view a reciprocity treaty with Hawaii similar to that which the United States Government was hesitating to renew. *The Times* stated that the affair concerned England as much as Canada "since the development of the Pacific trade of Canada and the opening of communications with the East along the Canadian Pacific route are matters of direct imperial interest." Moreover, it might be possible to extend the advantages of such a treaty to the United Kingdom by means of a supplementary convention stipulating most-favored-nation treatment.[9] In addition, San Francisco papers reported that the Hawaiian Government was negotiating in England a loan of two million dollars which was to be used for establishing a cable with the Pacific coast of Canada and for which the public revenues of the Kingdom were to be pledged as security.[10]

Although Carter assured Bayard that "no negotiations or proposals" had been "initiated by the Hawaiian government looking forward to a reciprocal arrangement with Canada,"[11] the Secretary harbored misgivings about the London loan. He informed the Minister that the President had heard of the proposal "to pledge the public revenues of the Hawaiian kingdom as a collateral security for that loan; that it seemed to him that to give even to a set of private creditors the necessary right of inspecting the exercise of the taxing power of the country would virtually be creating a mortgage on that country, or, to use the language of the treaty between Hawaii and the United States, to create a lien in favor of third parties." Such a course, Bayard felt, "was directly invasive of the rights and liberties of the Kingdom of Hawaii" and indirectly impaired the preferred rights of the United States under the Treaty of 1875.[12] Carter was of the same opinion and promised to communicate with his Government on the matter.

In an avowed effort to preserve the autonomy of the Islands and the "paramount influence" of the United States there, President Cleveland, in his annual message of December 6, 1886, recommended that the existing treaty stipulations be extended for a further term of seven years. He expressed his unhesitating conviction that the intimacy of American relations with Hawaii should be emphasized. As a result of the Reciprocity Treaty of 1875, "those islands, on the highway of Oriental and Australasian traffic, are virtually an outpost of American commerce and a stepping-stone to the growing trade of the Pacific. The Polynesian island groups have been so absorbed by other and more powerful governments, that the Hawaiian Islands are left almost alone in the enjoyment of their autonomy, which it is important for us should be preserved." Propositions to abrogate the treaty would be "most ill-advised. The paramount influence we have there acquired, once relinquished, could only with difficulty be regained, and a valuable ground of vantage for ourselves might be converted into a stronghold for our commercial competitors."[13] This manifestation of executive interest in the Islands encouraged those senators who had long favored the renewal of the treaty to revive Morgan's amendment for the acquisition of a coaling and repair station at the Pearl River lagoon.[14]

Opposition to the Amendment

SECRETARY OF STATE Bayard favored the extension of the Reciprocity Treaty with Hawaii, but disapproved of the proposed amendment. He perceived "how the exclusive commercial privileges exchanged" in the agreement expanded "themselves into political results of a most important character." The treaty "effectively answered propositions from maritime powers in Europe to gain a foothold" in the Islands, and he held "that the United States could not witness without great discomposure the transfer of any portion of the Hawaiian group to a European political owner. The vast importance, and our close and manifest interest in the commerce of the Pacific Ocean" upon which we held the most important seaboard, rendered "the Hawaiian Group of essential importance to us on every score," and he trusted that the foes of the treaty would not "allow a commercial question to outweigh political considerations so important as . . . the control of these contiguous Islands on our Pacific coast."[15]

After the Hawaiian Government modified the arrangement for the London loan by withdrawing the pledge of the revenues of the Kingdom and substituting the pledge of the Minister of Finance, Bayard expressed his opposition to the absolute cession of Pearl Harbor to the United States as a naval and coaling station. He explained to Cleveland that under the "favored nation" clause in the treaties Hawaii had negotiated with Germany and Great Britain since 1875, "if any exclusive commercial port were now to be granted to us, the claim would be instantly made for equal treatment by the other powers." English and German influences were strong in Hawaii and naturally adverse to and in competition with the United States. Canada, disposed to subsidize a line of steamships between Victoria and the Sandwich Islands, would gladly open new ports duty-free to sugar. Since Midway Island, about one hundred miles to the northwest of Hawaii and under United States possession since 1867, had as good a harbor for coaling as Pearl Harbor, the Secretary believed that free use of the former would serve American purposes and would not involve the United States or Hawaii with the other treaty powers. Moreover, Pearl Harbor, only a short distance from the sea, "would not be tenable against assault unless elaborately fortified, so that its control in the event of war would necessarily pass to the stronger *naval* power!—(which certainly the U.S. is *not*, at present)." Considering these facts as well as the disinclination of the Hawaiian Government to make the concession, Bayard objected to engrafting the Pearl Harbor amendment upon a treaty "which as at present framed merely gives a longer life to the present favorable status."[16]

There was also strong opposition to the Pearl Harbor amendment —though for quite different reasons—from senators representing the sugar, sorghum, and rice-producing states of the South, and the sugar-refining states of the East, who, regardless of their party ties, denounced this studied arrangement to extend American influence and interests still further in the Islands. To this group Senator Morrill of Vermont, a Republican unalterably opposed to the lowering of American trade barriers, added his weight and influence.

Meanwhile, in Honolulu there prevailed misunderstanding, uncertainty, confusion, and a verbal and press battle over the origin of the Pearl Harbor scheme, attributed to Henry Carter by its enemies. Carter was identified with the Benedict Arnolds of Hawaiian politics, and reference was made to his public speeches of 1873, when he approved of the cession of Pearl Harbor and carried the point of cession to its logical conclusion—annexation of Hawaii. The *Pacific Commercial Advertiser*, now the mouthpiece of Gibson, in an article of May 6, 1886, entitled "Treaty Making at Washington," observed that Hawaii was placed in the peculiar position of having a treaty made for its acceptance without the formality of consulting its Government, either through the United States Minister Resident in Honolulu or the Hawaiian Minister in Washington. No one in the country having an official right to be informed on the subject had received any diplomatic communication concerning it. The article concluded:

> . . . let us say that the idea of ceding an inch of Hawaiian territory never occurred to the present administration. Their policy and actions have been in an opposite direction. The King and the entire native people are opposed to it. All foreigners of good standing in the community, with a few exceptions, are likewise opposed to annexation to any power, and these few who favor it, fortunately for themselves and the country, have ceased to exercise the measure of influence upon Hawaiian affairs which made them formidable several years ago. The country is now in a position to take care of itself. It owes much to the United States Government and people and is very far from being ungrateful; but it must maintain its independence unimpaired, and this could not be done were any foreign power to raise its flag, and establish its naval force at a convenient harbor within ten miles of the Hawaiian capital. Once for all, let us say that Pearl Harbor will remain national property and share the fortunes of the Hawaiian nation in the future as in the past.

Walter Murray Gibson, Minister of Foreign Affairs and the dominant person in the Government, when requested by the leader of the opposition to furnish the Legislature with intelligence on the subject, replied that he had received no information concerning the question asked. Mr. Carter had not reported that the United States Government desired to make a new treaty; "neither had he conveyed any intimation regarding a proposition for the cession of Pearl River Harbor." To a further question as to whether the Hawaiian Govern-

ment had asked the United States for a treaty containing stipulations
for the cession of Pearl Harbor, Gibson replied that the Hawaiian
Envoy had been instructed to sign a renewal of the Reciprocity Treaty
without any changes whatever from the existing one. That had been
done, and the treaty awaited the ratification of the United States
Senate. He concluded by asserting that the cession of Pearl Harbor,
or any territory, had never been contemplated and that "this Ministry
would not be sitting here now if they had made any proposal of
the kind."[17]

The Minister of Foreign Affairs spoke with similar certitude to
James H. Wodehouse, the British Consul General, who expressed his
satisfaction with the assurance and stated that in the opinion of his
Government the independence of the Hawaiian nation could not be
maintained unimpaired were any foreign power to establish its naval
force within ten miles of Honolulu.

The *Hawaiian Gazette*, the weekly opposition organ, advocated
the cession of Pearl Harbor and even designated a minister to succeed
Gibson, who might be relied upon to carry out the cession. In refer-
ring to the influence that Claus Spreckels wielded over the Hawaiian
Cabinet, that newspaper averred on March 23, 1886, that "our treaty
will be in danger so long as the present men are in power." After
Gibson read in the Honolulu papers extracts from an article in
the *San Francisco Chronicle* of May 5 entitled "The New Hawaiian
Treaty," which contained the full text of the measure before the
Senate, he informed the Legislature that it was a forgery, and laid
before the members Carter's dispatch of April 27 which referred to
information in a previous dispatch of March 18, 1885, but not to the
exact terms of the proposal. Instead Carter wrote: "Bayard authorizes
me to say that alleged amendments to the treaty in the Senate wholly
without knowledge or concurrence by him. Trust no notice will be
taken in Honolulu. Think treaty can be maintained intact with care
and prudence." The Minister announced that he had had the
Frelinghuysen-Carter Convention translated into Hawaiian. Thus the
Assembly would learn that the new treaty embodied nothing but a
continuance of the old treaty, without any modification whatever.[18]

Gibson, however, was unalterably opposed to the renewal of the
treaty with the Pearl Harbor amendment. Both he and King Kalakaua
were determined that if the cession of an inch of territory were to
be the condition of the continuance of reciprocity with the United
States, the treaty must be relinquished. The former considered it

injurious to the nation's cause that an impression be created abroad that Hawaii could not do without the treaty—that she was wholly dependent upon it for prosperity and continued progress. He maintained that her natural resources had been proved to be so favorable, her chief industries had been so thoroughly established, and the cost of production of sugar had been so much reduced, that at worst the abrogation of the treaty could only cause a temporary embarrassment in the Islands and enforce the opening of new channels of trade. Specifically, Gibson had in mind a reciprocity treaty with Canada after which it might be found possible to extend the advantages to the United Kingdom by means of a supplementary convention.[19]

Wodehouse was of the opinion that in case the treaty were terminated, Japan, and not Canada and Australia, would be the country with whom closer economic ties would be established, opening a new market for Hawaiian sugars, and observed "but this policy would doubtless be viewed with jealousy by the United States and the American element here."[20] This was true, for the annexationists were as convinced as they had been in 1873–74 that political affiliation would be the natural concomitant of economic preferential treatment.

Treaty Ratified

THE supplementary convention was read the second time in the Senate on January 10, 1887, and considered as in the Committee of the Whole. After Article 1, the Pearl Harbor amendment was inserted and, on the motion of Morrill, further consideration was postponed until the following day.[21] The vote on the amendment was finally taken on January 20, when twenty-one senators voting against it were outnumbered by twenty-eight of their colleagues, principally Republicans. On the same day the Senate advised and consented to ratification of the supplementary convention together with the amendment, by an even larger majority of forty-three to eleven.[22]

The Pearl Harbor amendment was carried only by the votes of several opponents of the treaty who on former occasion had voted against the concession. The publicity given to the Hawaiian opposition to cession led the foes—after they realized that they did not have the votes to block the treaty—to do the next best thing, to make the convention so disagreeable to Hawaii that it would be rejected there. The action of the Senate in ignoring the President and Secretary of State by passing the Pearl Harbor amendment as though senators had the constitutional right to originate negotiations—a policy they had pursued in the fishery question with England and the Nicaragua Canal Treaty—naturally annoyed President Cleveland. His friends said that this procedure was a trap for him to fall into and thus compromise the dignity of the presidential office. The Hawaiian Minister was of the opinion that the majority of the House and Senate did not want a naval station in the Pacific Ocean and would not approve a direct vote to furnish means for such a base. He believed that the object of Senator Edmunds, a shrewd party man, was to put the Chief Executive in the wrong and to show that he was not alive to American interests in the Pacific. Certainly, Cleveland's enemies did not hesitate to impugn the motives of the administration's "British policy." The excitement engendered by the fishery troubles and the London loan contributed to Edmunds' success in passing the amendment which, however, could not have occurred if the opponents of the treaty had not joined its proponents. In Carter's words, "the vote was carried in the Senate by the aid of those who thought that if Hawaii gave it to the U.S. she would not give it to any other power, and by those who wanted to make the treaty obnoxious to us, a change of four votes would have defeated it."[23]

Seeking to amend the treaty with the Pearl Harbor article was considered a Mephistophelean act by Carter, who informed Bayard that there was no chance of its being accepted by the Hawaiian Government. The Minister was of the opinion that the amendment "would not have been adopted had it been made public, and an opportunity had been given to the friends of the Sandwich Islands or the Administration to express an opinion on the subject." The Secretary of State considered the amendment "not germane to the objects of the treaty, but in substance and effect a new treaty altogether" and a virtual annexation of Hawaii by the United States Government. Carter drew attention to the exceedingly vague language of the amendment, remarking that as it stood, "at the end of seven years, or the termination of the treaty, the cession of Pearl Harbor would also drop with it, so that no permanent establishment would have been gained by the United States."[24] He hoped that the President would return the treaty to the Senate with a statement of his objections to the amendment and that it would pass as originally signed. Seven senators expressed to the Minister their intention to change their vote if the treaty were returned. Bayard, however, was of the opinion that this could not be done without establishing a dangerous precedent. Believing that the better way was to send a new treaty to the Senate, he asked Carter's opinion of a convention providing that the termination of the treaty should take place only after two or three years' notice instead of twelve months, stating that such a modification would give the planters security from the sudden withdrawal of the commercial privileges and would also meet some of the objections to an extension for seven years. The Secretary did not like leaving the interests involved "to the hazard of termination in some sudden spasm of feeling created by purely selfish interests," nor did he want the idea to go out that the administration had lost its interest in the question of renewal or rearrangement on a more permanent basis. He did want to see what ground the House of Representatives would take on the question of its rights to participate in such arrangements. Carter promised to consider the matter and consulted some of Hawaii's friends in the Senate, among whom were Morgan and Frye, who thought such a convention as suggested by Bayard would be accepted.[25]

The House did not delay. On January 22, acting upon the motion of Representative N. D. Wallace of Louisiana, it instructed its Committee on the Judiciary to inquire into the facts and report whether a treaty which involves the revenues "can be valid and binding without the concurrence of the House of Representatives and how far the power conferred on the House by the Constitution of the United States to originate measures to lay and collect duties can be controlled by the treaty making power under said constitution."[26] In a comprehensive report of twenty-three pages presented on March 3, the Committee maintained that the procedure adopted in negotiating the Treaty of Reciprocity was "a radical change in the equilibrium of the Constitution, which, unless reversed, will become dangerous to the rights of the people, by promoting the intervention of foreign nations in our domestic policy of taxation, through the agency of a minority of the tax-payers of the country." The report, presented by John R. Tucker of Virginia, recommended a resolution to the effect that the President, by and with the consent of the Senate, could not negotiate a treaty which would be binding on the United States, "whereby duties on imports are to be regulated, either by imposing or remitting, increasing or decreasing them, without the sanction of an act of Congress," and it requested the President to withhold final action on the proposed treaty and to condition its final ratification upon the consent of that body.[27]

Meanwhile, the staunch foes of reciprocity assailed the action of the Senate in extending the convention. Henry A. Brown was inspired to release on January 21, February 7 and 17, three open letters to senators and representatives. He insisted that it was "a crime against the people to continue a treaty which grants the United States no advantage whatever which Great Britain and Germany cannot share free of cost; which annually filches enormous tribute . . . for the enrichment of the projectors and supporters of Hawaiian reciprocity schemes." He estimated that in ten years the treaty had cost American consumers and tax payers $70,314,537 in sugar duties, a figure of loss which became $71,314,537 with the addition of an estimated million dollars in the remission of duties on rice and molasses.[28] Opposition journals, including the New Orleans *Picayune* and the *Sugar Beet*, joined in the denunciation.

While Bayard waited to ascertain the position of the House of Representatives, his attitude toward the ratification of the amended treaty gradually underwent a transformation. Simultaneous with the Carter conversations on Pearl Harbor were those with the representatives of Great Britain, Germany, and Hawaii on Walter Murray Gibson's disturbing program of primacy in the Pacific, including John Edward Bush's mission to King Malietoa Laupepa in an attempt to secure a confederation of Samoa with Hawaii. If only an exchange of courtesies with the King was secured, the Envoy was to proceed to Tonga and negotiate a treaty of commerce and amity. If, however, he met with success in Apia, he was to urge Tonga to join the confederation; then, if successful at the latter archipelago, he was to extend a similar invitation to the Cook Islanders. Since Gibson considered the Gilbertese incapable of self-government, he recommended the annexation of their group to Hawaii. Thus he contemplated a Hawaiian-dominated Polynesian confederation, plus an extension of Hawaiian territory.[29]

The inexpediency of a Hawaiian-Samoan alliance, Germany's heightened interest and activity in Polynesia which created menacing international complications in the Pacific, particularly in Samoa, the weakness of United States naval power, and the militancy of the United States Congress, all combined to convince the Secretary of State that it would be wise to avoid any further discussion of the

Reciprocity Treaty. He hoped that even in its amended form it would be ratified in Honolulu. By early March, 1887, Carter doubted if Bayard would make any further propositions to the Senate. The Minister was also anxious to evade further debate, for two of Hawaii's bitterest foes, who were formerly in the House, in the following session would be in the Senate to add to the force of the debate and vote.[30] But he would not recommend ratification to his Government without an interpretation of Article II.

During this period, when the ratification of the amended treaty was pending, the United States Minister in Hawaii, George W. Merrill, reported a conversation with an official connected with the Canadian Pacific Railroad returning to Canada from Australia whence he had journeyed in the interest of the enterprise. Merrill described the plans for a line of swift steamers which would shortly connect the western terminus of the railroad with Japan and China, as well as with Australia, whereas another would run between Halifax and Liverpool, "thus encircling the globe with a line of commerce, via Canada." Moreover, he referred to and quoted at length from an article in *The Times* of January 20, 1887, which reviewed the history of the Hawaiian Kingdom and contained the following:

> Distance and the disadvantage of not having a treaty, similar to the American, operate greatly to the detriment of British trade with the islands. There is, however, every reason to hope that the completion of the Panama canal, the Canadian Pacific Railway, and the proposed British cable, to the Colonies, which is to touch at Honolulu and for which the Hawaiian Government have already granted a handsome subsidy, may have the effect of improving the commercial relations between Hawaii and Great Britain and her Colonies.

In commenting on the possibility of terminating the Reciprocity Treaty in case Pearl Harbor were not ceded, the Minister observed "that other influences may be easily engaged in endeavoring to control and change the sentiment of this country by more favorable terms, and cause the initiative notice of intent to terminate, to be given by the Hawaiian Government."[31]

The Secretary of State was unable to give Carter any definite assurance as to the action Cleveland would take in case the treaty were accepted by Hawaii. Unquestionably, as it stood, it was not the measure which had been approved by the executive branch of the Government and submitted to the Senate, but having come back with the approval of that body as amended, it was in the power of the President, in case it was approved by the Government of Hawaii, to proclaim it and exchange ratifications. Carter mentioned that Canada "was holding out to Hawaii all sorts of promises and offers to give the same advantages" for a treaty of free trade. Bayard reminded him that it was not within the power of Canada to give what the United States could. A fortnight later, when Carter referred to the debates in the British Parliament which seemed to reveal a desire on the part of Great Britain to "control the commerce of the Northern Pacific Ocean," the Secretary replied that "when it became necessary for Americans to protect their rights on that ocean," means would be found to do it. The Hawaiian Minister then commented "that if it could be understood that the cession of Pearl Harbor would terminate with the Treaty, . . . he thought there would be no difficulty about its ratification by Hawaii." Bayard revealed that the more he "reflected upon the terms of that cession the less valuable it appeared"; he did not believe "the United States would send its money and its engineers out there to fortify Pearl Harbor, when so many hundreds more important harbors were not fortified"; nor did he believe that if the cession were made the United States Government would act to make the harbor available to its national vessels. In the first place, no navy existed to base on it, and second, American merchant shipping did not need it. Carter, nevertheless, wanted some assurance for the continuance of the favorable duties. He was informed "that there could be no guarantee for the continuation of the sugar duty; that the treaty . . . went into force and continued for seven years more; that Pearl Harbor cession made no difference and that no additional guarantee would be given in either case, and that it was not worth while to ask it."[32]

On June 3, Carter repeated his inquiry as to whether the cession of Pearl Harbor was terminable with the treaty. Bayard promised to reexamine the treaty and again expressed the opinion that "there was not much in the cession of Pearl Harbor"; it seemed improbable, even in the event of cession, that the United States would improve and spend money upon it within the seven years and leave San Francisco unprotected; he believed that the United States did not "require a fortification in the Pacific Ocean; that coaling stations were peace establishments and could not be held in time of war."[33]

Carter called at the State Department a week later and asked that he be given a written guarantee that Article II of the pending treaty was in no sense intended as an invasion of the sovereignty of the Hawaiian Government. This should include a statement to the effect that "the right to hold Pearl Harbor would end when the commercial treaty was terminated." The Secretary thought it was not within the province of the executive department to interpret the treaty in that way, and he refrained from saying "what rights would survive on the termination of the commercial part of the treaty." But he told the Minister that he was "unable to see that it contained any words which could be construed into a grant of political power within the Kingdom of Hawaii to the United States, that it was simply the right to enter a certain harbor in Hawaii, and to establish there a coaling and repair station for the use of vessels of the United States, and nothing more." The clause was really of very little value to the United States, "as we had already a coaling station in Honolulu, and on those docks the jurisdiction of the United States over their own citizens is conceded by Honolulu. We had no trouble at all in getting facilities for repairing, coaling, etc., and, therefore, Pearl Harbor was entirely superfluous as far as that was concerned."[34]

Before further conversations were held on the amended treaty, the June 30, 1887 "Bloodless Revolution" occurred in Honolulu. Still without knowledge of this upheaval, Carter, on July 6, informed Bayard that "the state of affairs in Hawaii was very critical," and he wanted to know what action the United States Minister there might take in case other foreign powers landed forces for the purpose of protecting their citizens from the mob. Bayard inquired if it would not be wise for Carter to return to Honolulu for the purpose of procuring the acceptance of the treaty as it had passed the Senate, i.e. with the Pearl Harbor amendment. The Minister was not certain, but he thought "that until matters had settled down a little it would not be well to give any possible pretext to foreign powers for any interference in Honolulu." The Secretary could not understand how any pretext could be given, since the treaty was a thing entirely between the Governments of Hawaii and of the United States. Carter then referred to the conduct of the King and Gibson and claimed "that corruption, perfidy, and weakness were the chief elements in the Government of Hawaii." He reiterated that the Pearl Harbor question was not the most important one to consider. Bayard regretted exceedingly that the interpolation of the Pearl Harbor amendment had caused delay and might defeat the treaty.[35]

In Honolulu, the policy of the Hawaiian Government during

1886 and the first half of 1887 underwent no metamorphosis on the question of Pearl Harbor; its officials remained adamantly opposed to any cession of national territory. Nevertheless, the mounting opposition of the reform elements to Gibson's policies, including his propaganda of "Hawaii for the Hawaiians," his reckless expenditures for nationalistic and patriotic projects, his primacy in the Pacific program envisaging a "Calabash Empire," and finally his disapproval of the amended Reciprocity Treaty and his refusal to step down, culminated in his overthrow and the revolution of June 30, 1887.

This *coup d'état*, planned and precipitated by the secret Hawaiian League, not only eliminated Gibson from the political scene but also divested King Kalakaua of nearly all direct personal control in government. A large public meeting in the "Armory of the Rifles," addressed by seventeen men and dominated by Attorney Lorrin A. Thurston, grandson of the Reverend Asa Thurston of the first company of missionaries, resolved, among other things, that the administration of the Hawaiian Government had ceased, "through corruption and incompetence, to perform the functions and afford the protection to personal and property rights for which all governments exist." The King was requested to dismiss "at once and unconditionally" his cabinet and to invite one of four named persons to assist him in selecting a new cabinet, which would be committed to the policy of securing a new constitution. He was to make immediate restitution of seventy-one thousand dollars involved in the opium scandal, and a five-point pledge was required that in the future he would not interfere either directly or indirectly with the election of representatives, or attempt to influence unduly legislation or legislators, or interfere with the constitutional administration of legislators or of his cabinet, or use his official position or patronage for private ends. Kalakaua acceded to each of the specific pledges required and agreed to cooperate with the reformers in improving his government. Whereupon the new Ministry invited a number of capable men, including Chief Justice Albert Francis Judd, Justice Edward Preston, and Sanford Ballard Dole, to assist in the preparation of a new constitution, which was completed in five days and nights.

The object of the framers of this "Bayonet Constitution" was to end irresponsible personal government by making the Ministry responsible only to the people through the Legislature, and to widen the suffrage by extending it to male residents of Hawaiian, American, or European birth or descent, thus enfranchising white foreigners who had previously found naturalization difficult or undesirable. Americans, Englishmen, Germans, Norwegians, Portuguese, and Frenchmen were thus able to retain their original citizenship and at the same time enjoy all the privileges and immunities of Hawaiians, but Chinese and Japanese, working alongside the Portuguese, were effectively excluded from the benefits of the same. The powers of the legislators were greatly enhanced. The Cabinet members were to be appointed and commissioned by the King, "removed by him only upon a vote of want of confidence passed by a majority of all the elective members of the Legislature, or upon conviction of felony," and subject to impeachment. The Monarch remained "commander-in-chief of the army and navy, and of all other military forces of the Kingdom by sea and land." But he might not proclaim war or organize a military or naval force without consent of the Legislature. The veto of a bill by the King could be overridden by a two-thirds vote of the Legislature. Nobles were no longer to be appointed for life by the King, but were to be elected for a term of six years, and serve without pay, one-third going out of office every two years. A new and significant article (No. 78) provided: "Wherever by this constitution any act is to be done or performed by the King or the Sovereign, it shall, unless otherwise expressed, mean that such act shall be done and performed by the Sovereign by and with the advice and consent of the cabinet." Most of the changes incorporated in the Constitution of 1887 were intended to strengthen the power of the propertied class. Since the representatives of wealth were not strong enough in the Legislature to command a two-thirds majority of both houses, they turned to admittedly revolutionary methods to secure their ends. Thurston asserts: "Unquestionably the constitution was not in accordance with law; neither was the Declaration of Independence from Great Britain. Both were revolutionary documents, which had to be forcibly effected and forcibly maintained."[36]

After the revolution Minister Carter "changed front" on the Pearl River question and urged the King to ratify the new treaty. The "Reform Ministry" which came into power was divided on the question. Its recognized head, William L. Green, and Godfrey Brown, a Scotsman, who served as Minister of Foreign Affairs, reportedly objected to the cession, whereas Lorrin A. Thurston, holding the office of Minister of the Interior, and Clarence W. Ashford, the Canadian Attorney General, favored it. Apparently, in that situation, the King would have the deciding vote. He expressed himself as

opposed to the amendment and privately informed Wodehouse that
he would never ratify the treaty, and that the native Hawaiians would
be opposed to it.[37] Theo. H. Davies, the British vice-consul in Honolulu on leave in England, confided to Salisbury that "the proposal
would be strenuously opposed by the King and by every Hawaiian;
and although the new Constitution appears to have divested the King
and his people of any special voice in the national affairs," Davies
believed that Kalakaua "would find sufficient support to render any
tampering with the integrity of the Flag a troublesome step." Gibson,
the former Minister, also "would use this proposal with great political
effect" as he had in 1873.[38] In spite of the attitude of the King and
his people and the warning of Wodehouse to Minister Green that
in the event of his Cabinet urging the acceptance of the Pearl River
cession upon the King, they "might stir up a dangerous feeling
amongst the Hawaiians which might be difficult to quell," the pressure of the planter and commercial groups whose interests were well
represented in the Reform Cabinet proved sufficient to bring about
acceptance of the amendment on condition that Hawaiian sovereignty
and jurisdiction were not impaired. King Kalakaua, however, disclosed to Wodehouse that his "assent to a change in policy respecting
Pearl Harbour was most unwillingly given to his cabinet."[39]

British Opposition

THESE decisions reached in Washington and Honolulu caused some
concern in certain British circles. Manley Hopkins, who had visited
the Pacific archipelago, had served as Consul General for the Kingdom
of Hawaii in London in the late 1850's and early 1860's, and had
authored *Hawaii: The Past, Present, and Future of Its Island-King-
dom* (London, 1866), addressed, even before the action of the Senate,
a letter to the editor of *The Times*. He asserted that the United States
had long desired a lease of strategic Pearl Harbor, but England,
Russia, Germany, and France were "all concerned that no such
concession should be permitted. A United States navy station there
has the North Pacific in its grasp. Our own possessions on the north
west coast of America and the Russian settlements above them, with
their road eastward to Japan, China, etc., could be cut off from exit
and entrance." Although the extension of the Reciprocity Treaty

affected only the sugar planters of Hawaii and the sugar refiners and consumers of San Francisco, the grant of Pearl Harbor deeply concerned the nations of the world.[40]

In the meantime the British Secretary of State for Foreign Affairs was well apprised of the treaty situation by Sir Lionel Sackville-West, Her Majesty's Minister in Washington, who commented in general terms concerning Cabinet meetings on the subject, but reported the results of "secret" Senate committee meetings the day they were held,[41] and by Consul General Wodehouse, who was in close contact with King Kalakaua in Honolulu. Consequently, the Foreign Office communicated with the Colonial Office, which in turn contacted, on the subject of the cession, the Admiralty, whose Lordships responded that, "with the exception of Pearl Harbour . . . it does not appear . . . that any port exists in these Islands [Hawaiian] which could prove suitable as a coaling Station in time of war." Therefore, they were "of opinion that it would be desirable to convey an intimation to the Hawaiian Government to the effect" that the grant of exclusive territorial rights over that harbor "to any one Power would undoubtedly lead other Powers to demand a similar concession which the Government would probably find it difficult to refuse on any sound and substantial grounds."[42]

This representation led to an opinion expressed by Sir Henry Holland, Secretary of State for the Colonies, that "in view of the eventual development of the Pacific route starting from Esquimalt, a Coaling Station in the Sandwich Islands will become a necessity. Under these circumstances, it is most desirable that the Hawaiian Government should not grant concessions to the United States Government or any other Power which would hereafter prevent the establishment of a Coaling Station in Pearl Harbour."[43]

As a result of these exchanges of view, the Foreign Office took the position that "the acquisition by the United States of a Harbour or preferential concession in any part of the Hawaiian Kingdom would infallibly lead to the loss of its independence and the extinction of the Hawaiian nationality." Since "Her Majesty's Government could not view with indifference the cession of a Harbour to any Foreign Power," the Marquis of Salisbury requested Wodehouse to impress upon the King's ministers the danger to their country of such a course.[44]

After the disturbances attendant upon the June 30, 1887 revolution, Secretary of State Bayard was deeply concerned over the future destiny of Hawaii and American influence there. On August 12, George Porter showed him a letter written by William R. Castle to the Secretary of the Navy, which described the King "as utterly profligate" and the condition of affairs as "deplorable" and predicted that a republic would probably be proclaimed, followed by a scramble for the domination of the Islands by the great commercial powers. Bayard was disposed to believe that with the present treaty "the interests of the sugar growers will tend to alliance with the U.S., *but if our present Sugar Tariff is reduced*, as I think it will be, there is no saying what new trade arrangements will be made with Great Britain or Germany." The action of the Senate under the lead of Mr. Edmunds, in insisting upon a cession of Pearl Harbor, might have had important consequences. Although Carter had promised to procure the agreement of the Hawaiian Government to the treaty as amended, his success was rendered doubtful by the late disorders. The Secretary lamented, "We must await events (without a Navy)."[45]

In less than six weeks Bayard was informed by Carter that his Government would ratify the treaty, "but in order to allay any sensibilities on the part of the natives to the suggestion of their ceding a portion of their Kingdom and jurisdiction over Pearl Harbor," he proposed an exchange of notes to the effect that the jurisdiction of Hawaii over Pearl Harbor was not ceded to the United States, nor was the term of the treaty prolonged by the Pearl Harbor amendment. The Secretary insisted that he had no authority in law to interpret a treaty, and that the Senate must give its interpretation or the courts of law would do so subsequently. He saw no reason why the treaty should not be submitted to the Hawaiian Government for its acceptance as amended, and said that "if they thought it worth while, after consideration, to return it with their approval and acceptance, . . . they could accompany that acceptance with a statement of what they held to be an interpretation of the Pearl Harbor amendment."[46] Carter concurred in this suggestion.

Bayard sent to the Hawaiian Legation a formal note explaining the situation with reference to the pending treaty and enclosed a copy of the amended agreement. He stated that the President was desirous that the same be accepted by His Majesty. In reply Carter presented a detailed interpretation of what he considered the scope of the Pearl Harbor amendment, stating that the question of Hawaiian jurisdiction was "left untouched by the article, and that in the event of the United States Government availing itself of the rights stipulated for, the autonomous control of the Hawaiian Government remains the same as its control over other harbors in the group where national vessels may be," except that in accordance with Article IV of the existing instrument, the Hawaiian Government was prevented "from granting similar exclusive privileges during the continuance of the convention to any other nation." As no special jurisdiction was stipulated for in the article inserted by the Senate, Carter observed "it cannot be inferred from anything in the article that it was the intention of the Senate to invade the autonomous jurisdiction of Hawaii, and to transfer the absolute property in, and jurisdiction over, the harbor to the United States . . . ." On the point of the duration of the right granted by the interpolated article which mentioned no special term for the continuance of the privileges, the Minister wrote: "It follows, in the absence of any stipulations to the contrary, that its term of duration would be the same as that fixed for the other privileges given by the original convention."[47]

In answering Carter's communication, Bayard briefly remarked that the amendment relating to Pearl River was adopted by the Senate in its executive session and that he had "no other means of arriving at its intent and meaning than the words employed naturally import." No ambiguity or obscurity in that amendment was observable, and he could "discern therein no substraction from Hawaiian sovereignty over the harbor to which it related, nor any language importing a longer duration for the interpolated Article II than is provided for in Article I of the supplementary convention."[48]

This exchange of notes apparently removed any objections that lingered in the minds of the members of the Hawaiian Cabinet, and on October 24, King Kalakaua directed that the Minister in Washington be instructed to ratify renewal of the treaty with the United States. Wodehouse, who was immediately and officially informed of this action, addressed a note to Godfrey Brown entreating that no instructions should be given to Carter until Her Majesty's Government had had time to learn the importance attached to such a conditional measure and asked for a reply to be transmitted to him by 12:30 the following day. No answer was forthcoming within the stipulated period. The Foreign Minister had already stated in substance that as the United States was a near and friendly power with which Hawaii had necessary and intimate commercial connections, and as the United States had granted the original Reciprocity Treaty at a loss to its revenue, to the great advantage of Hawaii, it would seem that, consulting the best interests of the people and so long as the autonomy of Hawaii was not invaded, it was a proper and patriotic policy for the King to advise the ratification of the supplementary convention as amended. Wodehouse was informed that the British Government misunderstood the situation in regard to Pearl Harbor, that no cession of sovereignty or of jurisdiction would take place, the lease to be co-terminated with the treaty. Since no reference was made to preferential concessions, the Consul General addressed to the Hawaiian Government a letter on this point.[49]

The Honolulu *Bulletin* and the *Gazette*, at intervals during the autumn of 1887, engaged in a verbal controversy concerning the Senate amendment to the supplementary convention and coupled their articles and editorials with the discussion of independence; thus the two subjects became so closely interwoven that it grew difficult to separate one from the other. The *Bulletin* of September 23 reprinted an article from the *New York Herald* of August 4, entitled "America Must Hold Hawaii," and observed that "not only is it plain to see that this is the inevitable policy of Washington toward Hawaii, but it is also clear that when we can no longer stand alone our interests will be secured by annexation to the United States, and not to any other country. And although we, editorially, strongly object to the establishment of an independent republic here under any circumstances, yet we would hail with pleasure Hawaii's becoming a part of the Great Republic of America, when the proper time arrives."

A month later the *Bulletin*, in a well-reasoned editorial, declared that independence was unquestionably desired by the bulk of the people. But politicians had made considerable capital of the proposal to lease or cede Pearl Harbor to the United States Government, contending that the suggested cession or lease meant "virtual cession of the country and the end of Independence" and that the rank and file patriots had fallen readily into line. Another view of the question and one which the *Bulletin* maintained was entitled to consideration was:

> that the consummation of the proposition, as a condition of the continuance of the Reciprocity Treaty, would be a sure and substantial guarantee of our Independence. Let it be remembered that the United States is not an aggressive nation. She has more territory than she can occupy fully for generations to come, in one big block. She does not cross the seas to enlarge her posses-

sions. Some of her richest holdings extend many degrees along the Pacific Coast, the nearest continental land to the Hawaiian Islands. It is therefore her natural policy, while having no wish to annex these islands herself, to oppose their annexation to any other Power. In establishing a coaling station for her warships at Pearl Harbor, she would become in a special manner the Protector of Hawaii, to prevent annexation by any other country under any pretext whatever. This is, in brief, the argument of those who favor the scheme, and to us it looks sound.[50]

Treaty Renewed

ON NOVEMBER 5, Bayard was informed by Carter that he had received full power to exchange the King's ratification for that of the President of the United States. The renewal treaty, with the authorization to be signed by the Chief Executive to effect the exchange of ratification, was sent to Cleveland on November 7 by Bayard, who was "very glad that we have now this significant treaty to be proclaimed." The treaty was duly ratified by President Cleveland on November 9 and proclaimed on the same day.

In the meantime the British Minister in Washington had been kept informed of developments. On November 3, Carter called on Sackville-West to explain the exchange and nature of the qualifying notes on Pearl Harbor and stated that instructions to proceed with ratification formalities were anticipated. Sir Lionel pretended to be, and let Carter infer that he was, surprised at the nature of the instructions awaited, as he had understood that both Carter and Bayard disapproved of the Senate amendment to the treaty and that "the question of Pearl River Harbour had been dropped by that body." Then Carter explained how the actual situation had been induced. He returned on November 7 to say that he had received instructions to ratify. Sackville-West reported to the Foreign Office his opinion of what prompted the ratification of the amended treaty. He believed that Bayard wished to avoid the discussion of Hawaiian reciprocity at the approaching conference on Samoa and, by accepting the Senate's action which he still strongly deprecated, to render that body more conciliatory in dealing with Pacific matters. Cleveland and his cabinet, the British Minister surmised, had been induced to take this course in consequence of the aggressive action of Germany in the South Pacific and the reported endeavors of that power to obtain a footing in Hawaii. Also, in view of the presidential election, the administration was seeking to gain popular support by thus appearing to resist European intervention and by opposing joint action in affairs connected with the interests of the American continent.[51]

The Times of November 4, 1887, carried this terse announcement: "The Hawaiian Government has agreed to cede Pearl Harbour to the United States as a coaling station on condition that if the present reciprocity treaty be abrogated, the United States shall relinquish the harbour."

The major consideration in negotiating and renewing the Hawaiian Reciprocity Treaty was political, not economic; it was the resolve to make the Islands industrially, commercially, and strategically a part of the United States and to prevent any other great power from acquiring a foothold which might be adverse to the welfare and safety of our Pacific coast in time of war. The importance of Pearl Harbor as a place of refuge and of supplies for the American merchant marine and cruisers in wartime was well appreciated. Yet the greatest value of the treaty rested in the fact that our possession of Pearl Harbor prevented the possibility of an enemy using it against us.

This determination to acquire strategic posture in the Pacific did not escape the attention of the British Foreign Office and Admiralty who realized that Pearl Harbor would be very valuable to the power possessing it exclusively, but could possibly be a corresponding disadvantage to other powers. Retiring Rear Admiral Sir Michael Culme-Seymour wrote from Esquimalt, "However the Hawaiian Govt. may attempt to explain away the cession of Pearl Harbour to the United States as a 'Coaling Station,' and only for 7 years, it is undoubtedly the thin end of the wedge and it may be considered certain that they will never leave it. It is in my opinion most detrimental to British interest. . . ." The Admiral observed that it would be up to his successor, Rear Admiral Heneage, to decide whether it was desirable to show a larger force at Honolulu, "but unless Her Majesty's Government are prepared to take extreme measures to prevent Pearl Harbour being ceded to the United States, it would be unwise to send other ships, or for the Commander-in-Chief to proceed there himself.[52]

No extreme measures were taken. In fact, after the cession was a *fait accompli*, Sir Lionel informed his Government of the exchange of qualifying notes between Carter and Bayard and explained that Article II, as inserted in the treaty by the Senate, did not "confer any exclusive right to Pearl Harbour further than the right of the United States under it to establish a coaling station." He sent cuttings from the *New York Herald* of November 10, 1887, reporting that trade reciprocity had been extended for seven years, but no territory had been ceded.[53]

Furthermore, Theo. H. Davies, on his return to Honolulu in mid-November, attempted to allay suspicions in London by writing confidentially to the Marquis of Salisbury that he (Davies) had been "unable to meet with any one who desires or would approve the actual cession of territory, or would be satisfied with anything except the independence of the island." The Vice-Consul was confident "that so long as the United States or the Dominion of Canada will afford to the Hawaiian Kingdom the facilities regarding the produce of the islands, which are provided by the present Treaty with the United States, there will be no possibility of any real violation of the Independence of the Islands from within." He had seen a private letter from Carter which convinced "him that there was no occult motive at work, and no thought upon Hawaiian neutrality." Davies explained, "There is no proper harbour at P. River, inasmuch as the present entrance will not admit any vessel but a small schooner. The United States Government have only acquired the right to make a harbour, and then to use it exclusively for a term of 7 years. The cession, so called, conveys no land, for the Hawaiian Govt. owns none of the land bordering upon Pearl River." It appeared to him "to be most improbable that the United States will take any steps, unless in the event of war, to make this cession into a harbour, and it will probably revert to its former position without having undergone any change. The clause seems to be rather a token to justify an extension of the Treaty, than a serious effort to obtain a naval station."[54]

Nevertheless, apprehensive that the acquisition of the unexcelled harbor would inevitably lead to the annexation of the valuable key to the North Pacific, the British Government proposed to the United States that the neutrality and equal accessibility of Hawaii be jointly guaranteed by the powers interested in the navigation of the Pacific concurring in a joint declaration.[55] The position of the Foreign Office at the time was as untenable as had been its stand on the question of preferential concessions; the Secretary and Undersecretaries were well-aware of this fact and not sanguine of results. They knew that Great Britain and France were bound by their joint declarations of November 28, 1843, whereas they themselves had nothing to offer either to the United States or to Germany for a similar declaration on their part. Furthermore, the Marquis of Salisbury penetratingly and cynically observed: "No use—Germany wishes to abolish—not guarantee neutrality."[56] Undersecretary Sir Julian Pauncefote candidly minuted: "I do not suppose that we could oppose to extremities the cession of the whole Hawaiian Group to the U.S. while we are so particular about Islands 1,000 to 2,000 miles distant from Australia or New Zealand; and I understand that we have done what we properly can in directing Major Wodehouse to support or encourage the King in declining to cede Pearl R. H."[57]

Sackville-West's mild approach to Secretary of State Bayard on December 23, 1887, produced no joint declaration, for the latter statesman felt that nothing had taken place lately which menaced in any way the independence of the Islands and that such a step as was proposed hardly seemed called for at the moment. He disclaimed all intention to establish a protectorate over the Kingdom and denied that there was any question of annexation. The Secretary of State, in a private letter addressed to the British Minister on February 15, 1888, explained that the existing treaties of the United States with Hawaii created special and important reciprocities to which the material prosperity of Hawaii owed its existence. In view of these arrangements it did not "seem needful for the U.S. to join with other governments in their guarantees to secure the neutrality of Hawaiian territory, nor to provide for that equal accessibility of all nations to those ports which now exist." Bayard "held that there could be no comparison between our rights in the Hawaiian Islands, as secured by the treaties of 1875 and 1887, with those of other nations," and he would not consent that the United States should be put upon an equality with them.[58] No Secretary of State—Democratic, Whig, or Republican—ever went so far as to promise never to annex the Hawaiian Islands.

Commissioner Wodehouse's efforts to impress upon the Hawaiian Ministers the dangers to their country and the illegality in the "cession" of a harbor to a foreign power were no more successful. A final attempt was made in a dispatch of February 9, 1888, addressed to the new Minister of Foreign Affairs, Jonathan Austin, in which reference was also made to the 1851 treaty between Great Britain and the Hawaiian Kingdom that granted to the contracting parties the right "to come with their ships and cargoes to all places, ports and rivers in the territories of the other where trade with other nations is permitted."[59] In reply Austin stated that the British misunderstood the nature of the amendment and explained that the "cession of Pearl River Harbour," used by the Commissioner in his dispatch, did not occur in nor did accurately describe the effect of the convention, "for no cession of Territory has been made, and in reality there is no such thing as Pearl River Harbour in the sense of its being a place available to Ships of War, or to any deep water vessels. The only thing which has been granted to the Government of the United States, is the right to make a harbour at its own expense, at a place called Pearl River Harbour, and having so made it, the exclusive privilege of using it during the continuance of the Treaty." It could hardly be said that the treaty of 1851, referred to by Wodehouse, whereby the right was granted to British ships of war "to enter all harbours, rivers, and places, would extend to the right to use harbours created by a third party at its own expense, under an agreement with His Majesty's Government, whereby such third party has paid a valuable consideration for the privilege of so creating such harbour." The Hawaiian Government was of opinion that the treaty with the United States did not involve any cession of territory to that country or any release of sovereignty or jurisdiction by Hawaii and that therefore the convention "does not in any manner affect the Independence of this Kingdom, and, furthermore, that the privileges granted by that instrument to the U.S. Government, in return for the reciprocal privileges granted by it to this Kingdom are compensatory, and expire with the termination of the Treaty, and that this construction of the convention is also that adopted by the United States Government." The question of preferential concessions in reciprocal treaties was one which had been thoroughly settled in favor of the right to grant such concessions in return for grants of similar value. The Hawaiian Government did not wish that the British Government consent to forego any of the rights and privileges conceded to it by the treaty of 1851; instead, it was the former Government's intentions that these rights should be maintained unimpaired.[60]

The Foreign Office was satisfied with the assurance given by Austin, and a suggestion came from one undersecretary that "perhaps the Admiralty might be able to explain how the creation of this new

Harbour by the U.S. would affect British ships visiting that part of the coast of the Sandwich Islands."[61] Accordingly, on April 20, a communication was addressed to the Admiralty requesting the Lords' opinion on this subject. A reply succinctly stated "that as the anchorage and harbour of Honolulu, which is within a few miles of Pearl Harbour, will remain available for use by H.M. Ships when visiting the Sandwich Islands, it is considered that the exclusive right to use Pearl Harbour, recently granted to the United States, will not prejudicially affect British Naval Interests."[62] Thereafter the matter was dropped.

NOTES

1. Carter to Gibson, No. 101, March 18, 1885, AH, FO & Ex.
2. Carter to Gibson, No. 11, conf., April 27, 1886, *ibid.*; memo. written by Bayard after a conversation with H. A. P. Carter, May 7, 1886, Bayard Papers, LXXXVIII.
3. *Sen. Ex. Journal*, XXV, 419. Nowhere in the amendment is the word "cession" used in reference to Pearl River Harbor. Cf. *New York Herald*, June 30, 1890.
4. Carter to Gibson, No. 41, conf., April 27, 1886, AH, FO & Ex.
5. Memo. written by Bayard after a conversation with Carter, May 7, 1886, Bayard Papers, LXXXVIII; *New York Daily Tribune*, May 6, 1886. The *San Francisco Chronicle* beat the *Tribune* by a day, publishing the text of the treaty on May 5, 1886.
6. Thomas F. Bayard Letter Book, II, 128.
7. *New York Daily Tribune*, May 6, 1886. Miller died March 8, 1886.
8. *Evening Star* (Washington), Aug. 6, 1886.
9. *The Times* (London), Sept. 23, 1886.
10. Memo. written by Bayard after a conversation with Carter, Nov. 30, 1886, Bayard Papers, IC; *For. Rels.* (1887), pp. 558, 562. For a scholarly and well-documented treatment of Bayard's attitude toward the acquisition of Pearl Harbor, see Charles Callahan Tansill, *The Foreign Policy of Thomas F. Bayard, 1885–1897* (New York, 1940), pp. 359ff.
11. Carter to Bayard, Oct. 16, 1886, Bayard Papers, XCVI.
12. Memo. written by Bayard after conversation with Carter, Nov. 30, 1886, Bayard Papers, IC.
13. Richardson, *Messages and Papers of the Presidents*, (New York ed.), XI, 5085–86; *Sen. Ex. Docs.*, 52nd Cong., 2nd sess., No. 77, p. 166; *Cong. Rec.*, 49th Cong., 2nd sess., p. 4; *For. Rels.* (1886), p. vi.
14. *Sen. Ex. Journal*, XXV, 690, 694; *House Ex. Docs.*, 49th Cong., 2nd sess., No. 130, p. 2.
15. Bayard to William R. Morrison, March 16, 1886, Bayard Letter Book, II, 215; *Sen. Docs.*, 56th Cong., 2nd sess., No. 231, Pt. 7, p. 260; *Public Ledger* (Philadelphia), Feb. 1, 1891.
16. Bayard to Cleveland, Jan. 11, 1887, Papers of Grover Cleveland, CXLII, MSS, Library of Congress; Bayard Letter Book, IV.
17. Merrill to Bayard, No. 66, June 3, 1886, and encl. No. 4, USDS, Dispatches, Hawaii, XXII.
18. See note 17. Cf. *Pacific Commercial Advertiser*, "Pearl River Harbor Again," June 16, 1886; Wodehouse to FO, No. 11, May 10, 1886, FO 58/241, Hawaiian Islands, Designs of the United States on Pearl Harbour.
19. Gibson to Carter, No. 6, April 10, 1886, AH, FO & Ex., Letter Book, No. 63, p. 383. Cf. *The Times* (London), Sept. 23, 1886.
20. Wodehouse to FO, No. 11, conf., May 10, 1886, FO 58/241.
21. *Sen. Ex. Journal*, XXV, 690. Earlier Morrill had failed in an attempt to amend the supplementary agreement by an additional clause requiring legislation by Congress to carry the agreement into operation (*Sen. Ex. Journal*, XXIV, 709).
22. *Ibid.*, XXV, 25, 708–10. Those who voted in the negative were Jonathan Chase of Rhode Island, Francis M. Cockrell of Missouri, Richard Coke of

Texas, James B. Eustis and Randall L. Gibson of Louisiana, Justin S. Morrill of Vermont, Matt W. Ransom of North Carolina, William J. Sewell of New Jersey, John Sherman of Ohio, and George G. Vest of Missouri.

23. Carter to Gibson, No. 81, Feb. 2, and priv. and conf., Feb. 3, 1887, AH, FO & Ex., "H. A. P. Carter, Jan.–April, 1887."

24. Memos. written by Bayard after conversations with Carter, Jan. 22, 30, 1887, Bayard Papers, CII. For Senator Edmunds' views and notice to terminate the treaty, see the *New York Herald*, June 30, 1890.

25. Carter to Gibson, Nos. 81, 82, Feb. 2, 4, and priv. and conf., Feb. 3, 1887, in AH, FO & Ex.

26. *Cong. Record*, 49th Cong., 2nd sess., pp. 914–15.

27. *Ibid.*, p. 2721; *House Reports*, 49th Cong., 2nd sess., No. 4177, pp. 22–23.

28. These were published in Washington in the form of pamphlets entitled: *Revised Analysis of Hawaiian Treaty Blunders*, *Addendum to Analyses of Hawaiian Reciprocity Treaty Blunders*, and *Addendum No. 2 to Analyses of Hawaiian Reciprocity Blunders*. See the latter, p. 8.

29. Gibson to Bush, Dec. 24, 1886, AH, FO & Ex.; Bayard Papers, Feb. 5, 25, April 29, May 20, June 3, 14, 20, 1887, CII, CIV, CVII–CIX; cf. my "Hawaii's Program of Primacy in Polynesia," *Oregon Historical Quarterly*, XLI (1960), 377–407, and *The United States and the Hawaiian Kingdom*, pp. 74–81.

30. Carter to Gibson, No. 86, March 3, 1887 and priv. and conf., Feb. 3, 1887, AH, FO & Ex.

31. Merrill to Bayard, No. 110, March 14, 1887, with encls., USDS, Dispatches, Hawaii, XXIII.

32. Memos. written by Bayard after a conversation with Carter, April 29, May 13, 1887, Bayard Papers, CVII.

33. Memo. June 3, 1887, Bayard Papers, CIX. For similar opinions that the United States would not during the life of the treaty spend money on Pearl Harbor, see Davies to Salisbury, conf., Nov. 17, 1887, FO 58/241; Wodehouse to FO, No. 19, pol., May 7, 1891, FO 58/258; *San Francisco Chronicle*, May 5, 1886.

34. Memo. written by Bayard after conversation with Carter, June 10, 1887, Bayard Papers, CIX.

35. Memo. written by Bayard after conversation with Carter, July 6, 1887, USDS, Hawaii, Notes from, III (not in Bayard Papers).

36. Thurston, *Memoirs*, p. 153; cf. *ibid.*, pp. 129, 131, 137, 141–43, 150–52, 158–61, 608; Sanford B. Dole, *Memoirs of the Hawaiian Revolution* (Honolulu, 1936), pp. 47–49, 53–56; *For. Rels.* (1887), p. 578; *ibid.* (1894), pp. 602, 793–817; Ralph S. Kuykendall, *Constitutions of the Hawaiian Kingdom: A Brief History and Analysis*, HHS, *Papers*, No. 21 (Honolulu, 1940), pp. 46–48. For a general treatment of the Revolution of 1887, see my *The United States and the Hawaiian Kingdom*, pp. 81–95.

37. Wodehouse to FO, Aug. 2, 1887, FO 58/241. Merrill was of the opinion that the Green ministry would favorably consider a proposition to add the Pearl Harbor clause to the Treaty of Reciprocity. Merrill to Bayard, No. 139, Aug. 29, 1887, USDS, Dispatches, Hawaii, XXIII. In 1873 Green and Carter were strong advocates of the cession of Pearl Harbor and, if necessary, of annexation to the United States.

38. Davies to Salisbury, conf., Sept. 9, 1887, FO 58/241.

39. Wodehouse to FO, Oct. 29, 1887 (telegram), *ibid.*

40. *The Times* (London), Jan. 20, 1887; cf. *Pacific Commercial Advertiser*, March 1, 1887.

41. Sackville-West to FO, No. 229, Aug. 5, 1887, FO 58/241.
42. FO to CO, March 1, 1887, CO to Adm., April 21, 1887, Adm. to CO, No. 916, conf., May 12, 1887, FO 58/241.
43. CO to FO, conf., June 11, 1887, *ibid.*
44. FO to Wodehouse, No. 25, pol. and conf., Sept. 8, 1887, *ibid.*
45. Memo. written by Bayard after conversation with Carter, Aug. 12, 1887, Bayard Papers, CXI.
46. *Ibid.*, Sept. 21, 1887, Bayard Papers, CXII. On the question of the exclusive right to use Pearl Harbor terminating with the recession of the treaty, see the *New York Herald*, June 30, 1890.
47. Carter to Bayard, Sept. 23, 1887, USDS, Hawaii, Notes from, III.
48. Bayard to Carter, Sept. 23, 1887, USDS, Hawaii, Notes to, I.
49. Wodehouse to FO, Oct. 29, 1887 (telegram), FO 58/241. For the attitude of the United States toward differential or preferential treatment, see United States Tariff Commission, *Reciprocity and Commercial Treaties*, pp. 418–19; *For. Rels.* (1899), p. 404. For the British attitude, see Office of Committee of Privy Council for Trade to FO, Jan. 22, 1867, in FO 58/112; John Bassett Moore, *Digest of International Law* (8 vols., Washington, 1906), V, 264–65; Peirce to Evarts, Nos. 391, 395, May 21, June 13, 1877, and Comly to Evarts, No. 13, Dec. 3, 1877, USDS, Dispatches, Hawaii, XVII.
50. *Honolulu Daily Bulletin*, Oct. 18, 1887. A similar attitude toward annexation had been expressed by the *Hawaiian Gazette*, March 24, 1882; cf. *Bulletin*, Sept. 30, Oct. 5, 6, 7; *Gazette*, Oct. 6, 7, 1887.
51. Sackville-West to Salisbury, Nos. 303 and 309, Nov. 4, 7, 1887, FO 58/241.
52. Culme-Seymour to the Adm., No. 215, Nov. 7, 1887, encl. in Adm. to FO, Dec. 12, 1887, FO 58/241. In the summer of 1873, another commander of the British Pacific squadron, Rear Admiral Charles F. Hillyar, while visiting Honolulu in the iron-clad vessel *Repulse* en route to Vancouver, advised the Hawaiian Government against the cession of Pearl Harbor (Peirce to Fish, No. 212, July 3, 1873, USDS, Dispatches, Hawaii, XV).
53. Sackville-West to Salisbury, Nos. 309, 324, Nov. 7, 12, 1887, with encl. in the latter, FO 58/241.
54. *Ibid.*; Davies to Salisbury, conf., Nov. 17, 1887, FO 58/241; Confidential Memorandum respecting the Designs of the United States on the Hawaiian Islands, FO 58/241 and CO 537/136; cf. memo. written by Bayard after conversation with Carter, June 10, 1887, Bayard Papers, CIX.
55. Sackville-West to Bayard, Dec. 23, 1887, *For. Rels.* (1894), App. II, pp. 23–25; memo. written by Bayard after conversation with Sackville-West, Dec. 23, 1887, Bayard Papers, CXV.
56. Minutes on Sackville-West to Salisbury, No. 303, Nov. 4, 1887, FO 58/241.
57. Minutes on FO draft telegram to Wodehouse, Feb. 28, 1887, *ibid.*; cf. my "Australasian Monroe Doctrine," *Political Science Quarterly*, LXXVI (1961), 264–84; my "British Opposition to the Cession of Pearl Harbor," *Pacific Historical Review*, XXIX (1960), 381–94; my "Great Britain and the Sovereignty of Hawaii," *ibid.*, XXXI (1962), 333–36.
58. Bayard to Sackville-West, private, Feb. 15, 1888, USDS, British Legation, Notes to, XX; Confidential Memorandum respecting the Designs of the United States on the Hawaiian Islands, printed for the use of the Foreign Office, Nov. 29, 1889, FO 58/241 and CO 537/126, printed in *For. Rels.* (1897), App. II, 25.
59. Wodehouse to Austin, Feb. 9, 1888, encl. in Wodehouse to FO, No. 45, March 13, 1888, FO 58/241.

60. Austin to Wodehouse, Feb. 16, 1888, encl., *ibid.* Copies of both letters are also enclosed in Merrill to Bayard, No. 173, Feb. 24, 1888, USDS, Dispatches, Hawaii, XXIII, and are also available in AH. Nearly two months later the Commissioner informed the Foreign Office that Pearl Harbor had been surveyed by order of Rear Admiral L. K. Kimberly and "on very reliable authority," Wodehouse understood that the Admiral "strongly recommended that it be made available for the use of vessels of the United States Navy" (Wodehouse to FO, No. 153, April 4, 1888, FO 58/241). A Foreign Office minute on this dispatch indicated that the cost of improvement was estimated at $600,000.
61. Minutes on Wodehouse to FO, No. 45, March 13, 1888, FO 58/241.
62. Evan Macgregor to Undersecretary of State, FO, May 22, 1888, FO 58/241. For a later unofficial discussion of the establishment of a naval station at Pearl Harbor and annexation of the archipelago, see *Correspondence with Reference to Pearl Harbour, Reprinted from the Hawaiian Gazette for Theo. H. Davies, November 1892,* a 29-page pamphlet, copy in University of Hawaii Library and in FO 58/279.

8

HAWAIIAN PROSPERITY AND
TREATY MODIFICATIONS

Reciprocity and Profits to 1893

WE HAVE SEEN how the opponents of Hawaiian reciprocity, principally representatives of groups who considered their interests adversely affected by the competition of Hawaiian sugar and rice, lost their long, and at times vigorously contested, but not always well-coordinated, campaign against the treaty. The sugar planters of the South and the refiners of the East, whose main link was Henry Alvin Brown, were frequently at odds on the question of the tariff and the polariscope and often failed to cooperate in the battle against the Hawaiian Treaty. Their natural allies, the sorghum and beet sugar industries, were not yet strong enough to exert much pressure upon public opinion or on Washington. The rice growers of the South ended their active opposition to the treaty after 1885, when imports of Hawaiian rice declined by one-third and consequently ceased to enter into direct competition with the American product. Repeated arguments that the Louisiana sugar planters suffered from the competition of Hawaiian sugar failed to carry much weight in a Congress that during the 1880's indulgently granted both the sugar and rice interests of the United States an extraordinary amount of tariff protection. In fact, the sugar growers of Louisiana were made the beneficiaries of the most liberal, if not the most prodigal, legislation that was ever enacted by the Congress in the direct interest of a single class of producers.[1] During the long debate on the Mills Bill in 1888, many Republican congressmen began to oppose Louisiana's insistent demands for high tariff protection.

The arguments for the abrogation of the treaty based upon Treasury losses, eloquently expounded by John E. Searles, Henry A.

Brown, William R. Morrison, and others, were not especially impressive with successive congresses confronted with the perplexing problem of a treasury surplus. President Cleveland, who recommended the extension of the treaty on political grounds in one paragraph of his second annual message of 1886, devoted his entire message of December 6, 1887, to the surplus in the Treasury, and invited a general drastic reduction of tariff rates.

After the ratification of the supplementary convention, almost all resistance to it was abandoned. Surprisingly, Brown referred only casually to the treaty in his pamphlet *Sugar and the Tariff*, published in Washington in the spring of 1888, and thereafter remained silent on the subject. However, during the debate in the House of Representatives on the Mills Bill, Thomas M. Browne of Indiana and Joseph G. Cannon of Illinois demonstrated how the domestic tariff on sugar enabled Spreckels' sugar monopoly on the Pacific coast to take advantage of the Hawaiian Treaty and to exploit the poor and rich sugar consumers. In discussing the treaty, Cannon averred that if he were in the Senate he would "kick pretty lively"; he wished "he could get a lick at it" and thus help "to abrogate it."[2] That lick never came, for succeeding congresses, in their concentration on much more significant matters, devoted little attention to the Hawaiian Treaty. Eastern sugar refiners also had their interest and energies diverted by Claus Spreckels' sudden and unexpected plunge into the beet sugar industry in California and the refining business on the Atlantic seaboard "to fight the trust on its own ground and demonstrate it was not omnipotent."[3]

Hawaii's prosperity was dependent upon the continuance of the favored status enjoyed by the treaty grades of Island sugars. The principal beneficiaries of this boom in industry, banking, commerce, and the carrying trade were of American birth or ancestry. The constitutional changes of the summer of 1887 placed the preponderance of political power with the property owners; therefore, Hawaii seemed destined to enjoy both economic prosperity and political tranquility through an orderly, responsible government.

But the situation was changed completely by the presidential election of 1888 in which the tariff was the principal campaign issue. The Republican candidate, Benjamin Harrison, who stood for high protection, defeated Grover Cleveland. This victory was complete; the Republican Party for the first time in sixteen years controlled the Executive and both houses of the Legislature. The fifty-first Congress, which assembled in December, 1889, proceeded immediately to draft revised tariff legislation. A large section of the party wanted to place sugar on the free list, whereas another group, led by Secretary of State James G. Blaine, advocated reciprocity primarily in the hope of improving the political position of the United States abroad. The legislation finally prepared in the Ways and Means Committee, chaired by William McKinley, was to a large extent devised by Nelson Dingley, Jr. of Maine, whose ability to grapple with problems of finance and revenue made him one of the distinguished members of the House. This measure, known to the country as the McKinley Bill, was entitled "an act to reduce the revenue." With the aim of eliminating fifty to sixty million dollars of the Treasury's annual income, the tariffs on raw sugar and molasses were entirely remitted. A duty on refined sugar adequate to protect the handsome profits of the powerful sugar trust and a provision of an annual bounty of six or seven million dollars for American sugar planters saved the extremely vulnerable sugar schedule from serious attack. Under the urging of powerful lobbies who practically wrote their own schedules, high rates were maintained, raised, or initiated on all manufacturing commodities that were conceivably subject to foreign competition.

Secretary Blaine was opposed to placing sugar on the free list unless its exemption from duty was coupled with a proviso that the countries from which it was imported should grant some equivalent concession to products of the United States. Although he was engrossed in the sessions of the Pan American Conference while the McKinley Bill was being framed, Blaine attempted without success to press his objection to the sugar clause on the Republican members of the Ways and Means Committee. He sent two emissaries to the Committee, one of whom, John W. Foster, experienced in Latin American affairs, discussed thoroughly with McKinley the question of reciprocity to which the congressman had given very little consideration. Perhaps the putative author of the bill would have made some concessions, but Thomas B. Reed, Speaker of the House, was on unfriendly personal terms with the Secretary of State and exerted his influence to defeat Blaine's efforts to keep sugar off the free list.[4] Moreover, McKinley was unwilling that his protective tariff measure should be cluttered with arrangements for lowering rates and resented pressure from the State Department to modify it. This was a domestic, "not a foreign bill." He was of opinion that the United States had always lost when reciprocity had been tried and decided to leave the question to "the illustrious man who presides over the State Department."[5] Blaine's efforts in the Senate finally resulted in a mild compromise affected by a clause which in brief provided that if any country imposed "duties or other exactions upon the agricultural or other products of the United States," the President should have the power "and it shall be his duty to suspend by proclamation to that effect, the provisions of this act relating to the free introduction of sugar, molasses, ..."

While the bill was pending, informal discussions on the extension and broadening of Hawaiian-American treaty relations took place between Carter and Blaine, but the latter, whose attention was then directed to the Bering Sea seal controversy and the Pan American Conference, indicated little concern over Hawaii's trade. In a private personal letter addressed to the Secretary, Carter expressed a desire to discuss the tariff revision contained in the McKinley Bill. The proposed legislation, he indicated, would prove "very disastrous to all the interests between Hawaii and the United States, and to the commercial and industrial interests which have been built up and fostered by the admission of Hawaii into the protective policy of the United States."[6]

In spite of protests and warnings of impending disaster from the American Minister in Honolulu and from the Hawaiian Minister in Washington, the McKinley Tariff Bill was approved on October 1, 1890.[7] Either by clerical error or by intent, the section exempting imports from Hawaii from the operation of the new duties was deleted from the bill. This deletion did not in the least affect the Islands' prime export, sugar, which was on the free list, but it had the effect of reimposing duties on other products such as rice and tallow, which were on the free schedule under the Reciprocity Treaty. Thus Hawaii was threatened with the loss of whatever few advantages remained after the heavy blow dealt sugar. Moreover, Joseph N. Dolph's amendment to the Navy Appropriation Bill proposing to appropriate five hundred thousand dollars or less for establishing a coaling and repair station at Pearl Harbor, convinced Hawaiians that the United States, who had destroyed the real value of the treaty to the little Kingdom, intended to claim all its own privileges under the arrangement.

There was certainly no intention on the part of the administration to perpetuate the error or to inflict more damage upon the people and Government of the Polynesian Kingdom. In his second annual message on December 1, 1890, President Harrison referred to the "wrong" done to the Hawaiian Kingdom in the Tarriff Act which he was "bound to presume was wholly intentional." He hoped that Congress would "repair what might otherwise seem to be a breach of faith on the part of this Government."[8] The State Department forwarded Carter's protest to the proper committees of Congress. Appropriate bills to meet the case were immediately introduced in the Senate by John Sherman on December 2 and in the House by William R. McKinley on December 4.[9] In reporting favorably on the latter, the Committee on Ways and Means observed, "There are special reasons for the maintenance of the treaty at this time." Carter, nevertheless, warned the Secretary of State that if the error in the tariff law remained uncorrected, Hawaii would abrogate, an act which would result not only in the United States losing its exclusive privileges to enter in and use Pearl Harbor, but very probably in Hawaii's turning to Great Britain for a reciprocity convention with Canada and perhaps Australia.[10] The legislative slip was eventually corrected in an act approved March 2, 1891, which provided that nothing in the Tariff Act should be held to repeal or impair the provisions of the Treaties of 1875 and 1887 respecting commercial reciprocity with the Hawaiian Islands.

The McKinley Act, by removing the duty in the United States on sugars not above number 16 Dutch standard, placed Hawaiian sugars on the same level as that of other countries. American planters, however, were protected by a bounty of two cents a pound on their sugar. This elimination of preference to Hawaiian sugars by the free admission of all raw sugar into the United States resulted in a disappearance of the former excess of the Hawaiian price over the price of all other imported sugar. Whereas in other producing markets which exported sugar to the United States, the price of the commodity held its own after the enactment of the McKinley Tariff, in Hawaii the price fell by two and three-fourth cents, approximately the amount of the former duty.[11] When the new tariff had been in effect only seven months, Consul General Wodehouse estimated the annual loss to Hawaii at about four million dollars, the planters' loss being forty dollars on each ton of sugar. Later the United States Minister in Honolulu calculated that in two years the price of Hawaiian sugar dropped from one hundred to sixty dollars a ton and property depreciated not less than twelve million dollars.[12] Lorrin A. Thurston maintained that the price of sugar produced in Hawaii was reduced, in round numbers, from ninety to fifty dollars a ton. The same amount of sugar produced there, that sold for $12,159,048 in 1890, sold for only $6,963,504 in 1892, a reduction of $5,195,544 or forty-two and two-thirds per cent, and the effect was to reduce the selling price to less than the cost of production on all but a few of the most favorably located plantations.[13] While Americans cheered for "Protection, Patriotism and Prosperity," Hawaiian planters longed only for prosperity.

The whole basis of the Reciprocity Treaty, so far as the terms offered by the United States were concerned, was the sugar schedule which placed Hawaiian and American sugar growers on the same footing. The removal of the sugar tariff swept away all the benefits that Hawaii had derived from the treaty, though the free admission of all American goods into the Islands remained the same as before. The arrangement became an "entirely one-sided affair." It was never intended that the smaller country should concede all the benefits to the larger. The Hawaiian planters and businessmen knew that the United States, in making the treaty, not only expected to control the trade and commerce of the rich group, but indirectly to secure political advantage as well. It was unreasonable to expect Congress to restore the sugar tariff, but as the treaty had arranged for Hawaiian and American sugar growers to be on the same footing, the only compensating advantage that the United States could give the Kingdom for the removal of the sugar duties was the bounty of two cents per pound bestowed upon the domestic producers. The Hawaiian people, planters, and Government felt that they had an equitable claim to this bounty. But securing it was not easy. After the McKinley Act became law, the bounty could be extended to Hawaiian sugar only by the approval of both houses of Congress, whereas prior to the passage of the bill, Senate action alone would have been required to ratify a free trade treaty.

From the point of view of the sugar planters and the Hawaiian Government the American position after 1890 was untenable, for the compensations and the equivalents arranged in the Treaty of 1887 had been changed to the great disadvantage of Hawaii by the McKinley Act. By treaty stipulations, Hawaii was not allowed to grant special privileges in any of her harbors to any foreign power whereby she might take advantage of the importance of her peculiar geographical position and obtain concessions in return, nor even to negotiate a commercial treaty with any other country by which reciprocal advantages might be obtained. Meanwhile the United States continued to hold the chief political advantage of the treaty—the right to use Pearl Harbor—and in addition thereto, received a pecuniary bonus from Hawaii of $130,913 per annum, arrived at by the excess of advantage to the United States from duties remitted by Hawaii and from duties collected on imports from Hawaii, $435,526, over advantage to Hawaii from duties remitted by the United States and from duties collected on imports from the United States, $304,613. In other words, Hawaii was tied to the apron strings of the United States, was prevented from helping herself, and was paying the United States $130,000 a year for the privilege.[14]

Naturally, there was resentment of this state of affairs and demands for retaliation. The *Ka Leo*, in an editorial of May 5, 1891, declared that by the passage of the McKinley Bill, the United States injured beyond redemption the staple industry of the Hawaiian Islands, "and have thus incidentally broken faith with us, by rendering useless the Reciprocity Treaty which had been made for the sole purpose of protecting that said industry, and in exchange for which alone we had consented to cede the possession of Pearl Harbor." In the presence of this infraction by the United States to the promises of the Treaty of 1887, the Pearl Harbor clause became null and void, and the *Ka Leo* called upon the Foreign Office to so notify the United States Government. There was no objection to that Government's spending seven hundred thousand dollars if they chose, to cut an entrance into Pearl Harbor, but it must be understood that it would be at their risk and peril "and that no expenditure of money on their part will now be considered by us as giving them any title or right to a permanent occupation of that portion of our territory. It must also be well understood that, even if the present treaty does not come to an end through mutual understanding before its legal termination, . . . yet most assuredly it will never again be renewed with the Pearl Harbor clause, unless the United States have some advantages to offer us, more tangible than what we have received from them as yet; and here, let it be said that the occupation of Pearl Harbor would be of no benefit to these islands further than the personal interest of the few wealthy land-owners around its shores, who have already discounted by fictitious valuations the possible boom to their properties."

Hawaii wanted and thought she was entitled to the sugar bounties granted American producers. Since sugar could no longer find "a

profitable and privileged market in the States," the *Ka Leo* editor
observed: "We must look for some better markets elsewhere, and
it is the duty of our Foreign Office to now see whether such markets
cannot be obtained and opened by proper negotiations with the nearest
sugar consuming countries, which are Canada, New Zealand and
Australia."[15]

Negotiations to Modify the Treaty, 1889–1892

ACTUALLY, before the passage of the McKinley Tariff Bill, diplomatic efforts were directed toward broadening the treaty relations
of Hawaii and the United States. In spite of the unprecedented prosperity that followed in the wake of the Reciprocity Treaty of 1875
and its extension in 1887, the sugar planters in the Islands were concerned over the stipulated time limit in the treaty and the absence
of any permanent guarantee of their continued good fortune. Excitement and apprehension were produced in Hawaii early in 1889 with
the arrival of news of a proposed modification of the United States
tariff which would jeopardize the benefits of reciprocity. In a communication of March 8, Jonathan Austin, Minister of Foreign Affairs,
instructed Carter to warn the Secretary of State of the danger in
tariff revision. Specifically, Austin wrote:

> If it should become necessary for us to seek markets outside
> the United States for our products, intimate associations with
> foreign purchasers would naturally tend to the alienation of our
> feelings for the U.S., and sympathies would naturally prevail for
> the interests of those with whom we were in closer commercial
> relations, and while there is no thought of annexation to the
> United States, the desire is very strong that that country shall
> not permit of our absorption by any European power. If, how-
> ever, Canada—for example—should make successful offers for
> our products and put out lines of communication which would
> control the carrying trade now under the American flag to say
> nothing of the diversion of the passenger traffic, to Canadian
> ports and lines of railway, a feeling might be engendered that,
> if the refuge of annexation, or a protectorate should ever become
> necessary the United States would not command the favor of our

citizens to the same degree that it would if a question of that kind were to be settled at the present time.[16]

In submitting this warning to Blaine, Carter stated that it was not contended that there would be any technical violation of the terms of the Reciprocity Treaty existing between Hawaii and the United States by the proposed legislation, but there was no doubt that the intention of the Treaty of 1875 was to put the Hawaiian products included in its schedules upon the same footing as a similar American product. If, however, the pending Senate bill should become law without providing for the inclusion of Hawaiian sugars in the enjoyment of the bounty it probably "would tend to the destruction of the industries and trade created by the Reciprocity convention of 1875 and to the diversion of Hawaiian trade to other channels."[17]

The two officials pursued the subject in conversation. Apparently the return of James G. Blaine to the State Department was considered a propitious moment for the accomplishment of the cherished objectives of the sugar planters and commercial interests. This proponent of a vigorous policy in Hawaii was dissatisfied with the imperfect "cession" of Pearl Harbor and, like his predecessor, was concerned over the absorption of the islands of Polynesia by the maritime powers. Moreover, a year before, Carter and Samuel G. Wilder, president of the Hawaiian Steamship Line, had suggested to Bayard that the protection of the United States was desirable.[18] Blaine and the Hawaiian Minister found no great difficulty in reaching an agreement based upon unique privileges requested and extended to both parties. Defending the treaty seventeen months later, Carter implied that Blaine initiated the negotiations by asking that a greater degree of permanence be given to American rights in Pearl Harbor; the Minister countered that this could not be granted unless Hawaiian sugar growers were assured that they would share equally with Americans in any bounty that might be granted, a statement to which Blaine assented. The guarantee of independence was added to disarm critics who might suspect the United States of designs on the Islands.

On April 11, 1889, Carter submitted to the Secretary of State for confidential use a seven-article convention providing for the mutual application of provisions of any bounties or other favors to either contracting power, for complete reciprocal free trade except in articles which were prohibited by the laws of either country from being produced or imported into such country, and for an engagement on the part of the United States

> to guarantee positively and efficaciously the independence and autonomy of Hawaii in all its territory, and, in consideration of such guarantee and to enable the United States of America to more effectually fulfil this obligation, His Majesty the King of Hawaii agrees, that during the continuance of this convention he will enter into no treaties or engagements of any kind whatsoever with any foreign power, without the concurrence and assent of the Government of the United States of America and that in the event of any difficulties arising between the Kingdom of Hawaii and any foreign power, or of any domestic disturbance whereby the peace or tranquillity of the Kingdom of Hawaii should be threatened, the forces of the United States of America (exclusively) may take such steps as may become necessary to preserve the peace and to maintain the sovereignty of Hawaii over all the territory and ports of the Kingdom and to protect the just interests of foreign residents.

The treaty was "to remain in force until terminated by the mutual consent of both the high contracting parties or for a term of ten years and further till the expiration of two/three years after either party gives notice."[19] Thus it was proposed that Hawaii, in its commercial and productive interests, was to enjoy all the privileges of one of the states of the Union and in exchange become a virtual protectorate of the United States.

The Envoy forwarded this draft to his Government, ostensibly as emanating from himself—not from Blaine, whose hand did not appear in the business—but intimated that the provision for the exclusive use of American forces to maintain the sovereignty of Hawaii was probably undesirable.[20] Three members of the Cabinet—Jonathan Austin, Lorrin A. Thurston, and Samuel M. Damon, in the absence of Attorney General Clarence W. Ashford—were of the same opinion, cognizant of how seriously such a proposition would prejudice the treaty with King Kalakaua, his people, and the British element even though it was evident that the United States could and would land forces, as in the past, if the necessity arose. Carter returned home in May and during the summer conferred with the Cabinet on the proposed treaty. A modified draft was agreed upon, providing for the guarantee of the independence of Hawaii by the United States, for reciprocal free trade in the native products of each country, and for equality of treatment in respect to bounties. The extension of the right of the United States to enter and use Pearl Harbor was made contingent upon the passage by Congress of the necessary legislation to implement the reciprocity provisions. The treaty was to remain in force until terminated by the mutual consent of both parties.[21] This draft, instead of stipulating for the "concurrence and assent" of the Government of the United States to all treaties or engagements entered into between the King of Hawaii and any foreign power, merely provided that these should not be negotiated "without the full knowledge" of that Government. Two alternative clauses relating to the forces of the United States having "freedom of access to" and "action in" the territory of Hawaii were, according to a later statement of the Ministers, discussed and rejected by them.[22]

This modified treaty did not materialize. By some means, a copy of the draft containing the rejected troop action clauses found its way into the Honolulu newspapers hostile to the Ministry and caused a discussion of the subject in the public journals and in private and commercial circles.[23] The Rev. Sereno E. Bishop, however, reports that King Kalakaua was anxious to defeat the Reform Party in the approaching election and saw his opportunity to discredit it with the native people by portraying it as a sacrifice of Hawaiian autonomy. King Kalakaua reportedly communicated the offensive clauses to the reactionary "liberal" leaders ("National Reform Party"), who effectively used them "to fire the native mind." Their aim was to secure a majority in the Legislature and thus create a new cabinet whose members would join the King in resisting the constitution or, failing that, would proceed with reactionary amendments in the legal method.

This report may be true. There is, however, documentary evidence that on September 24 at eight o'clock in the morning, the King showed a draft of the convention to Wodehouse and asked his opinion of it. The British Commissioner responded that he hoped His Majesty "would never sign it, as it would involve the loss of the independence of his kingdom." On this draft, which the King later lent to the Englishman, were recorded the former's remarks on the margin of Article IV and the proposed additions to it, which the Cabinet, meeting later that morning, agreed to omit because of the King's objections. The article in question provided, in brief, that in order to enable the United States "to guarantee the sovereignty and independence of Hawaii efficaciously, and without danger of complications with other Powers," the Hawaiian Government agrees to negotiate no treaties, conventions, or agreements with any other power "without the full knowledge of the government of the United States." The note by the King read: "This appears to be coercion. I would omit this and the additional clauses of section 4." These proposed additions were:

> And the Hawaiian Government further agrees in consideration of such guarantee, and to enable the United States to effectually protect the independence and tranquillity of the Hawaiian Islands that the forces of the United States may have access to such parts of the Hawaiian dominions as may be necessary for that purpose.
>
> If (which God forbid) the independence and sovereignty or the tranquil administration of the Hawaiian Government should be threatened, it is agreed that the forces of the United States may have such freedom of action in the territory of Hawaii as may be necessary for the purpose of insuring the independence and peaceful administration of the Hawaiian Government. (Note by the King: "This amounts to a Protectorate.")[24]

In the meeting of September 24, the Cabinet and King Kalakaua agreed that Carter be instructed to open negotiations for an extension of the treaties subject to termination or modification by mutual consent; that there be put into effect between the two countries "complete reciprocal free trade": except in opium, spirits, and other prohibited articles; and that the products of Hawaii be embraced within the bounty system of the United States. As an equivalent for the foregoing, the United States should "positively and efficaciously guarantee Hawaiian independence, authority and sovereignty."[25]

The next day, Wodehouse and his French counterpart, M. d'Anglade, called upon Austin to inquire if the rumors were true that a new Hawaiian-American treaty providing for reciprocal free trade and also for placing the independence of the Islands under the sole guarantee of the United States was under negotiation. The Minister of Foreign Affairs replied that the Government had been for some time in favor of a mutual free-trade agreement, but the question of the United States' guaranteeing the independence of the Islands had not yet come up for discussion by the Cabinet; however, if it did, he should support it. At the same time he declared that the Cabinet as a unit was against anything that might impair Hawaiian independence. When the Commissioners inquired what had necessitated this proposed guarantee and against whom it was directed, they were assured that it was aimed neither at Great Britain nor France, but were told that "Germany, perhaps" was the power. Austin claimed that he was in possession of information which "showed that the question of the absorption of these islands by certain Powers interested in the Pacific had been under consideration during the past year." Wodehouse replied that he was not aware that such was the case and did not believe that Germany cherished any designs against the independence of this group. The two visitors observed that their "government would not approve of the independence of these islands being placed under the sole guarantee of the United States." Mr. Austin again asserted that no treaty had been submitted by the Cabinet to the King.[26]

Events moved swiftly. Pursuant to the call of John E. Bush, a public meeting attended almost entirely by native Hawaiians, with a sprinkling of whites and Chinese, was held in the auditorium of the Chinese Theatre the following evening, September 26. Bush, who was unanimously chosen chairman, announced his acquaintance with the context of the rumored protectorate treaty and denounced the scheme as a complete and absolute surrender of the independence of the Islands. The general tenor of the speeches was expressed in that made by J. L. Kaulukou, whose denunciation of the treaty included a characterization of its supporters as "black sheep." In each succeeding treaty with the United States, Hawaiians were asked for fresh concessions. They had given up Pearl Harbor; now they were requested to make further surrenders. He asked: "Would there be anything left of us eventually?" It was believed that a majority of the foreign population of the Islands sympathized with the Hawaiians in this matter. Attorney William A. Kinney, a spectator, assured the audience that the idea of landing foreign troops there was as revolting to whites as it was to natives.

A resolution was passed praying His Majesty to withhold royal assent to any agreement "which might affect the independence and autonomy of his kingdom," and before any final decision was arrived at on such a treaty, if submitted, "to allow the feeling of the nation to be expressed through their duly elected representatives in Legislature assembled for that special purpose."[27] The following morning a committee composed of Messrs. A. Rosa, J. L. Kaulukou, J. F. Colburn, and others presented this resolution to King Kalakaua, who replied that he would take the matter under advisement, that he was pleased to see his people indicating a warm interest in the welfare of their country and the protection of their independence. Two days later, the same committee, waiting on the Ministers, made certain inquiries, to which was promised a reply in writing.

The Cabinet published a full explanation of the Government's position in regard to the extension of the treaty, which in substance was as follows: As a result of nearly a year's consideration of the subject of extending treaty relations with the United States, the Cabinet had concluded that the history of Hawaiian staples during the preceding thirteen years had demonstrated the advantages secured by the Reciprocity Treaty. The development of the export trade from $2,241,041 in 1876 to $11,707,598 in 1888, "with its attendant advantages to all our citizens and residents, . . . and its beneficent influence upon our national welfare," were "fresh illustrations of the principle that no great material advantage can be enjoyed by any class dependent upon labor without the entire community partaking of such benefits." With only the certainty of a five years' continuation of that treaty, the experience of the interval between 1883 and 1887 when Hawaii's commercial well-being depended upon "the uncertain humor of the American Congress," and with the strong probability that renewed and strenuous efforts would be made by opponents in the United States to terminate the treaty at the end of five years, the Ministers considered it "the part of wisdom to prepare in the days of prosperity for the days that are to follow." In the preceding session of the United States Congress there was a strong movement for the reduction of sugar duties and the payment of bounties upon sugar of American production. The effect of such legislation would have been "to discriminate against Hawaiian sugars in favor of American, and materially reduce to us the value of the existing treaty without any corresponding benefit." The Ministry believed it to be the duty of their Government to endeavor to secure the placing of Hawaiian products upon the same basis as American products in respect to bounties and privileges. Moreover, the policy of annexation prevailing among the European powers interested in Polynesia had resulted in the rapid absorption of nearly all the Pacific islands. The observation was made that if it had not been for the good offices of the United States Government, Samoa probably would have been annexed by one or more European nations. Within the past year the question of the disposition and absorption of that group and the Hawaiian Islands had been the subject of serious consideration by certain powers interested in the Pacific. The latter were the only wholly self-governing islands in that ocean. "Our situation is peculiar. We have no military or naval strength of our own to maintain our autonomy against the pettiest naval power; and we have to-day no guarantee of our continual independence as against any foreign nation other than the sufferance or the mutual jealousies of the great powers." Since it had "long been the custom of European nations to form alliances with neighboring countries for purposes of defense, safety, and commercial exchange," the Ministers felt that the time had arrived when they "should follow a precedent so well established and form an alliance with some great nation." If an alliance of this character were desirable "it should be in the direction where our greatest interest lies. The proximity of the United States, the cordial friendship which has been from the commencement of our civilization a marked characteristic of our relations with the American people, and the extensive commercial exchanges which are the result of such relations, point inevitably to that great country as our best friend, our most valuable commercial colleague, and our natural political ally."

Therefore, animated by the desire to strengthen and extend the commercial ties and to "secure the safety and perpetuation of our institutions by an alliance," the Cabinet had instructed their representative in Washington to ascertain if the United States would be willing to negotiate a convention whereby four stated objects would be secured. These were concerned with bounties, reciprocal free trade, a positive and efficacious guarantee of independence, and restriction on treaties with foreign powers, but did not include the exclusive use of American forces to maintain the sovereignty of Hawaii. This "full explanation" contained the following sentence: "Any statements of objects or intentions, and any purported draft of a treaty stating more or other than is above indicated, which may have been published, are unfounded and incorrect."[28]

The British and French diplomatic representatives in Honolulu lost no time in calling upon the Minister of Foreign Affairs to point out the discrepancy in the assurances given them on September 25 and the statements made in the official reply to the committee. Austin endeavored, in this conversation of October 5, to explain that when he had said that the question of the guarantee of independence had not yet come up for discussion in the Cabinet, he had meant that no formal agreement had been reached by the Cabinet. M. d'Anglade remarked that with regard to Article IV of the proposed treaty stipulating that Hawaii should agree not to make treaties with other powers without the knowledge of the United States, the word "knowledge" meant "permission." Austin refused to admit this. The Frenchman pointed out that to continue in force all treaties and conventions now existing between Hawaii and the United States until they should find it mutually advantageous to abrogate such "would amount to a cession of Pearl Harbour to the United States, for, as had been well observed in a local paper, 'mutual obligations between a small nation of 80,000 people and a great nation of 65,000,000, are not what they seem.' "

Wodehouse observed that under such a treaty as that proposed "there would be very little independence left. That it would give the United States, through their Minister here, power to interfere in anything, even to the nomination of Hawaiian Ministers, and, in fact, to dominate the whole country." His strongest objection to the treaty, as he disclosed to Salisbury, was that the British might find themselves "shut out from Honolulu as a 'coaling station.' " The Commissioner could hardly believe Austin's statement that the King was ready to sign a treaty on such a basis as that projected. The diplomats were informed that it was the intention of the Government to submit the treaty to the Legislature of 1890.[29]

At a meeting of the Cabinet on December 20 the treaty extension was again considered and the King was strongly advised to sign an authorization to Mr. Carter to negotiate, conclude, and execute a treaty. Kalakaua called attention to the fact that Mr. Ashford was absent on the mainland and that the Cabinet was incomplete; he refused to authorize the negotiations. When reminded that instructions, with a draft of the project, were approved on September 24, and that he had given his full assent, he denied the fact. Further reminded that the Supreme Court had upheld the Ministry in its position that the majority of the members should determine policy, the King replied that the decision related only to internal affairs and not to his constitutional treaty-making prerogative.[30] Although Kalakaua and Thurston had heated words over this interpretation of the Sovereign's power, the former persisted in his refusal to sign the authorization.

Meanwhile, Ashford visited briefly the United States and his homeland. On his arrival on the East coast, he received a telegraphic invitation from Sir John Alexander Macdonald, Canada's first Prime Minister, to visit him at Ottawa. There Sir John reportedly expressed great interest in Hawaii and its relations with Canada, a country naturally sensitive about the ascendancy of her neighbor, the United States. The commercial interests of British Columbia, and particularly those of the Canadian Pacific Railway, anxious for a larger share in the trade with Australasia, appeared jeopardized. Moreover, the enormous cost of the transcontinental railway, running through a sparsely populated region, impelled its managers to make the most desperate efforts to procure freight and passengers elsewhere; hence its aggressive plan to secure Pacific commerce and if possible to gain political and commercial influence in the Hawaiian Islands. A close friend and associate of the Prime Minister at this time was Sir George Stephen, later Lord Mount Stephen, whose financial genius brought about the Canadian Pacific Railway and who served as its first president. This Scotsman came to Montreal in 1850 and distinguished himself in Canadian business and finance, becoming a director and in 1876 president of the Bank of Montreal. Stephen was interested in the national policies of Macdonald, and the Prime Minister often consulted him on national problems. In both men's eyes the Canadian Pacific was potentially a vast transoceanic and transcontinental system stretching all the way westward from Liverpool to Hong Kong, a "great northern imperial route for traffic and defence."[31] As indicated above, early in 1887 George W. Merrill warned Secretary Bayard of the globe-encircling plans of the Canadian Pacific system and the future prospects of improved commercial relations which *The Times* had forecast. That the commercial tribute of their sister colony in the Antipodes should be paid to the United States and not to themselves appeared unfair to Canadians. American influence in Hawaii was a barrier to Australian trade as well as an obstacle to Canadian influence in the Pacific. Macdonald's cordiality to the visiting Attorney General of Hawaii allegedly extended to tendering him a railroad pass to Vancouver and arranging for him to be a special guest of Mr. Stephen.[32]

From the date of his return to Honolulu, Ashford reportedly changed his attitude, which previously had been one of cooperation with the other Ministers, and encouraged the King to resist the advice of the Cabinet majority. After the spring elections in Hawaii, which resulted in a Legislature opposed to the Ministry, the Attorney Gen-

eral became an active and earnest opponent of the new treaty with
the United States and advocated a Pacific cable and a reciprocity
treaty with the Dominion of Canada. This policy aroused suspicion
in the capital that he was under the pay of the Canadian Pacific
Railway, if not an agent of the Canadian Premier.[33]

This writer has been unable to discover any documentary evidence
in the Public Archives of Canada or indications in the biographies
and memoirs of Sir John Alexander Macdonald or the histories of
the Canadian Pacific Railway that Clarence W. Ashford engaged
directly in fostering Canadian commercial relations with Hawaii.[34]
Kalakaua himself was certainly shrewd and nationalistic enough, and
had sufficient moral support from his people and the British and
French diplomatic representatives in Honolulu, to feel secure in
opposing this infringement of the sovereignty of his Kingdom. We
do have proof, however, that Theo. H. Davies, on his return journey
from London in the autumn of 1889, stopped in Ottawa, conversed
with Premier Macdonald on Hawaiian trade prospects, and saw other
interested officials.[35]

The Cabinet again, on April 10, discussed the advantageous
development of commercial relations between Hawaii and the United
States, and the majority advised the negotiation of the treaty. But
the Attorney General supported the King in his opposition and explained that he was not bound by the *ex parte* decision of the Supreme
Court that the majority of the Ministers should determine policy.
Subsequently, Ashford contended in the Legislature that to abdicate
the right to make treaties with other powers without the approval
of the United States was a surrender of independence unworthy in
itself and especially detrimental to some very probable advantageous
commercial arrangements with Canada, which he would communicate
upon a suitable occasion.[36]

Early in May, Austin notified Carter that the King and Cabinet
had decided not to authorize the negotiation and therefore no action
could be taken until after the meeting of the Legislature.[37] The treaty
had become a political issue in the biennial election of February 5,
1890, and so strong was the opposition to it that the "National Reform
Party" won every seat in Oahu and enough in the other islands to
make the control of the Legislature a matter of doubt until it actually
assembled on May 21.[38] When that body convened, the division in
the Cabinet combined with the general popular dissatisfaction with
the proposed treaty and the manner in which it had been handled,

particularly in Austin's withholding from an investigating committee of the Legislature all correspondence with Carter in the spring of 1889 on the ground that it was private and not public information, resulted in the June 16 resignation of the Reform Cabinet. A further extension of reciprocity was temporarily out of the question. The sugar planters were deprived of the prospect of the sugar bounty, and the United States Government, as the *New York Times* surveyed the situation, was "left without guarantees of permanent influence in Hawaii, except what they may be compelled to take by force."[39]

Although the Reform Ministry's proposal for reciprocal free trade in exchange for a protectorate failed in the autumn of 1889 and the spring of 1890, the new incumbents soon sought to secure an agreement which might save the Islands from the fatal blow inflicted by the McKinley Tariff. Only six months after the fall of the Austin Cabinet, the Legislature, on November 13, 1890, passed a resolution authorizing negotiations with the United States Government "for a treaty revision looking forward to the extention of the principle of reciprocity between the two countries . . . "; it, however, contained a precautionary stipulation that this should be done "while guarding most zealously the freedom, autonomy, and independent sovereignty of the Kingdom of Hawaii."[40] Carter believed that there was the possibility of extending the reciprocity principle to admit free all Hawaiian products instead of a limited list, but at first he counseled delay in negotiating such a treaty. Later, when he felt assured of favorable action in Congress, he advised that the attempt be made. The new Foreign Minister, Samuel Parker, instructed Carter to begin the negotiations for such a treaty as he believed would be acceptable to both Governments. In less than a month the Minister was able to forward to Honolulu a copy of a draft tentatively agreed to by Blaine and John Bassett Moore providing for complete free trade between the two countries (thus admitting free of duty refined as well as raw sugar) and the extension of existing treaties indefinitely until terminated by mutual consent.[41] Carter contemplated returning to Honolulu to discuss and defend the treaty, as he had done in 1889, but the precarious state of his health caused him instead to go to Europe. His illness resulted in a delay in the negotiations for months, and his untimely death[42] required the Hawaiian Government to dispatch John Mott Smith, Minister of Finance, to Washington in October, 1891, to complete the assignment.

This special Envoy submitted to Blaine a draft of a modification of the Treaty of 1875 and supplementay article of 1887 with points to bring to the notice of the Secretary. Complete reciprocity in trade, except in liquors, opium and preparations thereof, and other prohibited articles, and the extension to the Islands of the "bounties and immunities" granted to American domestic growers, were proposed. In addition, the United States was asked to agree that if on the expiration of five years from the date of signing this convention, she had not deepened the entrance to Pearl Harbor "sufficient for the passage of deep-sea ships, and have entered upon the 'use' of the harbor," Hawaii should have the right to give notice and to terminate the supplementary article. The Hawaiian Government also wanted an assurance on the part of the United States that it would promote the laying and operating of an ocean cable from San Francisco to Honolulu.[43] The former request was prompted, no doubt, by the speculative boom which had mushroomed in 1890 for the development of the Ewa and Pearl Harbor area. The latter project Carter had been urged to press the preceding September, and he did, by making a definite proposal that the two Governments join in laying a telegraphic cable between the coast of California and the Islands. Hawaii offered to contribute five hundred thousand dollars towards the cost of such a cable and to make such equitable arrangements as to the control and maintenance of the same and as to the exclusive rights to land such cables in Hawaii as the United States would deem satisfactory. At the same time the Minister pointed out that since the public interests involved were so great, it seemed to the Hawaiian Government that the two nations most interested should undertake the work either directly or by assisting and stimulating private industry. Moreover, he emphasized that the commercial interests to be benefited were, for the most part, American.[44]

Blaine and Mott Smith encountered no difficulty in reaching an agreement on the form and wording of the treaty which as finally negotiated provided for the extension of the reciprocity principle, a five-year time limit on the Pearl Harbor improvement, and an article binding the President and Queen Liliuokalani mutually "to urge upon their respective governments the speedy construction and operation of an ocean cable between California and the Hawaiian Islands."[45] The proposed treaty was promptly sent to President Harrison in whose office it remained. Although he was interested in the problems involved, by mid-October he had not yet considered them "sufficiently to have an opinion as to how far we can go in extending our trade relations; but the necessity of maintaining and increasing our hold and influence in the Sandwich Islands" was to him "very apparent and very pressing."[46] Blaine was anxious to do the same immediately. In writing the Chief Executive in regard to the purchase of the Danish colonies of St. Thomas and St. John, he opined, "I think that there are only three places that are of value enough to be taken, that are not continental. One is Hawaii and the others are Cuba and Porto Rico. Cuba and Porto Rico are not now imminent and will not be for a generation. Hawaii may come up for decision at any unexpected hour and I hope we shall be prepared to decide it in the affirmative."[47]

Twice in September the Secretary of State indicated his belief that there was "a good deal of mischief brewing in those Islands!" and that he felt "sure that American interests were in jeopardy"; yet, he did not see how far the United States could go and what action it could "take to thwart the schemes of those who are seeking to bring the islands under the control of European powers." In late November, Blaine prodded the Chief Executive to take up the Hawaiian Treaty which "he could settle in twenty minutes" and return it so that the anxious Mott Smith might forward the same to San Francisco where Charles R. Bishop was waiting to carry it to the Queen.[48] Harrison's indecision was due to a combination of reasons including, no doubt, the belief that the Senate would not advise ratification, the desire not to reopen the tariff question in that House by a proposal which would modify the McKinley Act, the appearance of inconsistency on the part of a party which espoused protection to propose free trade even for political reasons with a small nation, the fear of pressure from California's fruit and sugar refining interests and, finally, the effect of such a unique treaty on the presidential election of 1892.[49]

The Hawaiian Minister was apprised by the State Department as well as by Senator Nelson W. Aldrich that nothing could be done until after the election, but if the Republicans were victorious, they would reopen the negotiations.[50] With the return of the Democrats, Mott Smith again broached the subject to Secretary of State John W. Foster, who had succeeded the incapacitated Blaine in June, 1892, but was informed that the President would not again take up the treaty and that its chances would be better under the incoming Democratic administration of Grover Cleveland.[51] The sagacious Secretary knew that there were secret but powerful forces at work in the Islands aiming at nothing short of annexation, and he was unwilling to complicate further the confused Hawaiian situation. Before the new President was inaugurated and free trade negotiations could be renewed, the émeute of January, 1893 occurred.

This revolution was carefully planned and skillfully executed by a secret Annexation Club formed in early 1892 "to be ready to act quickly and intelligently, should Liliuokalani precipitate the necessity by some move against the constitution tending to revert to absolutism or anything of the nature."[52] In the spring of that year Attorney Lorrin A. Thurston journeyed to Washington to ascertain in advance the probable attitude of the United States Government to the objectives of the Club. Secretary of State Blaine was apprised of a certain line of proposed action, which was subject to radical change if circumstances required it.[53] Later, a clerk in the Court of Claims, acting as a contact with Washington officials, made and received a reply to an overture for the assignment to the United States of the sovereignty of Hawaii.[54] At the close of the year this agent assured Thurston that should "unexpected changes make it seem best for you to act immediately, everything possible to second your plans will be done at this end of the line in the short time that remains."[55] This assurance was all that Thurston and Company required.

The Queen was permitted to regain control of the Legislature, which passed the controversial Lottery and Opium Bills and ousted the Wilcox-Jones Cabinet that favored American interests. Liliuokalani, with a Ministry of her choice and at a time when the U.S.S. *Boston* had been temporarily withdrawn from Honolulu harbor, was cleverly enticed into a trap-announcement of her intention to promulgate a new constitution, for which her people had repeatedly petitioned.[56] The ensuing four days—January 14 to 17, 1893—of precision action on the part of the subversive and clandestine Annexation Club that publicly emerged as a Committee of Safety concerting with United States Minister John L. Stevens, and the appearance of overwhelming force in the landing of marines and bluejackets from the *Boston*, which had opportunely returned to port, were sufficient to cause Liliuokalani, under protest, to yield her authority[57] until such time as the Government of the United States should, upon the facts being presented to it, undo the action of its representatives and reinstate her in the authority she claimed "as the constitutional sovereign of the Hawaiian Islands." Her submission to force was prompted by three reasons: "the futility of a conflict with the United States, the desire to avoid violence and bloodshed and the destruction of life and property," and the certainty which she felt that Cleveland's government would "right whatever wrongs may have been inflicted upon us in the premises."[58] The leaders of the revolution, however, considered her abdication as final and irrevocable. A Provisional Government, ten of whose eighteen officers were drawn from the Committee of Safety, was established to exercise power until annexation to the United States could be achieved. A special commission of five members was hastily dispatched to Washington to negotiate the necessary treaty.[59]

NOTES

1. *Washington Post*, Feb. 25, 1892. In 1892 it was estimated that perhaps $12,000,000 would be distributed in the support of the sugar industry of Louisiana (*ibid.*, April 5, May 4, 1892).
2. *Cong. Record*, 50th Cong., 1st sess., pp. 3360, 5956.
3. *San Francisco Morning Call*, May 6, 1888. This was in retaliation against the trust's efforts to market sugar in Spreckels' domain. Convinced that with the latest in machinery, equipment, and technology he could process sugar at a lower cost than that of the trust—the American Sugar Refining Company—Spreckels completed a $3,000,000 refinery in Philadelphia in 1889 and fought a bitter price war with his competitors for two years. At the end of that period the two stubborn combatants ended the profitless battle by the trust obtaining a 45 per cent interest in Spreckels' Philadelphia Refinery and the following year a controlling interest. The sale of this stock yielded the interloper a profit of about $3,000,000, the original cost of his refinery. The trust also secured in 1892 a 50 per cent interest in the California Sugar Refinery which then became known as the Western Sugar Refinery. In the words of Professor Adler: "Though the results of the battle were thus something of a stalemate, Spreckels must be judged the victor when one considers the relative size of the opponents" (Adler, *Claus Spreckels*, p. 36).
4. John W. Foster, *Diplomatic Memoirs* (2 vols., New York and Boston, 1909), II, 3–5. For Blaine's concern over the proposed tariff legislation, see Ida M. Tarbell, *The Tariff in Our Times* (New York, 1911), pp. 204–06.
5. Margaret Leech, *In the Days of McKinley* (New York, 1959), p. 46.
6. For the compromise achieved, see Taussig, *Free Trade, the Tariff, and Reciprocity*, pp. 126–30; cf. *Democrat Chronicle* (Rochester), June 23, 1890 (editorial).
7. Carter to Blaine, April 25, 1890, USDS, Hawaii, Notes from, III; *U.S. Statutes at Large*, 51st Cong., XXVI, 583–84. Passage of the bill was delayed during the summer of 1890 by the recalcitrance of the Republican senators from six newly created western states, who made silver-purchase legislation the price of their support of the McKinley Tariff.
8. Richardson, *Messages and Papers of the Presidents*, IX, 10.
9. *Cong. Record*, 51st Cong., 2nd sess., pp. 15, 109.
10. Blaine's memo. of conversation with Carter, Jan. 6, 1891, USDS, Hawaii, Notes from, III; cf. Carter to Blaine, Feb. 1, 1891, *ibid.*
11. United States Tariff Commission, *Reciprocity and Commercial Treaties*, p. 130.
12. Wodehouse to FO, No. 19, May 7, 1891, FO 58/258; Stevens to Foster, No. 74, Nov. 20, 1892, USDS, Dispatches, Hawaii, XXV, printed in *For. Rels.* (1894), App. II, 282.
13. Thurston, "The Sandwich Islands, I, The Advantages of Annexation," *North American Review*, CLVI (1893), 278.
14. *Ibid.*; cf. Mott Smith to Blaine, Aug. 1, 1892, USDS, Hawaii, Notes from, III.
15. *Ka Leo* (Honolulu), May 5, 1891. Although this article was published as an editorial, Wodehouse believed that it was written by the late Attorney

General Ashford who was a contributor to the paper. The British Commissioner recognized "his style and his views on the Pearl Harbour question which are, in the main, correct" (Wodehouse to FO, No. 19, May 7, 1891, FO 58/258).

16. Austin to Carter, March 8, 1889, encl. in Carter to Blaine, priv. and conf., March 29, 1889, USDS, Hawaii, Notes from, III.

17. Carter to Blaine, priv. and conf., March 29, 1889, *ibid.*

18. Memo. written by Bayard after a conversation with Carter and S. G. Wilder, Jan. 5, 1888, Bayard Papers, CXIX. Before Bayard left the State Department, Carter again spoke freely of the various influences tending to bring the King under British control and the Minister said that he had in mind "the suggestion of the United States dealing with the question by means of a treaty through which they could form a protectorate, taking control of the foreign affairs" and the revenues "of the Sandwich Islands" (memo. written by Bayard after a conversation with Carter, Jan. 5, 1889, Bayard Papers, CXXX).

19. Carter to Blaine, conf., April 11, 1889, USDS, Hawaii, Notes from, III.

20. Sereno E. Bishop, "The Hawaiian Queen and Her Kingdom," *The Review of Reviews*, IV (New York, 1891), 153. This is not the place to present the details of the unsavory controversy as to the origin of the troop action clause. Mr. Austin, in his June 13, 1890 reply to the Committee on Foreign Relations, claimed that this clause had been merely suggested by Carter as something which the United States might perhaps ask in the course of the negotiations, not as a subject already discussed between him and Blaine. Three months later, Carter, in a letter to J. A. Cummins, Austin's successor, stated that the clause had never been mentioned between himself and Blaine, but had been prompted by occurrences in Honolulu in *July, 1889*, which was actually three months after *April 11*, the date Carter sent his draft to Blaine (Carter to Cummins, Sept. 21, 1890, AH, FO & Ex.). From the point of view of the United States there was nothing sinister or unique in the proposed protectorate arrangement. See the provisions of the treaty negotiated by Benjamin A. Bidlack, on December 12, 1846, with New Granada (Colombia) and one by Elijah Hise, in June 1849, with Nicaragua (Samuel Flagg Bemis, *A Diplomatic History of the United States* (3rd ed., New York, 1951), pp. 245, 248).

21. A copy of this modified treaty is in AH, FO Letter Book II, pp. 83–86. Copy in Spaulding Collection.

22. Carter to Blaine, priv. and conf., March 29, 1889, USDS, Hawaii, Notes from, III.

23. Stevens to Blaine, No. 3, Oct. 7, 1889, USDS, Dispatches, Hawaii, XXV, printed in *For. Rels.* (1894), App. II, 292.

24. Encl. in Wodehouse to Salisbury, No. 11, conf., Sept. 27, 1889, in Confidential Memorandum respecting the Designs of the United States on the Hawaiian Islands, printed for the use of the Foreign Office, Nov. 29, 1889, BPRO, FO 58/241 and CO 537/136. Published in *Pacific Commercial Advertiser*, Sept. 30, 1889.

25. Cabinet Council Minute Book, 1874–1891, Sept. 24, 1889; Thurston, *Memoirs*, p. 207.

26. Bishop, p. 153.

27. *Pacific Commercial Advertiser*, Sept. 27, 1889; Wodehouse to Salisbury, No. 11, conf., Sept. 27, 1889, with encl., FO 58/241.

28. "A full explanation of the Government position in regard to the treaty

Question," Oct. 4, 1889, printed by the *Pacific Commercial Advertiser*, encl. in Stevens to Blaine, No. 3, Oct. 7, 1889, USDS, Dispatches, Hawaii, XXIV; encl. in Wodehouse to Salisbury, No. 11, conf., Sept. 27, 1889, FO 58/241, (published in *Pacific Commercial Advertiser*, Oct. 5, 1889).

29. Wodehouse to Salisbury, No. 13, conf., Oct. 19, 1889, FO 58/241.

30. Thurston, *Memoirs*, p. 208.

31. Donald Grant Creighton, *John A. Macdonald, the Old Chieftain* (2 vols., Toronto, 1955), p. 441.

32. Merrill to Bayard, No. 110, March 14, 1887, USDS, Dispatches, Hawaii, XXIII; cf. *The Times* (London), Jan. 20, 1887. Thurston, *Memoirs*, p. 209; Bishop, "The Hawaiian Queen," p. 153.

33. Stevens to Blaine, No. 25, May 28, 1890, USDS, Dispatches, Hawaii, XXV, printed in *For. Rels.* (1894), App. II, 231.

34. There is no mention of Ashford's meeting with Macdonald and Stephen or the tendering of the railroad pass in Creighton's comprehensive biography of Sir John A. Macdonald or in the following: *Memoirs of . . . Sir John Alexander Macdonald*, ed. Joseph Pope (London, 1894); A. Mercer Adam, *Canada's Patriot Statesman . . .* (London and Toronto, 1891); George R. Parkin, *Sir John A. Macdonald* (Toronto, 1908). Neither John Murray Gibbon, in *Steel of Empire, A Romantic History of the Canadian Pacific, the North West Passage of Today* (Indianapolis, 1935), nor Harold A. Innis, *A History of the Canadian Pacific Railway* (London and Toronto, 1923), mentions the visit to Canada of Attorney General Ashford. See my "Canada's Interest in the Trade and the Sovereignty of Hawaii," *Canadian Historical Review*, XLIV (1963), 28–30.

35. Davies to Salisbury, conf., Nov. 17, 1889, with encl. article from *Daily Colonist* (Victoria, British Columbia), Nov. 3, 1889, FO 58/258.

36. Bishop, p. 153. These commercial arrangements were never communicated but they probably concerned cable landings on Necker Island. Cf. *Sen. Ex. Docs.*, 53rd Cong., 2nd sess., No. 16, pp. 8–10.

37. Austin to Carter, May 3, 1890, AH, Treaty Documents, (copy in Spaulding Collection); cf. *Minority Report, Committee on Foreign Relations*, presented by Hon. H. P. Baldwin, June 14, 1890; Thurston, *Memoirs*, pp. 209–14.

38. H. W. Mist to Carter, Feb. 13, 1890, (copy in Spaulding Collection), printed in *For. Rels.* (1894), App. II, 203–303.

39. *New York Times*, Sept. 15, 1891. In summarizing and commenting upon Bishop's article published a year earlier, this journal criticized Canada's "artful trick" in hindering American policies in Hawaii and held the Dominion responsible for the defeat of Blaine's treaty, saying, "Her influence had thus been about as detrimental to the sugar interests of Hawaii as it had been to the seal-fur interests of Alaska and London and probably with even less benefit to Canada itself."

40. Stevens to Blaine, No. 8, Nov. 14, 1890, USDS, Dispatches, Hawaii, XXV, printed in *For. Rels.* (1894), App. II, 339.

41. Carter to Cummins, Nov. 27, Dec. 5, 21, 1890, Feb. 15, 1891, AH, FO & Ex., file (Spaulding Collection); Parker to Carter, March 10, 1891, *ibid.*; Carter to Parker, April 6, 1891, *ibid.*

42. Carter died on November 1, 1891.

43. Mott Smith to Blaine, Nov. 18, 1891, USDS, Hawaii, Notes from, III; cf. Mott Smith to Blaine, Aug. 1, 1892, *ibid.*

44. Carter to Blaine, Dec. 13, 1889, *ibid.* Similarly, two years earlier Rear

Admiral L. A. Kimberly, of the U.S.S. *Vandalia*, then stationed in Honolulu, communicated to the Secretary of the Navy: "If the Government of the United States desires to impress its views, power, and intentions, in the future, on the Government of these islands, the effect of a cable in promoting such influence is obvious." (Kimberly to William C. Whitney, Nov. 14, 1887, N. A., U.S. Navy Dept., R. G. 45, Naval Records Collection of the Office of Naval Records and Library, Area 9 file, 1814–1910, Jan.–July, 1887).

45. Carter to Blaine, Dec. 13, 1889, USDS, Hawaii, Notes from, III; Mott Smith to Parker, Dec. 2, 1891, AH, FO & Ex.

46. Harrison to Blaine, Oct. 14, 1891, Benjamin Harrison Papers, CXXXI, MSS, Library of Congress.

47. Blaine to Harrison, Aug. 10, 1891, *ibid.*, CXXVII.

48. *Ibid.*, Sept. 16, 18, Nov. 20, 27, 1891.

49. Mott Smith to Parker, Jan. 30, Feb. 10, 1892, AH, FO & Ex. (copy in Spaulding Collection).

50. *Ibid.*, April 22, May 6, July 15, 1892.

51. Mott Smith to Robinson, Dec. 30, 1892, *ibid.*

52. Thurston, *Memoirs*, p. 229.

53. Memo. encl. in Thurston to Blaine, May 6, 1892, USDS, Misc. Letters, May, 1892, Pt. 2.

54. Archibald Hopkins to Thurston, Nov. 15, 1892, AH, Thurston Papers, printed in Thurston, *Memoirs*, p. 233.

55. *Ibid.*, Dec. 29, 1892, AH, FO & Ex.; Misc. Local Officials, printed in Thurston, *Memoirs*, pp. 242–43.

56. Liliuokalani, *Hawaii's Story by Hawaii's Queen* (Boston, 1898), pp. 383, 384, 391; cf. memo. from the *Hui Kalaiaina* to J. H. Blount, showing why the people urged the Queen to promulgate a new constitution, *House Ex. Docs.*, 53rd Cong., 2nd sess., No. 47, *Report of Commissioner to the Hawaiian Islands*, pp. 17–18; cf. *ibid.*, pp. 581–90. (Hereafter cited as *Blount Report*).

57. Liliuokalani, pp. 384–93; Thurston, *Memoirs*, pp. 129, 249–56, 261–69, 270, 274, 276–79, 608–21; Dole, *Memoirs*, pp. 70–78, 82–87; 53rd Cong., 3rd sess., *House Ex. Docs.*, No. 1, Pt. 1, App. II, *For. Rels.* (1894), *Affairs in Hawaii*, pp. 208, 387–90, 493–95, 498–503, 582, 584–86, 590, 739, 769, 819, 1028, 1031, 1034, 1038–39; 53rd Cong., 3rd sess., *Sen. Reps.*, No. 227, pp. 183, 185, 202, 222, 343, 345, 368, 444–46, 448, 450–51, 453, 585–86, often referred to as the *Morgan Report*.

58. Liliuokalani, pp. 387–90.

59. For the background of the revolution and the course of events January 14–18, 1893, see my *The United States and the Hawaiian Kingdom*, Chaps. 4 and 5.

9

SUGAR AND ANNEXATION

Misjoinder of Wealth and Political Power

ONE OF THE adverse effects of the prosperity in Hawaii coincident with commercial reciprocity was the aggravation of an already serious socio-politico-economic phenomenon which had gained momentum for over a decade. The Hawaiian Kingdom had presented an anomalous and unparalleled situation since the 1860's. The majority of white residents with millions of dollars invested there, appeared content "under the domination of a primitive and inferior race," satisfied to share in the Government and hoping to improve it, instead of overturning it altogether.[1] The enterprising capitalist class long had been apprehensive over the absence of representation of their capital in the Legislative Assembly and their inability to control appropriations. Concern was voiced by the independent *Pacific Commercial Advertiser* as early as April, 1864, over the danger of the Legislature "being filled with men totally unfit to represent at least the foreign population and its capital, or to enact laws for the kingdom." The editor went so far as to advocate "a change in the organic law of the land" even if the constitution itself had to be revised.[2]

Deeply underlying the opposition to the policies of King Kalakaua was the mounting dissatisfaction of the propertied class—largely American, Hawaiian-American, and British—who had gradually acquired and developed the major resources of the Kingdom, had prudently conserved and invested their income, owned nearly all the real and personal estates, and conducted nearly all the substantial business. This group—not the native Hawaiians—controlled the combination of labor and capital which organized the industry and commerce and provided much of the revenue of the archipelago. Yet they had only an indirect, uncertain, and precarious voice in policy. With the unprecedented prosperity and industrial expansion incident to reciprocity, the disparity between invested capital and political power became more pronounced, for American capital in Hawaii increased more rapidly than did the American population. During the first seven years of the Treaty of Reciprocity's operation, property-value increases ranged from twofold to tenfold, and general extravagance in government was the natural result.[3] The propertied foreigners, numerically the smallest but economically the wealthiest element in the Kingdom, paid the highest taxes to support a government which they were unable to manipulate and in which the native Hawaiian, owning practically no property, legislated the rate of taxation and the amount of expenditure. Even under the most favorable circumstances, this single misjoinder of the producing with the expending power would be looked upon with apprehension. But conditions in Hawaii were otherwise not favorable; they were "actively and menacingly unfavorable."[4]

A statistical analysis of the taxation of the Hawaiian Kingdom for the year 1881 indicates that of 31,032 taxpayers paying a total of $389,648.81, 1,243 Americans (including 357 naturalized, over two-thirds of whom were born in the Kingdom) paid $101,863.88. This amount was over thirty thousand dollars more than the $71,189.70 paid by the 1,361 British and German residents in the Islands.[5]

There was such a state of anxiety in the minds of American residents that a number of the most prominent planters and businessmen earnestly pressed Minister James M. Comly for some assurance that the United States Government would protect American citizens against legislation that amounted to a practical confiscation of a large share of their estates. He informed these gentlemen that however exceptional and irregular their condition might be, in having their property at the mercy of a legislative body beyond their control and inimical to their interests, the same comity was due to the Hawaiian Government "that would be paid by the government of the United States to any stronger and more powerful state," and expressed the conviction that Secretary of State Frelinghuysen "would not approve of any interference with the rights of the Hawaiian Kingdom as a sovereign State."[6]

When Attorney Lorrin A. Thurston, as agent of the secret Annexation Club of Honolulu, visited Washington in the spring of 1892 for the purpose of ascertaining the possibility of the United States acquiring the Kingdom, he also pointed to the misjoinder of wealth and political power there. Four-fifths of the property was owned by foreigners, whereas out of an electorate of fifteen thousand only four thousand voters were foreigners, thus placing the natives in an overwhelming majority. The situation in the southern states was duplicated in Hawaii, to wit, "An overwhelming electoral majority in one class, and the ownership of practically all the property in another class." The only way that the foreigners had been able to protect themselves against being taxed out of existence, Thurston explained, was by securing and maintaining control of the House of Nobles by means of the property qualification for electors thereto, which, with the few representatives that they were able to secure, gave them the control of the Legislature. This fact was recognized by native Hawaiians, and in conjunction with their natural jealousy of foreigners, it had "tended to draw the line closely between parties on the color line, giving rise to much bitterness of feeling on the part of the natives against the foreigners."

This antagonism had increased and was also directed against Queen Liliuokalani because some native Hawaiians felt that she catered more to foreign support than to that of her own people, and "appearances are such as to justify this belief." In addition to this disturbing element, the extreme diversity of nationalities prevented any continuity of concerted action among the foreigners. Permanent foreign residents believed that there was no prospect of stable government except by some form of union with the United States or England.[7]

The influential Hawaiian sugar planters and leading businessmen knew from long experience that their prosperity was dependent upon a combination of partial treaty terms and favorable tariff legislation in the United States. A treaty providing for free trade and bounties in exchange for a protectorate, ratified before the McKinley Bill became law, would, no doubt, have prevented or delayed for years the secret machinations of the annexationists. But, in their precarious situation, after failing to secure the Carter-Blaine Convention, they saw possibilities of relief only in annexation. Consequently, both open and covert agitation for union with the United States intensified in 1892 and led to the revolution of January, 1893. After that event, an American resident of the Islands, and one of the Queen's last ministers but not a member of the annexationist party, testified to Commissioner James H. Blount that the depression in the sugar business brought on by the passage of the McKinley Bill, which played havoc with the handsome dividends enjoyed by the planters since 1876, and the loss of power by the Reform Party "were the only and true reasons for the revolution." The prospect of the sugar bounty was "the main motive for the desire to be annexed on the part of a handful of responsible men."[8]

Julius A. Palmer, Liliuokalani's secretary, also maintained that the Constitutional Monarch would never have given place to the sugar baron tyranny and that the commissioners of the latter would never have knocked at the gate of President Harrison, had it not been for the Reciprocity Treaty. This opinion was not confined to the former Queen's supporters, but was frequently voiced in American journals. The independent Washington *Evening News* maintained that the revolution was engineered by parties desirous of improving their financial condition by inducing the United States to restore to them the advantages they received under the Reciprocity Treaty previous to the passage of the McKinley Bill. Under this treaty the planters made from seventy-five to one hundred per cent on their plantation investments, or about six million dollars a year. After the McKinley Tariff not more than ten per cent could be realized on sugar cultivation; consequently, they were anxious to secure the two cents a pound bonus.[9]

Annexation Fails in *1893*

THE Hawaiian Commissioners, who arrived in Washington in February, 1893 to negotiate a treaty of annexation, encountered the popular belief or suspicion, often voiced in the American press, that the sugar planters and the western sugar trust controlled by Claus Spreckels were behind the annexation scheme. In the words of William R. Castle, "Our bitterest enemies are those who charge a job against us—that sugar has done this thing—or Spreckels, or someone else. It is not admitted that we can be honest or patriotic."[10] The *New York Herald*, no doubt borrowing the phraseology from the Albany *Times-Union* which earlier had observed that the Hawaiian sugar interest "is the nigger in the fence, the cat in the meal tub, the milk in the coconut," queried six times on its editorial pages of February 7 and 10: "Is Spreckels & Co. the nigger in the fence of the sugar islands?" Later the same journal commented that "there is more sugar than statesmanship and more jingoism than patriotism in the hasty movement."[11] The *New York Post* characterized the overthrow of Queen Liliuokalani as a "revolution of sugar for sugar," and was echoed the following week by the *Nation* decrying the revolution "of sugar by sugar and for sugar" carried through by "a plutocracy of merchants and planters." Similarly, the *St. Louis Republican* asserted that the revolution was "for the benefit of Claus Spreckels to help him make a dollar."

This suspicion of the role played by sugar in the revolution, and in the desire of Hawaiian planters to enjoy the big United States free trade market and at the same time to share in the two cents a pound bounty, together with the opposition of senators from states producing both cane and beet sugar to the entry of Hawaiian coolie labor into competition with their products in the American market, resulted in the omission of any reference to sugar in the annexation treaty of February, 1893. From the beginning of the negotiations with the Commissioners, Secretary of State John W. Foster was of the opinion that the bounty on sugar, if incorporated in the treaty, would be one of the most serious obstacles to its passage. Perhaps a half-cent or six-tenths of a cent per pound might be assented to by the Senate.[12] But, after further consideration and consultation with President Harrison, his cabinet, and members of the Committee on Foreign Relations, the Secretary concluded that it would be utterly impossible to get Senate consent to any bounty. By omitting a reference to it and the tariff, the greatest cause for opposition would be eliminated.

The Envoys agreed, for they had no choice; there was no other market for their sugar. Attorney Thurston, leader of the Commission, admitted to Foster that the planters of Hawaii "searched the world over; they made the most detailed investigation, in London, in Germany and in Australia, and there was nothing else for them to do, except make a contract with the sugar trust."[13] In his first dispatch to Honolulu as Minister Plenipotentiary, Thurston confided that he could see nothing in sight for Hawaii in the direction of England, and other countries were out of the question. He observed,

> Suppose that England does accept our overtures and that we can get everything that we ask for and become a crown colony, under the British system, which would be the form of government best suited for us, then where are we? We need expect no favors from the United States, for whether they have treated us rightfully or wrongfully, fairly or unfairly, there will be an

undefined feeling against us, and it is not at all likely that we could count upon continued reciprocity relations. If anything were needed to kill the sugar industry, that would do it. The only possible sugar markets outside the United States would be England, Canada and Australia. The distance of England puts her out of the question; Australia supplies her own sugar, with the exception of a small margin which she gets from Fiji and other adjacent Islands; and Canada's total consumption is less than a hundred thousand tons, with a prohibitory railroad tariff between us and the bulk of her population. The simple fact is that we have got no market for anything except the United States. It seems to me that it is the United States or nothing.[14]

Lorrin A. Thurston, William R. Castle, and Charles L. Carter grasped every opportunity to educate the American public in the direction of annexation. Thurston and Castle made a special effort to meet the editors of the most influential journals, particularly those opposed to annexation, among which were the *New York Post*, the *Nation*, the *New York World*, the *Chicago Herald*, and the *Chicago Post*. All made their strongest fight on the ground, as the *Nation* put it, that the proposed treaty was "a job by, of and for sugar." After hearing Thurston's convincing explanation of the sugar situation, most editors expressed themselves satisfied and modified their attack somewhat. E. L. Godkin, editor of the *New York Post* as well as of the *Nation*, explained that, although he did not believe in annexation and would continue to oppose it, he would thereafter eliminate the sugar job from his argument.[15] Pressure was thus removed from Claus Spreckels and the sugar planters as fomenters of the revolution, and the whole blame placed upon the Queen. Defamation of her character and an exposé of the rottenness of the monarchy in general were resorted to as a means of achieving the desired end.

The Senate did not act on the treaty during the few remaining days of the Harrison administration and the incoming Grover Cleveland withdrew it for further study.

Concerned over events in Hawaii, Claus Spreckels made his eighteenth visit to Honolulu, arriving there on April 18, 1893. That afternoon, Minister John L. Stevens, anxious to get the annexation business settled before May 24, when he planned to leave, attempted to enlist the sugar king's support through his influence on Paul Neumann, the Queen's agent. Once Liliuokalani was induced to accept annexation she could persuade the Kanakas to do the same.[16] Spreckels, in an interview on April 20 with her at her Washington Place home, reportedly answered her request for assistance by saying he would help by not making loans to the Provisional Government and "they would naturally collapse."[17]

On the other hand, according to the *Hawaiian Star*, the Californian assured President Dole that he would support the Provisional Government. Actually Spreckels had not come to a clear decision and wanted to consider the idea of a republic, which he hoped to control as he had King Kalakaua for almost five years. He told a *Star* reporter: "I have not yet made up my mind about the thing; I am not here to tear down the Provisional Government, but I am here to see justice done to all parties, and when I have determined what I regard as justice I will be heard fast enough."[18]

The sugar magnate's greatest anxiety was over the future of contract labor. He told an Associated Press correspondent that "the labor question is the all-important one and constitutes my only objection to annexation. Whites could not and Kanakas will not work in the cane fields. Negroes have been spoken of for laborers, but it is impossible to keep them in the country; they always want to go home." The monarchy could not be restored. If he could find a man of ability whom he could trust he would favor a republic—the thing was to find the man. The Provisional Government could not remain in power always. "Give the United States a place at Pearl Harbor in fee simple—that is all they want. They would keep their ships there and protect us if we couldn't take care of ourselves. . . . Uncle Sam wouldn't allow any power to take these islands. . . . The Kanakas, though, are easily influenced, and I can't be here all the time. Some smooth talker from the States, Australia or the South Seas could come here and lead them astray."[19]

Soon after his arrival in Honolulu, Claus Spreckels invited William G. Irwin and Henry P. Baldwin to his home to discuss the effects of annexation on the planters. Irwin drafted a letter which was presented, over Spreckels' signature, to a group of several planters and sugar agents at a meeting on April 25 in the office of Attorney William O. Smith, an extensive owner of sugar plantation stock and one of the ring leaders of the revolution. The letter dealt with the contract labor experiment and problem in Hawaii, set forth the system's advantages to the planter and the laborer, and concluded that it was the only arrangement on which the planters could rely.

Disturbance of the contract labor system would cripple the sugar industry and bankrupt the Islands. After discussing the political outlook, the prospects of the sugar industry, and the contract labor question, the planters referred the letter to a committee of three that reported two days later to a second meeting. Since the planters' endorsement of the letter was not unanimous, it was decided that a formal statement be made to Commissioner James H. Blount on the effects of annexation on the sugar industry.

Having failed to secure the support of the planters, Spreckels aired his views in an interview with Charles Nordhoff, a correspondent of the *New York Herald*. The conservative millionaire, who had the largest property holdings and paid the highest taxes of any planter in Hawaii, did not agree with some annexationists that political stability was impossible without annexation. He felt "sure that stable, orderly, and economic government" was possible in the Islands. He explained that he had not at first opposed annexation. The revolution, occurring so suddenly, was a complete surprise to him. "Many planters were brought to acquiesce in it by delusive promises that they would get the sugar bounty if annexation came, and that the labor system would not be disturbed; that the United States was so eager to possess the islands, that any terms demanded here would be at once granted, and other nonsense of that kind."[20]

Spreckels continued to advocate an independent republic, attempting to win over the Rev. Sereno E. Bishop, mouthpiece of the annexationists, Samuel M. Damon, managing partner of Bishop and Company and Finance Minister, and others who would listen.[21] When interviewed by Blount on June 5, the sugar king asserted that most of the planters did not want annexation if they could not get contract labor. He reported a conversation with President Dole, who had studied the immigration laws of the United States, but believed that Washington would give Hawaii separate legislation so that the planters could import labor. In answering pertinent questions posed by the Commissioner, Spreckels clearly stated his opinion that the revolution was "largely a struggle to take political power from the natives and put it in the hands of the whites"; that "seven-eighths at least" of the former "would be opposed to annexation"; that if the native Hawaiians had arms they "would bring the Queen back to the throne"; and that "the Provisional Government would never be there if the United States troops were not landed, and they knew that long before they landed."[22]

Between the interviews with Nordhoff and Blount, the magnate determined a course of action intended to bring about the collapse of the Provisional Government. On May 29, the cashier of Claus Spreckels and Company demanded payment that afternoon of a ninety-five-thousand-dollar loan made during Liliuokalani's reign and covered by notes which had been signed by officials of the Hawaiian Postal Savings Bank. The Provisional Government had assumed responsibility for these notes. This demand was unexpected as it was understood that Spreckels' bank was in no hurry to collect the principal. Since the Government did not have the money in the treasury for an immediate payment, Finance Minister Damon and his colleagues faced a crisis. Realizing that failure to pay would cause a loss of confidence in the Provisional Government, they acted quickly and obtained pledges from Honolulu businessmen for the entire amount. On June 1, forty-five thousand dollars plus fourteen hundred dollars in interest was paid to Spreckels and Company; the balance of fifty thousand dollars plus eighteen hundred dollars in interest was forthcoming two days later.[23] This quick settlement and the prompt payment of thirty thousand dollars semi-annual interest on the London loan bolstered the confidence of the supporters of the Provisional Government, chagrined the supporters of the Queen, increased the annexationists' attacks on the royalists in the press, and led to "an idiotic trick" of posting a placard on the sugar king's Punahou mansion, threatening his assassination in blood red letters which read: "Gold and Silver will not stop lead!"[24]

Thwarted in his scheme for a republic, ridiculed by the *Hawaiian Star* and the *Gazette*, and frightened by the threat to his life, Claus Spreckels left Honolulu with his family on July 19, vowing to carry on his war against the Provisional Government in Washington, D.C.[25]

After a thorough investigation of the causes and course of the revolution, President Cleveland decided not to resubmit the treaty. The mid-Pacific group was not annexed; neither was the Queen restored. The establishment of a so-called republic, which was in fact an oligarchy, did not serve to terminate the Reciprocity Treaty which remained in effect. But the Cleveland administration encouraged and increased Hawaii's economic dependence upon the United States through the Wilson-Gorman Tariff of 1894. This act, by abolishing the domestic sugar bounty and restoring the tariff on sugar importations, permitted Hawaii to regain her original advantageous position under the Reciprocity Treaty which had been practically nullified by the McKinley Tariff.[26] After the passage of the new act a margin between the Hawaiian import price and the import price of all sugar in favor of the Hawaiian commodity reappeared. Under this fortunate stimulus the Hawaiian sugar industry prospered and expanded,[27] yet the sugar planters could not rest content.

Annexation Achieved

THE news of McKinley's election, which was received in Honolulu on November 16, 1896, via Japan, revived hope and activity among jubilant annexationists and was a welcome relief to President Sanford B. Dole and his colleagues, who still considered the matter of annexation to be of vital importance to the country. The Republican victory coincided with an increasing anxiety over the possibility of the revision of the United States tariff in such a way as to jeopardize the advantages of reciprocity or to destroy it completely. There had been fear that if the United States was not concerned enough to promote annexation, there would not be sufficient interest in Congress to continue the Reciprocity Treaty. If the United States let go of the Islands, they would immediately become a prize for England, Japan, or Russia. Dole was convinced that without United States aid the Republic could not remain independent.[28]

William N. Armstrong, writing from San Francisco on December 28, 1896, warned the Hawaiian planters of the danger to their sugar cane economy from beet sugar competition and urged them to get into the Union before any new questions were raised. He reported that California had turned to the sugar beet for a money crop; Nebraska was rapidly learning how to make this sugar; beets could be grown successfully in many Atlantic states; the reason that they had not been planted there was that the farmers had no faith in the business. Success in California and Nebraska would eventually have an effect in the East. Those who had put large capital into the business might at any time "raise a cry against the cane product and fire the hearts of the farmer and laborer." Hawaiian planters hardly realized the changed conditions of sugar production. The British West Indies were on the verge of bankruptcy and were clamoring for relief or annexation to the United States. The policy of the American legislators would be to protect the home production in some form; that reciprocity would bring the Hawaiian Islands within that protection for any period of time was doubtful. "Under these conditions, the Hawaiian planter should see the supreme need of getting into the American fold. Delay is dangerous."[29]

This warning was timely, for both beet and cane sugar interests objected strenuously not only to the acquisition of tropical islands, but also to the extension of the Reciprocity Treaty. The *Washington Post*, formerly friendly to Hawaii but now supporting the sugar trust, attacked the treaty "savagely" and contended that the United States had paid for permanent rights in Pearl Harbor which existed without regard to a reciprocity treaty. Editorially, this journal asserted that "the real question is whether this treaty operates to the advantage of either the producing or consuming classes in this country, and the demonstrated fact that it benefits neither furnishes all the answer that Congress ought to need."[30] Henry Oxnard, a beet sugar producer and a national representative of the sugar trust, conducted a "house to house canvass" among congressmen early in May, 1897 and, by claiming that he was friendly to Hawaii, induced the press to allow him space for statements.[31]

Nevertheless, McKinley submitted a second annexation treaty to the United States Senate on June 16, 1897, which embodied the essential features of the one of February 15, 1893. The new (Dingley) tariff was made inoperative as to Hawaii on the last day of June; that is, the exemption clause in favor of Hawaii which had been removed in the Finance Committee was replaced. Since duties were raised on raw sugar from elsewhere, Hawaiian planters in the two years which were to elapse before the Reciprocity Treaty could be abrogated would get double-duty benefits. Minister Hatch was certain that their "sugars would have been put on the dutiable list if the President had not come forward with annexation."[32]

The sugar trust, determined that its monopoly should not be jeopardized, persisted in its opposition to annexation. The Western Sugar Refinery Company of San Francisco, jointly owned by the Spreckels family and the sugar trust, controlled the entire market for refined sugars in all the United States lying west of the Missouri river. This monopoly was so complete that it prevented any raw sugar from being sold by the grocers in the area. With annexation that refinery would lose control of the Hawaiian crop, and yellow sugars and washed sugars from the Islands would at once be put on sale throughout the Pacific states. Every pound of that sugar consumed would displace an equal number of pounds of refined sugar. Consequently, the company would lose its refining profit on exactly that quantity of sugar, the aggregate of which would be considerable. With annexation there would be nothing to prevent the establishment of refineries at the Hawaiian Islands, and in this way the monopoly of the Western Sugar Refinery Company would be broken.[33]

Spreckels and Oxnard joined forces to fight annexation. John Spreckels, former Senator Charles N. Felton of California, and Henry Oxnard spent two months of the summer of 1897 in Washington, lobbying against the new treaty. The elder Spreckels purchased the *San Francisco Call* in the name of his son for the purpose of fighting annexation and, beginning with the issue of December 1, 1897, mailed free copies of that newspaper to each member of Congress. Spreckels and Oxnard also conducted an anti-annexation campaign in Sacramento.[34] While the sugar magnate sent agents up and down the West coast to get petitions and resolutions against annexation, Oxnard attempted to create confusion and dissension among the beet sugar growers by offering California growers fifty cents a ton more for their beets if annexation were defeated and by telling the beet growers of Nebraska that they would get fifty cents a ton less for their beets if annexation were accomplished.[35]

The Beet Sugar Association of Nebraska launched a vigorous campaign against the treaty in the latter part of 1897 by flooding the country with circulars urging the people to oppose annexation and to write their congressmen to that effect. The association maintained that annexation was the only thing that threatened the success of the beet industry. Offers were made to start beet factories all over the country, a move which proved effective and one that the Hawaiian Commissioners found impossible to meet.[36]

Senator William Vincent Allen from Nebraska presented to the Senate, on January 5, 1898, a memorial of the American Sugar Growers Association remonstrating against the annexation of the Hawaiian Islands. This petition called forth a resolution from Henry Cabot Lodge directing the Secretary of Agriculture to inform the Senate of the amount of sugar then imported into the United States, and the amount of beet sugar produced in the country, "with what sugars imported or domestic, the beet sugar of the United States comes into competition, what effect, if any, the importation of Hawaiian sugar has or could have upon the beet sugar production of the United States." Senator John M. Thurston brought forward, on February 7, a resolution of the Beet Sugar Association of Nebraska also remonstrating against the acquisition of Hawaii, a resolution which was followed by a similar one of the citizens of that state, presented on July 9.[37]

For a combination of reasons, including the inability to secure a two-thirds vote in the Senate, the annexation treaty was abandoned and for it was substituted a joint resolution, which, in its ten paragraphs embodying the terms of a treaty, stipulated the conditions that should obtain in the Hawaiian Islands until "Congress shall provide for the government of such islands."[38] Thus the subject was brought within the reach of Congress under the precedent established in the annexation of Texas. While the treaty was under consideration and during the delay in passing the joint resolution, the planters of Hawaii maintained an agent in Washington to watch over the Reciprocity Treaty. Attorney William A. Kinney, as well as Lorrin A. Thurston, was back in the capital lobbying for Hawaii. In case annexation failed, every effort was to be made to continue reciprocity.

While the joint resolution was pending, the sugar trust moved "heaven and earth to get an adjournment," believing that if they could cause consideration of annexation to be deferred until the next session, they would have accomplished their purpose; in that session, a short one expiring by limitation on March 3 or 4, 1899, ordinary routine business would occupy all the time.[39] The House voted down a substitute resolution proposing to guarantee the independence of the Hawaiian Islands, and passed the Newlands resolution on June 15; a similar resolution was carried in the Senate on July 6, 1898.[40]

Hawaii passed under the sovereignty of the United States the following August 12.[41] The sugar planters and allied commercial interests, at last, could feel secure in their investments. Cane sugar production, under the most favorable combination of circumstances in the world, leaped forward[42] only to be surpassed in the territory's economy by activities associated with defense, including the belated development of the dormant Pearl River lagoon into a strategic naval base.

NOTES

1. Captain William Reynolds commented upon this condition as early as 1868 (Reynolds to Secretary of the Navy Gideon Welles, No. 3, Jan. 20, 1868, U.S. Navy Dept., Captains' Letters, 1868).
2. April 23, 1864, *ibid.*; cf. *ibid.*, May 7, 1864.
3. Minister Daggett to Secretary of State Frederick Frelinghuysen, No. 144, April 20, 1884, USDS, Dispatches, Hawaii, XXI.
4. James Comly to Frelinghuysen, No. 217, May 8, 1882, *ibid.*, XX, printed in *For. Rels.*, 1882, pp. 342–43.
5. See encl. in Daggett to Frelinghuysen, No. 29, Nov. 18, 1882, *ibid.*; cf. my *The United States and the Hawaiian Kingdom*, pp. 52–54, 58–59, 341.
6. See note 4.
7. Memo. encl. in Thurston to Blaine, May 6, 1892, USDS, Miscellaneous Letters, May 1892, Pt. II.
8. Statement of William H. Cornwell to James H. Blount, April 24, 1893, 53rd Cong., 3rd sess., *House Ex. Docs.*, No. 1, Pt. 1, *For. Rels.* (1894), App. II, 495.
9. *Washington Post*, Jan. 30, Feb. 1, 1893, April 23, 1897.
10. W. R. Castle Diary, Feb. 24, 1893. Cf. Feb. 22, March 2, 1893. Transcript copy in University of Hawaii Library.
11. *New York Herald*, Feb. 24, 1893.
12. USDS, Protocol of Second Conference between the Secretary of State and the Hawaiian Commissioners, February 7, 1893; Castle Diary, Feb. 7, 1893.
13. William R. Castle, Jr., "John Watson Foster, Secretary of State, June 29, 1892–February 23, 1893," in S. F. Bemis, ed., *American Secretaries of State and Their Diplomacy* (10 vols., New York, 1927–29), VIII, 216.
14. Thurston to Dole, conf., accompanying dispatch No. 1, June 13, 1893, AH, U.S., Minister and Commissioners to Washington (printed in Thurston, *Memoirs*, pp. 296–301, p. 300 quoted).
15. Thurston to Dole, Feb. 9, April 7, 1893, AH, U.S., Minister and Commissioners to Washington. The latter is printed in Thurston, *Memoirs*, pp. 291–95.
16. 53rd Cong., 3rd sess., *U.S. House Ex. Docs.*, No. 1, Pt. 1, App. II, *Affairs in Hawaii*, p. 973.
17. Liliuokalani's Diary, April 20, 1893, AH. Five days later the Queen complained of "much maneuvering and wire pulling with Mr. Spreckels," that the Provisional Government was trying to turn him against her (*ibid.*, April 25).
18. *Hawaiian Star*, April 21, 1893.
19. *San Francisco Chronicle*, May 4, 1893, Honolulu date line April 26, 1873.
20. *Hawaiian Gazette*, May 23, 1893.
21. S. E. Bishop to Gorham D. Gilman, May 17, 1893, HMCS Library. Gilman, an ardent annexationist and an American merchant resident for years at Lahaina, Maui, had returned to Massachusetts.
22. 53rd Cong., 3rd sess., *U.S. House Ex. Docs.*, No. 1, Pt. 1, App. II, *Affairs in Hawaii*, pp. 989–90.
23. *Hawaiian Star*, May 29, 30, 1893; *Pacific Commercial Advertiser*, June 2, 1893; *Hawaiian Gazette*, June 6, 1893; *New York Times*, June 7, 1893. A. B. Spreckels claimed that the funds to pay the loan came mostly from S. M. Damon (*New York Advertiser*, June 30, 1893).

24. *Hawaiian Star*, June 9, 1893; *Bulletin* (Honolulu), June 22, 1893; *New York Tribune*, July 5, 1893. A radical suggestion was made by some ardent annexationists that if Spreckels attempted to embarrass the government, martial law should be proclaimed and every dollar worth of his property confiscated (*San Francisco Chronicle*, May 4, 1893).

25. For the details of Spreckels' eighteenth visit to and his dramatic departure from Honolulu, see Adler, *Claus Spreckels*, Chap. 21.

26. See my *United States and the Hawaiian Kingdom*, Chap. 7, for a treatment of Cleveland's policy towards Hawaii.

27. See Appendix II.

28. Dole to his brother, George H. Dole, Nov. 21, 1896, Letters of Sanford Ballard Dole to George H. Dole 1859–1912, MSS, Collection of Robert E. Van Dyke Foundation, Honolulu.

29. *Pacific Commercial Advertiser*, Jan. 8, 1897; cf. "England and the West Indies," *Morning Advertiser* (New York), Nov. 26, 1896, editorial; "Beet Sugar Industry," *Commercial Advertiser* (New York), Dec. 17, 1896, editorial; "Sugar Industry Injured, England Alarmed at Condition of West India Trade," *New York Times*, Dec. 19, 1896.

30. "A Good Treaty to Abrogate," *Washington Post*, April 26, 1897.

31. *Pacific Commercial Advertiser*, May 19, 1897.

32. Hatch to Cooper, personal, July 1, 1897; cf. Hatch to Cooper, July 7, 1898, AH, Hawaiian Officials Abroad, U.S. Minister at Washington.

33. "Sugar Trust and Annexation," statement of H. M. Hatch, Dec. 27, 1897, *ibid.*

34. Adler, *Claus Spreckels*, pp. 254–55.

35. *Washington Star*, June 11, 15, 1898.

36. Hatch to Cooper, personal, Dec. 22, 1897, *ibid.*

37. *Journal of the Senate of the United States of America*, 55th Cong., 2nd sess., pp. 36, 50, 90.

38. *Cong. Record*, 55th Cong., 2nd sess., p. 4600; *U.S. Statutes at Large*, XXX, No. 259, p. 750.

39. Hatch to Cooper, May 22, 26, June 9, 1898, AH, Hawaiian Officials Abroad, U.S. Minister at Washington.

40. *Cong. Record*, 55th Cong., 2nd sess., pp. 6019, 6140–57, 6347; *New York Times*, July 7, 1898.

41. See *House Docs.*, 55th Cong., 2nd sess., No. 3, *Annual Report of the Navy Department for the Year 1898*, Appendix to the *Report of the Chief of the Bureau of Navigation*, pp. 145–47.

42. For the creation "of a new system of agriculture built around the fat progeny of one tiny cane seedling, H-109 cane," the chemical analysis of soils, and the application of chemical fertilizers, see Jared G. Smith, *The Reorganization of the H.S.P.A. Experiment Station and the Origin of H-109 Cane* (Honolulu, 1928).

10

BENEFITS OF RECIPROCITY

Native Hawaiians

IN THE PROLONGED and sometimes fervid discussions of the phe-
nomenal results, indisputable advantages, and hideous evils that
emanated from the Reciprocity Treaty with Hawaii, this writer has
not discovered a single official report, periodical article, or speech
in the United States Congress or in the Hawaiian Legislature devoted
exclusively to the benefits accruing to native Hawaiians. Theoretically,
under the "trickle down" economic theory, the planters, by pursuing
their own interests, promoted the welfare of the Hawaiian society
more effectually than they might have intended. By directing the
sugar industry in such a manner so that its product might be of the
greatest value, they may have envisioned only their own gain, but
in their activity they were "led by an invisible hand to promote an
end which was no part of their intention."[1] Consequently, what was
good for the planters was good for the nation; all the inhabitants of
the Islands shared in the treaty's benefits which trickled down in the
form of employment at increased wages to those on the lowest rung
of the economic ladder. The *Hawaiian Gazette* of May 24, 1882, in
evaluating the results of the treaty, asserted that "the interests, material interests, of the Hawaiian, the American, and the Englishman are
one; prosperity for one is prosperity for all." The treaty which had
enabled Hawaii to double its income in six years had raised the King's
civil list from fifty thousand to one hundred thousand dollars and
had also raised the Hawaiian laborers' wages from one to two dollars
and even to two dollars and fifty cents per day. The unanimous verdict,
according to the *Gazette*, was that this was "something worth working for and striving to keep."

One of the purported objects of the treaty as stated in 1875–76,
when it was under debate in Congress, was "to help the natives build

up and populate the islands with a happy, prosperous people." Yet, after six years of satisfactory operation of the treaty, not one Hawaiian of pure blood in all the Islands owned or operated exclusively a sugar or rice plantation. Some put in small lots on shares, others served as contract laborers for foreign proprietors, but none was affluent enough to possess large agricultural holdings. Rice cultivation was almost exclusively in the hands of the Chinese. Cattle ranches were largely operated by the Portuguese. There was no mercantile or manufacturing business in the Kingdom that was owned and managed by a Hawaiian of pure blood. The thousand little shops, bakeries, restaurants, and laundries were the property of the Chinese, Portuguese, and other foreigners.[2]

Moreover, official statistics indicate that the Hawaiian population, which stood at 44,088 in 1878, during the following six years under the extraordinary prosperity incident to reciprocity, declined to 40,014, a decrease of 4,074. During the same period the increase in population other than indigenous was 26,667. The population of the Hawaiian Kingdom in 1890, the end of the period of preferential treatment, was 89,000, but far less than half—34,436—were native Hawaiian. Thus during the flourishing years of reciprocity their numbers declined by 9,653. Hawaiian-born foreigners in the Islands increased from 947 in 1878 to 2,040 in 1884 and to 7,495 in 1890. The greatest augmentation of population came from Asians, with the Chinese numbering 15,301 (they had been 17,939 in 1884) and the Japanese 12,360.[3] Consequently, John E. Searles and others argued that reciprocity had not benefited, only demoralized and destroyed "the native population by substituting Chinese and other Asiatics."[4] The informed reader, however, is well-aware that the causes of the Hawaiian nation's decline were varied and that decline was apparent even before the first Reciprocity Treaty was negotiated.

There were only 1,326 Hawaiians out of a total force of 35,908 laborers engaged in 1899 on the fifty-nine large sugar estates. Charles H. Dietrich biasedly and incorrectly observed that only this number of Hawaiians can be supposed to have acquired "prosperous, happy homes." To accomplish this, Dietrich claimed, cost the United States $89,549,053, or just $67,533.22 per home, and he concluded "we would have saved money by keeping our tariff intact, importing the entire population, and boarding it in New York City."[5]

United States and Its Citizens

IN SPITE OF the fact that the Reciprocity Treaty in 1875 did not inaugurate genuine commercial reciprocity, the United States, especially after the supplementary convention was amended in 1886, supposedly secured commensurate political advantages. When the original treaty had been in operation less than fifteen months, Minister James E. Comly reported to the State Department that the "advantages to the United States in every political aspect, are unquestionably very great. In all matters of reciprocal feeling and amity, and in all the advantages resulting therefrom, the United States has under the Treaty every benefit practically that it would have if the Hawaiian Kingdom were a state of the Union."

In addition to the political benefits, the Minister Resident commented on the productive properties created by the treaty and held by Americans, namely, the inter-island mercantile marine, two railroads and equipment, a marine railway, warehouses, and so forth, estimated at the very low value of $1,500,000, which far exceeded the sum of their mortgages and capital stock indebtedness. The shipbuilding enterprise was almost completely monopolized by Americans. Within two years after the treaty had gone into effect twelve or fourteen vessels were added to the Hawaiian merchant marine from American builders.

The most neglected opportunity under the treaty was in the field of heavy agricultural and sugar machinery. With an unprecedented demand for agricultural implements and sugar plants, growing out of and favored by the reciprocity agreement and with the advantages of freedom from tariff and convenience of carriage, American manufacturers appeared to abandon that field to the British, with a tariff to pay and the inconvenience and expense of thousands of miles of additional carriage.[6]

According to the Collector General of Customs in Honolulu, the treaty gave a tremendous impetus to trade in almost all branches, "particularly in lumber, machinery, hardware, agricultural implements, iron and steel, and all staple goods." There was also a largely increased importation of livestock of all kinds, such as valuable stallions, mares, carriage horses, bulls, rams, ewes, pigs, and fowls. Naturally, with the horses came carriages and harnesses. "Indeed," reported the Collector, "there is no business that has been done with the United States, but has been largely increased, as under the good effects of the treaty many new industries have been undertaken here, in all of which the greater part of the machinery and tools have been imported from the United States."[7]

Both Elisha H. Allen and H. A. P. Carter in the 1870's, 1880's, and 1890's emphasized repeatedly to successive Secretaries of State the returns to American citizens and to the United States of reciprocity with Hawaii, and they amassed and interpreted statistics to prove that the economic gains were not all confined to the Islands, but were no less valuable to the richer party. Besides the political benefits, there were direct financial advantages accruing to the United States and its citizens, particularly in the opening of a field for investment of their capital, for making loans, and in the carrying trade, commission, and insurance business, which they would not have received but for the treaty. The profits to this country had been widely distributed in the purchase of Hawaiian exports, freights, and other earnings of vessels, insurance premiums, commissions, interest, dividends, and other miscellaneous profits passing into the wage fund and capitalized profits of the United States.

In the 1882 hearings before the Ways and Means Committee on the bill to terminate the Hawaiian Treaty, Elisha H. Allen and George S. Boutwell produced the following statistics on the increase in trade with and the arrival of American vessels at Hawaii:[8]

YEAR	INCREASE OF TRADE BETWEEN THE TWO COUNTRIES	INCREASE IN IMPORTS OF AMERICAN GOODS	ARRIVAL OF AMERICAN VESSELS AT HAWAII	
			arrivals	tonnage
1875	$1,922,555	$ —	74	41,350
1876	2,191,845	343,831	130	75,000
1877	4,092,225	1,100,643	140	90,947
1878	4,524,779	1,619,988	183	110,671
1879	5,632,856	1,820,355	177	99,102
1880	6,692,614	2,026,558	179	99,614
1881	8,373,075			

Minister Rollin M. Daggett in 1883 reported to the State Department that of the fifty-nine sugar plantations in the Islands, forty-nine were credited mainly to American ownership with a valuation of $10,235,464 out of an aggregate valuation of $15,886,800.[9] Carter exhibited statistics to Secretary Blaine in 1889 to prove "conclusively" that with an original investment of thirty million dollars, less than one-third of which was coin or its equivalent—i.e., foreign exchange —American citizens had in "nine years gained seventy-two millions of dollars, drawing the value of fifty-four millions in sugar and rice," and had "acquired profitable vested properties in the Hawaiian Islands, to the extent of eighteen millions."[10]

American residents in the archipelago and visiting officers of the United States Navy also indicated to the State Department the extent of American investments there. Captain C. E. Dutton, after a visit of seven months in Hawaiian waters in 1882, informed the Secretary of State that the ownership of the plantations was very nearly three-fourths American and the indebtedness in the form of mortgages, secured notes, and bonds was still more largely so. The paid up par value of these American investments was a little over $15,000,000, although their market value, principally in the form of stock, was at least fifty per cent higher or would be if there were a prospect of the continuation of the treaty. The commerce for the year ending June 30, 1882, carried about $11,000,000 of merchandise, and on this traffic almost $1,900,000 was paid for freight commissions and minor charges, of which $1,500,000 was net profit. About $340,000 was expended as interest on American loans, and nearly $1,200,000 in dividends to American stockholders.[11]

After the revolution of 1893, Lorrin A. Thurston, one of the Hawaiian commissioners sent to Washington to negotiate an annexation treaty, produced a comprehensive study of the benefits of reciprocity from January 1, 1876, to January 1, 1891, the end of the period of preferential treatment.[12] When the treaty went into effect there were but a few scattered, poorly equipped sugar plantations, most of which were on the verge of bankruptcy, the export of sugar in 1875 having been but 12,543 tons. "But for the treaty," he maintained, "the sugar business would have continued in the same condition, or, with the aid of East Indian coolies, would have passed under British control, with the consequent development of British influence. The commerce of the country was inconsiderable. The total value of all imports from all countries for 1875 was only $1,505,000. There were no commercial corporations other than five sugar plantations." There were no regular steam communications with the rest of the world, and inter-island trade did not support one small steamer. There was so little insurable property and so few people who could afford to insure, that insurance played an insignificant part in the Kingdom's business.

The total capital invested in the sugar business in 1875 was approximately $2,000,000, of which about three-fourths, or $1,500,000, belonged to United States citizens.[13] In January, 1891, the total capital invested in the same business was $33,455,990, of which $24,735,610, or about four-fifths, was held by United States citizens; thus, the increase of sugar property owned by Americans from 1875 to 1891 was $23,235,610. The profits from sugar on different estates and in different years varied from actual loss to a profit of fifty dollars a ton. Thurston estimated conservatively that the average profit during the treaty period was twenty dollars per ton. The total export of sugar from January, 1876, to January, 1891, was 1,002,085 tons. The profit thereon at twenty dollars a ton amounted to $20,041,700. The proportion of the total sugar property owned by Americans was seventy-four per cent, the profits on which amounted to $14,830,858. In addition, Thurston estimated the total commissions collected by American agents on sugar sales during the treaty period as $3,006,000.

The total exports from the United States to Hawaii were valued at $947,260 in 1875 whereas in 1890 they stood at $5,265,051. The value of all exports from the United States to Hawaii from January, 1876, to January, 1891, was $47,603,670. There was every indication, according to the Hawaiian Commissioner, that, but for the Reciprocity Treaty, the imports from the United States would have continued to decrease as they had prior to 1876. If, however, they had continued at the same rate during the sixteen years following 1875, they would have amounted to only $15,156,160. This shows that by reason of the treaty the United States had exported to Hawaii at least $32,447,510 worth of goods more than would have been exported without reciprocity.

During the period of the treaty, American ship-builders constructed thirty-nine vessels for the inter-island and twenty-six for Hawaiian foreign trade, a total of sixty-five which would not have been built but for the treaty and for which Americans received the sum of $3,189,500. A minimum profit on these transactions would be ten per cent, amounting to $318,950. The amount received by American vessels from Hawaiian freight during the same period was $6,707,521. But this by no means represented the total. Thurston pointed out that from 32.3 per cent in 1881, to 51.48 per cent in 1890, with a fair average of ten per cent of foreign freights, was carried in vessels under the Hawaiian flag. Practically all these ships were actually owned by Americans, the Hawaiian ownership being nominal in order to secure Hawaiian registry. The estimated profit received by Americans engaged in the inter-island trade for the fifteen years 1876–91 was $1,152,000.

With the exception of a few incorporated sugar plantations, there were in 1875 no commercial corporations in Hawaii, whereas in 1890 there were, other than sugar and shipping companies, forty-three commercial corporations with a paid-up capital stock of $5,610,421, of which $3,973,505, or over seventy per cent, was owned by Americans. In addition, Americans owned large amounts of other property in Hawaii, most of which was acquired after 1875. The value of unincorporated property, other than sugar plantations, actually owned by Americans and children of Americans, Thurston estimated at $5,000,000.

The insurance business in Hawaii in 1875 was scarcely worth considering. During the period from January, 1876, to January, 1890, the premiums collected on fire, marine, and life insurance in the archipelago by American insurance companies was $2,189,350. The amount of insurance alone in American companies in force in the Kingdom during 1890 was $6,400,000.

The total amount of sugar exported from Hawaii to the United States under the Reciprocity Treaty from January 1, 1876, to January 1, 1891, was 1,002,085 tons; molasses amounted to 1,693,981 gallons. The average duty on sugar remitted by the United States was approximately forty dollars a ton and on molasses, four cents a gallon. The total loss from remission of duties on Hawaiian products, sugar, molasses, rice and paddy, amounted to $42,680,796. Against this figure Thurston placed $70,973,464, representing the total American gains under the treaty and thus figured the American net profit as $28,292,668. This estimate, however, did not include all of the profits made by United States citizens. Omitted were the dividends of American stock holders in the commercial corporations other than sugar, the passenger receipts of American ships between the Islands and California, the profits made by Hawaiian merchants on the sale of $47,603,670 worth of imports from the United States, and subsidies paid by the Hawaiian Government to American steamships, along with other sources of profit, evidently large, but not easily reducible to exact figures.[14]

The Hawaiian Patriotic League questioned Thurston's estimates of the total capital engaged in sugar (in corporations and in un-incorporated plantations), out of which $24,734,610 were claimed to be American. This "fantastic array" was contradicted by the mere fact that out of a total of $537,757 for internal taxes, Americans paid only $139,998, or one-fourth, while, according to Thurston's statement, American plantation stock alone, outside of commercial firms and other American taxable property, ought to have paid over $247,000. The League asserted that it was an undeniable fact that, except for Claus Spreckels,

> no American has ever brought into this country any capital worth mentioning, but many have sent away fortunes made here; most of our present American capitalists, outside of sons of missionaries, came here as sailors or schoolteachers, some few as clerks, others as mechanics, so that, even if now they own or manage, or have their names in some way connected with property or corporations, this does not make their wealth of American origin. Those who are now independent run their plantations or business firms on money made here, out of the Hawaiian people and from Hawaiian soil, through coolie labor.[15]

The Senate Foreign Relations Committee in 1894, observed that the House Committee on Ways and Means found that United States exports to Hawaii for the nine years 1876–85 indicated an invoice value of $23,000,000, whereas our imports amounted to $54,000,000, and hastily concluded that the $31,000,000 visible trade balance against us had to be liquidated in coin and exchange. The Senate Committee claimed that this apparent discrepancy between the exports and imports vanished when full account was taken of the fact that the whole carrying trade and mercantile business were American in both directions. Reciprocity created a new mercantile marine, employing American-built steamers and sailing vessels constructed expressly for the service and costing over $3,500,000. Of this total tonnage, over ninety per cent was American built, and the rest was bought. A commerce amounting to $12,000,000 was in American hands. It was the only foreign commerce in the 1880's and 1890's which we could call our own. Before the treaty the sugar and rice imported at San Francisco came chiefly from Asia and the East Indies, where it was bought with London exchange and shipped in foreign vessels.

Reciprocity developed a trade with the Hawaiian Islands, which, relative to the population, was enormous and of which the returns to the United States were exceedingly large, "so large that it seems at first unaccountable." These profits did not, as was generally supposed, accrue to the great sugar monopoly, but went chiefly to American shipping which was promoted by the treaty, to the mercantile houses which handled the merchandise, and to the investors who advanced the capital to open and develop the productive properties. These profits, the authors of the report insisted, were nearly double the remitted duties and four or five times as great as the probable loss of revenue. Actually, only about $13,000,000 of the balance of trade was liquidated in coin, and the remaining $18,000,000 was paid to Americans and might be reckoned as a gross profit already realized. Over $9,000,000 went to American shipping; nearly $3,000,000 to San Francisco commission houses; nearly a million to the banks; over $2,000,000 for interest on loans and advances; and over $3,000,000 as dividends and miscellaneous profits. In addition, Americans held $6,500,000 of Hawaiian debts which they were compelled to liquidate out of future shipments.

The value of plantation properties held by Americans was assessed by the Hawaiian Government in 1883 as $10,180,164. This was assumed to be about two-thirds the real value. Thus it was estimated that Americans held approximately $15,000,000 worth of magnificent production properties. "This value," the report claimed, "has been created almost wholly since 1876 out of the grounds, buildings, and machinery, out of the soil by the combined action of capital and labor. It would be difficult to find in the annals of trade and production a result more gratifying."[16]

Holding quite a different opinion was Charles H. Dietrich, who found that the treaty had resulted in a net loss of millions to the United States and its citizens. From 1875 to 1900 the total American importations from Hawaii were valued at $238,486,346. During the same period American exportations to Hawaii amounted to $103,916,427. The amount of money which the Hawaiian producers would have paid in customs tariff to the United States Government on the goods let in free, if they had paid the same duties which were exacted from other countries, would have been $89,549,053. Thus it was evident that with each dollar's worth of goods sold the Islands, the United States had given someone a present of eighty-six cents in tariffs. If American manufacturers made ten per cent net profit on the goods they sent to Hawaii, that trade between 1876 and 1900 netted them $10,391,647 profit, leaving a net loss to the country of $79,157,388. In Dietrich's opinion the Reciprocity Treaty had failed in every respect, except that it had "enabled a few Americans, including Mr. Claus Spreckels and his sons, to exploit the Islands and make themselves millionaires at the expense of the American and Hawaiian people."[17]

Whether or not anti-annexationists and patriotic Hawaiians accepted Thurston and the Foreign Relations Committee's findings, the general effect of the treaty appeared to make the Islands an area for the very profitable investment of American capital. Reciprocity created a demand for American produce to an amount which might seem small—$23,000,000 in nine years—in comparison with total exports to the group of $54,000,000—but which, in view of the fact that the population making that demand was less than 80,000, was remarkably large, amounting to four or five times as much per capita as England or Canada bought from the United States.[18]

Lorrin Thurston and the Senate Committee were in agreement that in addition to securing a political benefit, the direct financial advantages that accrued to the United States and its citizens, which they would not have received but for the treaty, had more than repaid, dollar for dollar, all loss by the United States through the remission of duties under the reciprocity treaty. By the extension to Hawaii of the benefits of the American protective tariff, the United States had secured, without any effort on her part, "an enormous addition to her ship-building and foreign export and carrying trade, and there had been created a prosperous, progressive American community, which is no less American because it is across the ocean and under a tropical sky."[19]

NOTES

1. Adam Smith, *An Inquiry into the Nature and Causes of the Wealth of Nations* (Everyman's Library, Ernest Rhys (ed.), 2 vols., London, Toronto, New York, 1910), I, 400.
2. Comly to Frelinghuysen, No. 213, April 10, 1882, USDS, Dispatches, Hawaii, XX, printed in *For. Rels.* (1882), p. 333.
3. *For. Rels.* (1885), p. 472, citing the census of 1878 and of 1884; *San Francisco Morning Call*, Jan. 21, 1893. The Portuguese were next after the Asians, numbering 8,602. See Appendix III.
4. *San Francisco Chronicle*, Feb. 27, 1886.
5. *Sen. Docs.*, 57th Cong., 2nd sess., No. 206, p. 2.
6. Comly to Evarts, Nos. 13, 19, Dec. 3 and 28, 1877, USDS, Dispatches, Hawaii, XVII. The latter is printed in *For. Rels.* (1878), pp. 379–81.
7. Collector General's office to Comly, Nov. 20, 1877, encl. No. 2 in Comly to Evarts, No. 13, Dec. 3, 1877, *ibid.*
8. *Remarks of Mr. Elisha H. Allen, Hawaiian Minister, and Geo. S. Boutwell, Counsel, on the Bill for the Termination of the Hawaiian Treaty*, Washington, 1882, pp. 14–15, Allen Papers.
9. Daggett to Frelinghuysen, No. 92, Oct. 13, 1883, USDS, Dispatches, Hawaii, XXI.
10. Encl. in Carter to Blaine, priv. and conf., March 29, 1889, USDS, Hawaii, Notes from, III.
11. Dutton to Secretary of State, Feb. 6, 1883, USDS, Misc. Letters, Feb. 1883, Pt. 1. Captain Dutton, of the Ordinance Corps of the United States Army was in the Hawaiian Islands under the auspices of the Smithsonian Institute and the Geological Survey for the purpose of making a study of some of the volcanoes (Frelinghuysen to Comly, between Nos. 117 and 118, May 11, 1882, USDS, Instructions, Hawaii, II).
12. Thurston, "The Sandwich Islands," pp. 265–81. The reader should bear in mind that Thurston was representative of the extreme point of view of the American Party, was personally interested in sugar culture and the commerce of the Islands, and was a ring leader in the annexationist movement. His statistics correspond closely with those in *Sen. Reps.*, 53rd Cong., 2nd sess., No. 227, App. X, "The Hawaiian Treaty: A Review of its Commercial Results," pp. 465ff. In both, prepared by annexationists, the statistics were arranged to prove the desired point. Some of the same figures were interpreted differently by Charles H. Dietrich in "History of the Hawaiian Treaty, with a Report to Terminate the Treaty signed by Justin S. Morrill, Daniel W. Voorhees, and Nelson W. Aldrich," *Sen Docs.*, 57th Cong., 2nd sess., No. 206.
13. Thurston used the terms "Americans" and "United States citizens" in a broad general sense, meaning people of American birth or ancestry.
14. Thurston, "The Advantages of Annexation," pp. 272–76.
15. Statement of the Hawaiian Patriotic League, *For. Rels.* (1894), p. 921.
16. *Sen. Reps.*, 53rd Cong., 2nd sess., No. 227, App. X, pp. 467, 468, 475. An American citizen was defined in this report as one "who had the right to vote in the United States without naturalization and had the right to the protection of our government under public law."
17. *Sen. Docs.*, 57th Cong., 2nd sess., No. 206, pp. 1–3.
18. *Sen. Reps.*, 53rd Cong., 2nd sess., No. 227, App. X, p. 468; Thurston, "Advantages of Annexation," pp. 275, 279.
19. Thurston, p. 277.

APPENDIXES,
BIBLIOGRAPHICAL NOTE,
AND INDEX

APPENDIX I

EXPORTS OF SUGAR FROM HAWAII 1856–1890
(1 ton = 2,000)

YEAR	TONS	YEAR	TONS	YEAR	TONS
1856	277	1868	9,156	1880	29,352
1857	350	1869	9,151	1881	46,894
1858	602	1870	9,391	1882	57,088
1859	913	1871	10,880	1883	57,052
1860	722	1872	8,479	1884	70,826
1861	1,283	1873	11,064	1885	85,675
1862	1,502	1874	12,283	1886	108,111
1863	2,646	1875	12,540	1887	106,380
1864	5,207	1876	13,026	1888	117,944
1865	7,659	1877	12,783	1889	121,082
1866	8,869	1878	19,206	1890	129,899
1867	8,563	1879	24,279		

Lorrin A. Thurston, "Sugar: Its Status and Development," *Pacific Commercial Advertiser*, July 2, 1906, p. 37.

APPENDIX II

GROWTH OF HAWAIIAN COMMERCE

YEAR	TOTAL IMPORTS	TOTAL EXPORTS	DOMESTIC PRODUCE EXPORTED
1844	$ 350,347	$ 169,641	$ 109,587
1850	1,035,058	783,052	536,522
1860	1,223,749	807,459	480,526
1870	1,930,227	2,144,942	1,514,425
1880	3,673,268	4,968,455	4,889,194
1890	6,962,201	13,142,829	13,023,304
1899	16,069,577	22,628,742	22,324,865
1905	14,718,483	36,174,526	36,126,797
1915	26,416,031	62,464,759	62,195,586
1925	81,802,547	105,599,819	105,504,292
1935	84,552,884	100,033,996	93,431,000
1944	198,509,464	85,140,640	82,619,000

APPENDIX III

POPULATION OF THE HAWAIIAN ISLANDS BY NATIONALITIES

NATIONALITIES	1884 ALL ISLANDS TOTAL	1890 ALL ISLANDS TOTAL	1890 ALL ISLANDS MALES	1890 ALL ISLANDS FEMALES	1890 HONOLULU, OAHU MALES	1890 HONOLULU, OAHU FEMALES
Native Hawaiians	40,014	34,436	18,364	16,072	4,494	4,068
Mixed Parentage Hawaiians	4,218	6,186	3,085	3,101	1,257	1,346
Hawaiian-Born Foreign Parents	2,040	7,495	3,909	3,586	1,250	1,236
Chinese	17,937	15,301	14,552	779	3,950	457
Portuguese	9,377	8,602	4,770	3,832	933	799
Americans	2,066	1,928	1,298	630	767	431
Germans	1,600	1,034	729	305	261	105
Britons	1,282	1,344	982	362	529	267
Norwegians	392	227	155	72	55	21
French	192	70	46	24	25	23
Japanese	116	12,360	10,079	2,281	277	111
Polynesians	956	588	404	184	49	23
All Others	416	419	371	48	151	22

Compiled from the Census of 1890.

Admiralty dealing with the cession of Pearl Harbor, preferential treatment in reciprocity treaties, and threats to the independence of the Hawaiian Kingdom, were read in the British Public Record Office, London. The volumes especially informative were FO 58/136, 58/241, United States Designs on Pearl Harbour, 58/258 and CO 523/136.

In the manuscript division of the Library of Congress pertinent information was secured from the papers of the following statesmen: William L. Marcy, Hamilton Fish (including his diary), Frederick T. Frelinghuysen, Chester A. Arthur, Grover Cleveland, Thomas F. Bayard, James G. Blaine, John Sherman, Benjamin Harrison, and Elisha Hunt Allen. In addition, the Armstrong-Chapman Papers yielded valuable and interesting material. Unfortunately, this collection does not contain the replies of Judge Ruben Chapman to his brother-in-law.

The manuscript division of the Harvard College Library now houses the Hawaiian Club of Boston papers, including minutes of meetings and letter books; the correspondence of Edward P. Bond, who was a member and officer of both the Hawaiian Club and the Boston Board of Trade; the correspondence of Charles Sumner; and the larger portion of the James Hunnewell papers, the remainder being in the Baker Library of the Harvard University Graduate School of Business Administration, as are also the tariff papers of Justin S. Morrill.

In the Hawaiian Collection of the University of Hawaii Library are the transcript copies of the Gregg Collection which contain David L. Gregg's dispatches, without enclosures, his private letters in two parts, and the eight extant volumes of his diaries, together with some miscellaneous papers. The diaries are a rich storehouse of observations on mid-nineteenth century life and society in Honolulu as well as a revelation of Gregg's innermost convictions and intentions, especially on the subject of annexation. A transcript copy of the Diary of William R. Castle is also in the Hawaiian Collection. Several master of arts theses of the University of Hawaii in the field of history lead to the further investigation of certain aspects of United States-Hawaii relations.

The *Papers* and *Reports* of the Hawaiian Historical Society are readily available in the Mission-Historical Library in Honolulu.

The printed sources used in the preparation of this study, far too numerous and varied to be listed, included government documents, especially *Papers Relating to the Foreign Relations of the United States*, for the applicable years, James D. Richardson, comp.; *A Compilation of the Messages and Papers of the Presidents* (10 vols., Washington, 1896–99?); the *Congressional Globe*; *Congressional Record*; the *Journal of the Executive Proceedings of the Senate of the United States*; *United States Statutes at Large*; and United States Tariff Commission, *Reciprocity and Commercial Treaties* (Washington, 1919). Mention should be made of United States *House of Representatives Executive Documents*, 53rd Congress, 3rd session, No. 1, Part 1, or *Foreign Relations of the United States* (1894), Appendix II, "Affairs in Hawaii." This volume of 1437 pages comprises various Senate and House documents, with some duplications, dealing with Hawaii. Three other comprehensive volumes frequently consulted were: *House of Representatives Executive Documents*, 53rd Congress, 2nd session, No. 47, *Report of the Commissioner to the Hawaiian Islands*, often cited as the *Blount Report*; United States *Senate Reports*, 53rd Congress, 2nd session, No. 227, frequently referred to as the *Morgan Report*, as well as volume II of that report, which is not in the congressional series; and *Senate Executive Documents*, 52nd Congress, 2nd session, No. 77, which is correspondence respecting relations between the United States and the Hawaiian Kingdom from September, 1820, to January, 1893, together with a report upon the official relations of the United States with the Islands from the first appointment of a consular officer there by this Government. United States relations with Hawaii prior to annexation are summarized in John Bassett Moore, *Digest of International Law*, volume I, pages 475–520. Also valuable for printed official sources are the *Reports of the Minister of Foreign Relations*, Honolulu, for the applicable years; and the *Report of the Historical Commission of the Territory of Hawaii . . . December 31, 1926*, and for December 31, 1928.

Of the general histories covering part of the period, Ralph S. Kuykendall, *The Hawaiian Kingdom 1778–1854: Foundation and Transformation* (Honolulu, 1947) and *The Hawaiian Kingdom 1854–1874: Twenty Critical Years* (Honolulu, 1953), are, and perhaps will remain for all times, the most comprehensive, objective, and scholarly works. Research scholars in every area of Hawaiian history will always be deeply indebted to Professor Kuykendall. On the other hand, William D. Alexander, *History of the Later Years of the Hawaiian Monarchy and the Revolution of 1893* (Honolulu,

1896), and Lorrin A. Thurston, *Memoirs of the Hawaiian Revolution* (Honolulu, 1936) are slanted in favor of the annexationists.

Mention can be made of only a few of the most frequently consulted periodicals. For official proclamations, announcements "By Authority," and information and reports on activities of the Legislature, the *Polynesian*, once the official organ of the Hawaiian Government; the *Pacific Commercial Advertiser*, at times in opposition to and at other periods controlled by the Minister of Foreign Relations; the *Hawaiian Gazette*; and the Honolulu *Bulletin* were informative. The following newspapers: the *Alta California*, the *Chronicle*, the *Commercial Advertiser*, the *Herald*, the *Evening Bulletin*, and the *Merchant* (all of San Francisco), the Portland *Oregonian*, the *New York Times*, the *New York Herald*, the *New York Tribune*, the *American Grocer*, the *Washington Post*, the Washington *Evening Star*, the *Chicago Tribune*, the *Boston Globe*, the New Orleans *Daily Picayune*, and the New Orleans *Times-Democrat* were the most frequently used American newspapers, whereas *The Times* and London *Post* proved superior for England. The *North American Review*, the *Review of Reviews*, *Nineteenth Century Review*, the *Pacific Historical Review*, and the *American Historical Review* provided scholarly articles on special topics pertinent to Hawaiian-American relations.

INDEX

Adler, Jacob, Prof., on Claus Spreckels, 128, 238n3
Admiralty, and cession of Pearl Harbor, 201, 209 f.
Agency system and sugar agents or factors, 121 f., 126 f., 157 f., 220, 245, 304; petition for reciprocity, 101
Alabama (Confederate cruiser), 69
Alaska, 163
Albany *Times-Union*, on sugar and Revolution of 1893, 245
Aldrich, Nelson W., Sen., for abrogation of Rec. Tr., 162, 235
Alexander, B. S., Brigadier General: visits and gathers information on Hawaii, 84, 88; reports on Pearl Harbor, 93 f.
Alexander Liholiho, Prince, 13 f.
Alexander, Samuel T., pioneer in large-scale sugar production, 119 f.
Alexander, William P., Rev., 8
Allen, Elisha H., 10, 13, 32; mission to U.S., 37 ff., 47 f., 67, 69 f., 91, 101, 108 ff., 111, 123, 155; lobbies for reciprocity, 67, 131n12; before Committee on Foreign Affairs, 149 f.; death of, 170; and Spreckels' ring, 179n31; on advantages of reciprocity, 260
Allen, William Vincent, Sen., 253
Allis: and reciprocity, 83; oppose cession of Pearl Harbor, 97; and crown lands, 124
Almanac, 1834–62, 6
Alta California (San Francisco): and reciprocity, 72; King Kalakaua's visit, 109
American Board of Commissioners for Foreign Missions, 5 ff., 8
American contacts, influence, interest, and views in Hawaii, 3 ff.; missionaries and, 5 ff.; political and economic, 8, 12 ff., 22, 39, 48, 51, 67, 87, 169; allegedly endangered by British, French, and Germans, 12 ff., 115, 187; decline of political influence, 13; Adm. Belknap on, 153 f.; Cleveland on, 187; Bayard's concern for, 187 f., 201 f.; *New York Times* on, 233; Adm. Kimberly on, 241n44
American Grocer (*New York Grocer*), 142, 146
American investments in Hawaii, whaling, 40; shipping, shipbuilding, carrying trade, banking, insurance, and mercantile business, 163, 167 f., 171 f., 262 ff.; sugar plantations, 163, 264 f.
American Pacific Cable Co., 128
American Pacific Mail Steamship Co., 128
American population, best Hawaiian market, 104, 246, 266
American population in Hawaii, 273; *see also* American contacts, influence, etc.
American Sugar Co., 165, 168
American Sugar Growers' Association, opposes annexation, 253
American Sugar Refining Co., 238n3
American trade and interest in the Pacific, 62 f.; L. M. Morrill on jingo empire in the Pacific, 161 f.; Rec. Tr. of 1875, instrument of American policy in the Pacific, 183; Cleveland on, 187; Bayard on, 187
Americans in Hawaii, 3 ff., 173, 198 f.; citizens of, 199; in total population, 273
Andrews, Lorrin, 9, 11
Anglade, M. d', 226; opposes cession of Pearl Harbor, 230
Anglo-French (Eden) commercial treaty, 89

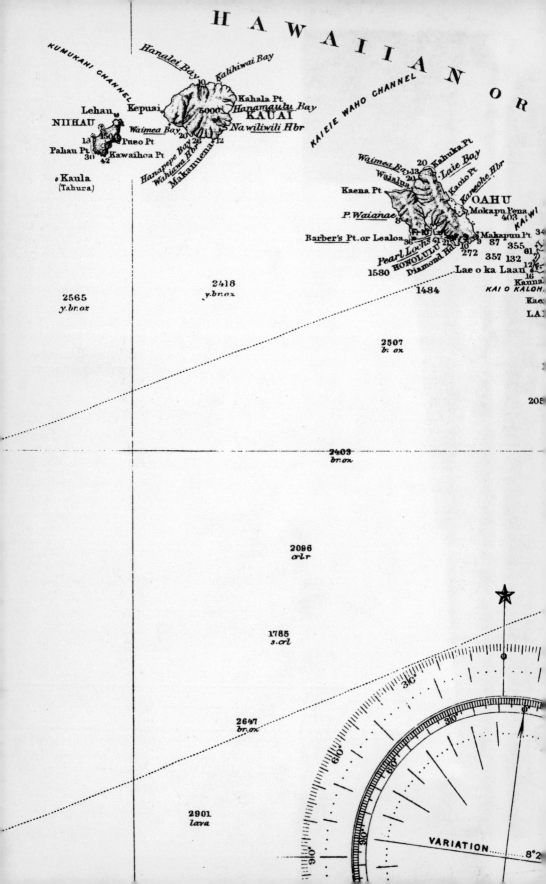